Advocacy for Paralegals

SECOND EDITION

JoAnn Kurtz

Ashlyn O'Mara

Arlene Blatt

 ▪ Toronto, Canada ▪ 2017

Emond Montgomery Publications Limited
60 Shaftesbury Avenue
Toronto ON M4T 1A3
http://www.emond.ca/highered

Printed in Canada.

We acknowledge the financial support of the Government of Canada.   Canadä

Emond Montgomery Publications has no responsibility for the persistence or accuracy of URLs for external or third-party Internet websites referred to in this publication, and does not guarantee that any content on such websites is, or will remain, accurate or appropriate.

Vice-president, publishing: Anthony Rezek
Acquisitions editor: Lindsay Sutherland
Managing editor, development: Kelly Dickson
Senior editor, production: Jim Lyons
Production supervisor: Laura Bast
Copy editor: Francine Geraci
Typesetter: Christopher Hudson
Proofreader: David Handelsman
Indexer: Paula Pike
Cover designer: Tara Agnerian
Cover image: Christopher Meder/Shutterstock

Library and Archives Canada Cataloguing in Publication

Blatt, Arlene, author
    Advocacy for paralegals / JoAnn Kurtz, Ashlyn O'Mara, Arlenne Blatt. — 2nd edition.

Includes index.
Revision of: Advocacy for paralegals / Arlene Blatt, JoAnn Kurtz.
ISBN 978-1-55239-596-7 (paperback)

    1. Trial practice—Canada.   2. Legal assistants—Canada.   I. Kurtz, JoAnn, 1951-, author   II. O'Mara, Ashlyn, 1984-, author   III. Title.

KE8422.B53 2017   347.71'075   C2016-905271-0
KF8915.B53 2017

To Ely, Max, Jacob, and Danny Henry.
—JK

To my parents for all their love and support throughout the years.
—AO

To Leonard and Felicie Blatt.
—AB

Brief Contents

PART I

INTRODUCTION

PART II

OVERVIEW OF THE LITIGATION PROCESS

PART III

PREPARING FOR A TRIAL OR HEARING

PART IV

THE TRIAL OR HEARING

PART V

FINAL PREPARATION

APPENDIXES

Detailed Contents

PART I

INTRODUCTION

1 Advocacy and the Litigation Process

2 The Paralegal as Advocate

PART II

OVERVIEW OF THE LITIGATION PROCESS

3 Steps in the Litigation Process

4 The Courtroom Experience

PART III

PREPARING FOR A TRIAL OR HEARING

15 Additional Submissions

16 Objections

PART V
FINAL PREPARATION

17 Final Preparation for the Trial or Hearing

APPENDIXES

A Selected Paralegal Rules of Conduct

B **Selected Paralegal Professional Conduct Guidelines**

Preface

Advocacy for Paralegals was designed to help paralegals prepare and present a case before a court or tribunal. The text starts with a discussion of advocacy and an overview of the litigation process. It then takes students through the parts of a trial or hearing and tells them how to prepare for each of those parts. The text concludes with a discussion of final preparation for the trial or hearing. Throughout the book we discuss relevant ethical issues in advocacy, including an examination of the *Paralegal Rules of Conduct*.

The text covers the competencies required by the Law Society of Upper Canada in the advocacy portion of an accredited paralegal education program, and deals with advocacy before the courts and tribunals where licensed paralegals are permitted to appear. While the book makes specific reference to courts and tribunals in Ontario only and to Ontario rules of professional conduct, the general principles apply throughout Canada.

This second edition has been expanded in a number of ways. The first edition of this text used a Small Claims Court fact situation to illustrate each stage of a trial. The second edition now includes both a Landlord and Tenant Board and a Provincial Offences scenario. It also contains a number of new chapters. One provides an expanded discussion of the role of the paralegal as advocate, including an examination of the paralegal licensing process and the scope of practice for paralegals. Another new chapter discusses interviewing witnesses as part of trial preparation. The second edition also includes expanded chapters on presentation skills and courtroom etiquette, as well as additional end-of-chapter exercises and discussion questions.

Acknowledgments

We would like to thank the following people for their help in writing this book: The Honourable M. Donald Godfrey of the Superior Court of Justice—Small Claims Court (retired) and His Worship Justice of the Peace Luigi Muraca of the Ontario Court of Justice, both of whom allowed us to observe them in court and then kindly took the time to meet with us and answer our questions; and our colleagues Linda Pasternak, Kent Peel, Michael Gulycz, Sandra Kingston, Gilda Berger, and Charles Granek, each of whom provided support and answers to our questions.

JoAnn Kurtz, JD
Arlene Blatt, JD
Ashlyn O'Mara, BA, LLB, BCL

January 2017

About the Authors

JoAnn Kurtz carried on a general practice with an emphasis on family law and real estate before joining Seneca College, where she is the program coordinator for the Law Clerk Diploma program of the School of Legal and Public Administration. She has taught various topics, including contract law, family law, residential tenancy law and advocacy, and is the author or co-author of many general interest and academic texts. She attended New York University and holds a JD from Osgoode Hall Law School.

Ashlyn O'Mara is a full-time professor in the School of Legal and Public Administration at Seneca College where she teaches a variety of subjects, including advocacy, tribunal practice and procedure, legal drafting and communication, computer applications for paralegals, ethics and professional responsibility, and real estate. Ashlyn also coaches Seneca's Paralegal Moot Team and helps paralegal students prepare for the Paralegal Cup Mooting Competition and the Osgoode Cup National Undergraduate Mooting Competition each year. For several years, Ashlyn worked as a practising lawyer in the areas of family law, estate planning and administration, estate litigation, and real estate law. She is an active member of the Ontario Bar Association where she serves on the executive of both the Young Lawyers Division (Central) and the Sole, Small Firm and General Practice Division. Ashlyn is a graduate of McGill University's Faculty of Law, having obtained degrees in both civil law and common law. Connect with her on Twitter: @AshlynOMara.

Arlene Blatt is a full-time professor in the School of Legal and Public Administration at Seneca College and teaches a variety of legal subjects to paralegal and law clerk students. She obtained her JD degree from Osgoode Hall Law School and is a member of the Ontario Bar. She has co-authored four Emond publications: *Advocacy for Paralegals*, *Residential Real Estate Transactions*, *Legal Entities and Relationships*, and *Legal Research: Step by Step*. She has also contributed a chapter on residential landlord and tenant law to an introductory legal textbook. Her areas of academic interest include landlord and tenant law, real estate law, and legal research.

PART I

Introduction

CHAPTER 1

Advocacy and the Litigation Process

When you read a case report it is often hard to imagine that the case—whether heard in a civil court, a criminal court, or an administrative tribunal—involves real people with a real dispute. A case report sets out the decision of the judge, justice of the peace, or adjudicator, which he or she arrives at by applying the relevant law to the facts of the case. While this process may sound simple, it is not. The parties involved—the plaintiff and the defendant in a civil case, the Crown and the defence in a criminal or provincial offences case, the applicant and the respondent in a tribunal case—typically disagree about the facts of the matter. This disagreement results in a trial or hearing and, after hearing the conflicting evidence of both parties, the judge, justice of the peace, or adjudicator has to determine which version to believe—in other words, the facts of the case. The judge, justice of the peace, or adjudicator has to make findings of fact and then apply the relevant law in order to reach a decision.

It is helpful to look at an example of each type of case in order to understand how the facts in an actual dispute are dealt with through the litigation process. What follows are three fact situations: a Small Claims Court case, a provincial offences case, and an administrative tribunal case. Throughout this text we will revisit these fact situations as we discuss each step of the litigation process.

FACT SITUATION 1

Small Claims Court: The Kitchen Renovation Case

Tina Fey and her husband, Tommy, hired Baldwin Brothers Construction to make some minor renovations to the kitchen in their home for a total contract price of $7,500. The work is now completed, but the Feys and the Baldwins have a disagreement about payment for the installation of three pot lights. Tina and Tommy claim that the contract price included the installation of all necessary lights in the kitchen. Baldwin Brothers Construction, on the other hand, claims that the contract required them to install five pot lights only, and that three additional pot lights were installed at Tommy's request as an extra to be paid for separately. Tina and Tommy have paid the original contract price but refuse to pay more.

The parties cannot resolve this disagreement, so Baldwin Brothers Construction has started a Small Claims Court action claiming $750 for the cost of supplying and installing the three disputed pot lights.

At the trial of this case, the judge must decide whether to grant judgment to the plaintiff, Baldwin Brothers Construction (Alec Baldwin and Stephen Baldwin, carrying on business as Baldwin Brothers Construction), for the $750. The first part of the decision-making process is to determine what, exactly, the parties agreed to. Of course, the judge was not present when the contract was entered into, so he or she must make this decision based on the evidence presented by the parties in court.

As often happens, the parties in this case did not have a written contract. Tina Fey and Alec Baldwin were the only people present when the oral contract was made, and they each have a very different understanding of what they agreed to.

FACT SITUATION 2

Provincial Offences Court: The Liquor Licence Case

Treetop Catering and Victoria Levens, its sole director, officer, and shareholder, have been charged with an offence under the *Liquor Licence Act*. Treetop Catering was hired by the Simpson Advocacy Club to organize and manage a party for its members being held at the Simpson Academy student lounge. The lounge included an indoor bar and a fenced outdoor patio area. In addition to a bartender, Treetop Catering hired a security guard who was to ensure that guests did not take alcohol outside the fenced patio. The party became quite noisy, and a neighbour, Patrick Elder, called the police to complain. When the police officer, Constable Matthew Lee, arrived, he found empty beer bottles and plastic wine glasses on the lawn outside the patio. He therefore charged Treetop Catering and Victoria Levens with the offence of permitting the removal of alcohol from the premises as prohibited under RRO 1990, Regulation 719 of the *Liquor Licence Act*.

At the trial, the justice of the peace will have to decide whether the defendants are guilty or not guilty. To secure a conviction, the prosecution must first prove beyond a reasonable doubt that the defendants permitted the removal of alcohol from the licensed area of the premises. If the prosecution does so, the defendants must then prove, on a balance of probabilities, that they had taken all reasonable steps to comply with the law.

Administrative Tribunal: The Landlord and Tenant Dispute

Alice and Arlo Guthrie were tenants in a two-unit building owned by Jim Croce. At the end of their one-year lease, Jim served a notice of termination of their tenancy so that Jim's daughter Cynthia could move into the apartment. Alice and Arlo could not find a similar apartment for the same rent, but did find a suitable apartment in the same neighbourhood at a higher rent. Alice and Arlo moved out, but Cynthia did not move into the apartment. Instead, Jim put it up for lease at a higher rent than Alice and Arlo were paying. Jim says that Cynthia changed her mind about moving into the apartment because she got a job in Ottawa. Arlo and Alice do not believe Jim. They think that he terminated their tenancy in bad faith, intending all along to re-rent to a new tenant for a higher rent.

Arlo and Alice have started a proceeding before the Landlord and Tenant Board under section 57 of the *Residential Tenancies Act*, claiming that Jim's notice of termination was given in bad faith and asking for an order that Jim pay their increased rent for one year ($100 per month × 12 = $1,200) plus their moving costs of $750, for a total of $1,950.

At the hearing, the adjudicator will have to decide whether to order Jim to pay Alice and Arlo $1,950. The first part of the decision-making process is to determine whether Cynthia ever intended to move into the apartment and, therefore, whether Jim acted in good faith in terminating Alice's and Arlo's tenancy. The adjudicator must make this decision based on the evidence presented by the parties at the hearing.

In each of these cases, the decision-maker (judge, justice of the peace, or adjudicator) will listen to each party's retelling of the events and choose which version to believe. Sometimes the parties' versions of events differ because one of them is lying, but more often their versions differ simply because they remember the events differently. So, how does a decision-maker choose between the different stories of two honest witnesses? The decision-maker will believe the story that makes more sense—the one that is more likely to have happened. It is the role of the advocate to present the client's story in the more persuasive—more believable—way.

After determining the facts of the case, the decision-maker will arrive at a decision by applying the relevant law to the facts. It is the role of the advocate to advise the decision-maker of the applicable law and also to suggest how that law should be applied to the facts so that the advocate's client wins.

Advocacy is the term used to describe the process of presenting a case or defence at a trial or hearing before a civil court, a criminal court, or an administrative tribunal. An **advocate** is a person who pleads the cause of another before a court or tribunal. Advocates are often lawyers but, at tribunals and lower-level courts, paralegals may also act as advocates.

---

advocacy: process of presenting a case or defence at a trial or hearing

advocate: person who pleads the cause of another before a court or tribunal

To appreciate the role of advocacy in the trial or hearing process, it is important to understand the relationship of advocacy to substantive law, procedural law, and the law of evidence.

Substantive law defines legal rights and obligations. Substantive law can be divided into categories, such as contract law, tort law, family law, real estate law, and criminal law. It is substantive law that determines whether you have a civil cause of action or a defence to a civil action. It is also substantive law that defines the elements of a criminal offence and the defences available to that offence. Substantive law also determines the facts that you must establish to constitute your claim or defence. The Kitchen Renovation Case involves the substantive law of contract. The Liquor Licence Case involves the substantive law of liquor licensing regulation. The Landlord and Tenant Dispute involves the substantive law of residential tenancies.

Procedural law, both criminal and civil, deals with the way in which a dispute first comes to a court or tribunal, and is then brought forward to a final resolution at a trial or hearing. Procedural law is for the most part concerned with what occurs before the actual trial or hearing, and afterward. The procedure in the Kitchen Renovation Case is governed by the procedural law of the Ontario Small Claims Court. The procedure in the Liquor Licence Case is governed by the procedural law of the Ontario Court of Justice (Provincial Offences Court). The procedure in the Landlord and Tenant Dispute is governed by the procedural law of the Landlord and Tenant Board.

Table 1.1 lists these distinctions for each of the three fact situations.

TABLE 1.1   Substantive Law and Procedural Law Aspects of Three Fact Situations

Fact Situation	Substantive Law	Procedural Law Venue
1. The Kitchen Renovation Case	Contract law	Ontario Small Claims Court
2. The Liquor Licence Case	Liquor licensing regulation	Ontario Court of Justice (Provincial Offences Court)
3. The Landlord and Tenant Dispute	Residential tenancy	Landlord and Tenant Board

You will not be successful in asserting your claim or defence when you get to the trial or hearing unless you can establish the facts that support your client's claim or defence. The **law of evidence** deals with how the facts, as required by substantive law, are to be proved.

---

substantive law: the law that defines legal rights and obligations

procedural law: the law that deals with the way a dispute comes to a court or tribunal and then continues to its final resolution

law of evidence: the law that determines the way in which the facts are to be proved, as required by substantive law

Advocacy has been described as both a science and an art. The key to successful advocacy is preparation, which is the science of advocacy. The art of advocacy lies in the performance. Some people are naturally better than others at public speaking, but this art can be developed. However, no amount of art can take the place of thorough preparation. If you go to the court or tribunal prepared and organized, and are courteous, you will be way ahead of most paralegals (and perhaps some lawyers) you will meet in opposition.

Good advocacy does not mean that you will win every trial or hearing. There are some cases that you cannot win, no matter how good an advocate you are. But you never want to lose a case that you *should* win. That is where good advocacy comes into the picture.

This book is not about evidence or about civil, criminal, or tribunal procedure. It assumes that you already have a basic understanding of those areas and an understanding of substantive law. This book will teach you the skills necessary to become a good advocate. It starts with a discussion of the paralegal as advocate, including an overview of the relevant *Paralegal Rules of Conduct* and *Paralegal Professional Conduct Guidelines* of the Law Society of Upper Canada. Then, after an overview of the litigation process, it takes you through the steps necessary to prepare and present a case at a trial or hearing, including an examination of the ethical issues that may arise.

Because this book is written for paralegals, it deals with advocacy before the courts and tribunals in which paralegals may lawfully appear. Trials can involve civil or criminal or provincial offence matters, and hearings can also take place before administrative tribunals. The advocacy skills involved in all of these trials and hearings are the same.

KEY TERMS

advocacy, 6
advocate, 6
law of evidence, 7
procedural law, 7
substantive law, 7

REVIEW QUESTIONS

1. What is advocacy?

2. What is an advocate?

3. What is substantive law?

4. What is procedural law?

5. What is the law of evidence?

6. What is the key to successful advocacy?

CHAPTER 2

The Paralegal as Advocate

Paralegals who appear as advocates before a court or tribunal in Ontario must be licensed by the **Law Society of Upper Canada** (LSUC) by successfully completing its licensing requirements. Once licensed, paralegals are regulated by the LSUC and must abide by its by-laws[1] and the *Paralegal Rules of Conduct* (the Rules),[2] which set out a paralegal's professional and ethical obligations. Paralegals who appear as advocates before a court or a tribunal have an important impact on the administration of justice and are therefore subject to increased scrutiny and responsibility when appearing on behalf of clients. As advocates, paralegals owe duties to their clients, the courts, tribunals, other licensees, court staff, and the Law Society of Upper Canada.

This chapter provides an overview of the paralegal licensing process, the permitted scope of paralegal practice, and the *Paralegal Rules of Conduct* that apply to advocacy-related matters.

Paralegal Licensing

Since 2007, the Law Society of Upper Canada has been responsible for the regulation of all paralegals in Ontario. The LSUC is authorized to educate and license Ontario's paralegals and to regulate their conduct. In order to qualify for admission as a licensed paralegal, an applicant must graduate from a LSUC-accredited paralegal education program, successfully pass the Paralegal Licensing Examination, and be of good character as determined by the LSUC. The licensing application form includes questions relating to the applicant's character. If an applicant's answers raise questions as to the applicant's character, the LSUC will conduct an investigation, and the matter may be referred to the LSUC's Hearing Panel for a hearing.

Law Society of Upper Canada: a self-governing body created by statute that educates, licenses, regulates, and disciplines paralegals and lawyers in Ontario in accordance with the *Law Society Act*,[3] its regulations, by-laws, and rules

Permitted Scope of Paralegal Practice

The **permitted scope of practice for licensed paralegals** is limited to the representation of clients before certain courts and tribunals as advocates. By-Law 4, section 6(2) authorizes licensed paralegals to represent parties before the Ontario Small Claims Court, the Ontario Court of Justice for proceedings under the *Provincial Offences Act* and for summary offences under the federal *Criminal Code*, and various administrative tribunals established by provincial or federal legislation, such as the Human Rights Tribunal and the Landlord and Tenant Board. Licensed paralegals are also eligible to represent clients in limited areas of immigration and refugee law, including hearings before the Immigration and Refugee Board.

Paralegals are not authorized to appear in the Ontario Superior Court of Justice (other than the Small Claims Court), nor are they authorized to appear on behalf of a client in any family law proceeding, including a proceeding in the Ontario Court of Justice.

The LSUC has signalled its commitment to study the expansion of the paralegal scope of practice over the coming years as part of its commitment to provide increased access to justice.[4] In 2016, the Ministry of the Attorney General and the Law Society of Upper Canada appointed the Honourable Justice Annemarie E. Bonkalo to lead a review into whether paralegals and other non-lawyer legal service providers should be permitted to handle certain family law matters.

Paralegal Advocacy Rules and Guidelines

Licensed paralegals are required to abide by the LSUC's ***Paralegal Rules of Conduct***. The Rules set out a paralegal's professional and ethical obligations and include rules that provide specifically for advocacy-related matters. Rule 2 sets out a paralegal's duties of professionalism, including integrity and civility, while Rule 4 sets out a paralegal's duties toward clients, courts, tribunals, other licensees, and the administration of justice. The LSUC has also created ***Paralegal Professional Conduct Guidelines***[5] to assist paralegals in interpreting and applying the Rules.

What follows is an overview of some of the provisions of Rule 2 and Rule 4. Specific provisions of the rules will be discussed in more detail throughout this text as we discuss the steps in the proceedings to which they apply. Appendixes A and B contain the Rules and Guidelines that are relevant to advocacy-related matters.

---

permitted scope of practice for licensed paralegals: areas of law in which licensed paralegals may represent clients as set by the Law Society of Upper Canada in its by-laws and rules

Paralegal Rules of Conduct: set of rules created by the Law Society of Upper Canada that establish ethical and professional standards of conduct for licensed paralegals in Ontario

Paralegal Professional Conduct Guidelines: Guidelines created by the Law Society of Upper Canada to assist paralegals with the interpretation of their professional obligations under the *Paralegal Rules of Conduct*

The Duty of Civility (Rule 2)

Licensed paralegals are officers of the court and, as such, owe important duties to the courts and tribunals before which they appear, to other paralegals and to lawyers. One of those duties is the duty of civility. Rule 2.01(3) of the Rules explicitly sets out a paralegal's mandatory obligations to be courteous, civil, and act in good faith with anyone he or she deals with. As set out in Guideline 1, that duty extends to the judge or adjudicator, court clerk and staff, other paralegals and lawyers, and clients and other parties including self-represented litigants. Paralegals are expected to conduct themselves with the highest standards of professionalism and civility in accordance with the Rules. Failure to do so can result in disciplinary action by the LSUC.

Civility refers to the manner in which a paralegal conducts himself or herself during the course of his or her practice, including conduct before a court or a tribunal. Civility demands that a paralegal communicate politely and respectfully with the court, opposing advocates and all persons he or she comes into contact with in the course of practice. A paralegal's general duty of civility is further elaborated in Rule 7: Duty to Licensees and Others and specifically Rule 7.01: Courtesy and Good Faith. Rule 7.01 details specific types of behaviour that a paralegal is prohibited from engaging in.

Examples of incivility include the following behaviours:

- Making personal attacks on an opposing advocate
- Making uninformed criticism of the competence, conduct, or advice of another advocate
- Lying to an opposing advocate and the court
- Failing to consult with an opposing advocate regarding the scheduling of dates
- Refusing to agree to reasonable requests from an opposing advocate, such as reasonable requests for time extensions and adjournments
- Using offensive, rude, or profane language
- Making faces, rolling eyes, tapping fingers or shoes, or engaging in other distracting behaviour during a hearing or a trial

There is nothing to be gained by engaging in rude and demeaning conduct. A paralegal can be a zealous advocate for his or her client without resorting to rude and disrespectful behaviour. While a paralegal is not required to help his or her adversary, neither should he or she take advantage of an adversary by attempting to wear him or her down using offensive and derogatory language or making unfounded allegations. This kind of behaviour adversely affects the administration of justice because it takes the adjudicator's attention away from resolving the legal issues. It also causes delay in the legal proceeding by distracting the advocates who may become embroiled in a war of words and animosity, thereby leading to a breakdown in communication. Finally, incivility in the courtroom can decrease the public's confidence in the justice system. (See Guideline 17.)

If a paralegal encounters rude and disrespectful conduct by another advocate in the courtroom, he or she should not engage. Rather, civility requires that the paralegal demonstrate patience and respect even when dealing with rude and disrespectful behaviour from another advocate.

The Duties of a Paralegal in the Role of Advocate (Rule 4)

Rule 4 of the *Paralegal Rules of Conduct* and Guideline 12 provide specifically for advocacy-related matters, including the paralegal's duties toward clients, tribunals, other licensees, and the administration of justice while acting as an advocate. Special duties also arise with respect to witnesses and unrepresented persons and in the context of negotiating a guilty plea on behalf of a client in a quasi-criminal or criminal matter.

Duty to Clients, Tribunals, and Others

When acting as an advocate, a paralegal is expected to act in a way that favours his or her client rather than the opposing party. A paralegal has no obligation to assist the opposing party. The Rules are clear that paralegals have a duty to represent their clients fearlessly. For example, Rule 4.01(4)(a) requires a paralegal to raise every issue, put forward every argument, and ask every question that the paralegal thinks will help the client's case, however distasteful that issue, argument, or question may be.

However, in representing his or her client fearlessly, a paralegal cannot behave in any manner that he or she wishes. The paralegal also has a duty to represent the client *within the limits of the law*. In other words, a paralegal cannot break the law or violate the Rules while advocating on behalf of his or her client (Rule 4.01(1); Guideline 12).

In addition to the paralegal's duties to his or her client, Rule 4.01 sets out his or her duties to the tribunal, the tribunal process, and other paralegals and lawyers. Under this rule, a paralegal is required to treat the tribunal and other licensees with "candour, fairness, courtesy, and respect" at all appearances and proceedings before all tribunals in which the paralegal may appear. "Tribunal" is defined in the Rules to include "courts, boards, arbitrators, mediators, administrative agencies, and bodies that resolve disputes, regardless of their function or the informality of their procedures" (Rule 1.02). A paralegal therefore should never assume that a different standard of behaviour applies to appearances before administrative tribunals, boards, and agencies. All bodies that resolve disputes, including administrative boards and agencies, should be treated with the same respect as a court.

The following behaviours may constitute failure to treat the tribunal with candour, fairness, courtesy, and respect:

- Repeatedly failing to attend mandatory court appearances
- Habitually arriving late to mandatory court appearances
- Engaging in disruptive behaviour in the courtroom

- Failing to stand when addressing the court
- Relying on evidence that is inflammatory or unreliable
- Arguing with the judge or adjudicator after a ruling has been made

In addition to duties to the tribunal itself, a paralegal appearing as an advocate also has duties to the tribunal process and the administration of justice. Rule 4.01(5) explicitly prohibits certain types of behaviours when appearing before a tribunal, including the following:

- Abusing the tribunal process by instituting or prosecuting proceedings that, although legal in themselves, are clearly motivated by malice on the part of the client and are brought solely for the purpose of injuring the other party
- Knowingly assisting or permitting the client to do anything that the paralegal considers to be dishonest or dishonourable
- Knowingly attempting to deceive a tribunal or influence the course of justice by offering false evidence, misstating facts or law, presenting or relying upon a false or deceptive affidavit, suppressing what ought to be disclosed, or otherwise assisting in any deception, crime, or illegal conduct
- Deliberately refraining from informing the tribunal of any binding authority that the paralegal considers to be directly on point and that has not been mentioned by an opponent
- Appearing before a judicial officer when the paralegal, a partner of the paralegal, a paralegal employed by the paralegal firm, or the client has a business or personal relationship with the officer that gives rise to, or might reasonably appear to give rise to, pressure, influence, or inducement affecting the impartiality of the officer
- Knowingly asserting as true a fact when its truth cannot reasonably be supported by the evidence or as a matter of which notice may be taken by the tribunal
- Endeavouring or allowing anyone else to endeavour, directly or indirectly, to influence the decision or action of the tribunal or any of its officials in any case or matter by any means other than open persuasion as an advocate
- Knowingly misstating the contents of a document, the testimony of a witness, the substance of an argument, or the provisions of a statute or like authority
- Knowingly permitting a witness or party to be presented in a false or misleading way or to impersonate another
- Needlessly abusing, hectoring, harassing, or inconveniencing a witness
- Dissuading a witness from giving evidence or suggesting that a witness be absent
- When representing a complainant or potential complainant, attempting to gain a benefit for the complainant by threatening the laying of a criminal charge or by offering to seek or to procure the withdrawal of a criminal charge

- Appearing before a court or tribunal while under the influence of alcohol or a drug

Disclosure, Witnesses, and Guilty Pleas

Under Rule 4, a paralegal appearing as an advocate in a proceeding also has duties with respect to the disclosure of information and documents to the opposing party, the interviewing of witnesses, the communication with witnesses giving testimony, and the entering of a guilty plea in a quasi-criminal or criminal matter.

A paralegal representing a client in a court or tribunal proceeding has a duty to comply with the rules of that court/tribunal that require one or both sides to provide information or documents to the other side. The paralegal's duties with respect to the disclosure of documents are discussed more fully in Chapter 7.

A paralegal can contact and interview all possible witnesses for both sides of a proceeding, subject to the rules regarding communications with represented persons, in order to prepare a theory of a case, to advise his or her client regarding possible and likely outcomes and settlement options, and, if necessary, to prepare for a hearing or trial. A paralegal's professional obligations with respect to interviewing and communicating with witnesses are discussed more fully in Chapter 7.

As set out in Rule 4.03, once a matter reaches a hearing or a trial, a paralegal's ability to speak with a witness giving testimony is very limited. The purpose of these limitations is to ensure that a witness's testimony is not influenced in a manner that would mislead the tribunal. Whether a paralegal can speak to a particular witness during the trial or hearing depends on two factors: (1) the stage of the witness's testimony and (2) whether or not the witness is providing evidence that supports the paralegal's case. Where the rules prohibit a paralegal from communicating with a witness giving evidence, the paralegal must not do so unless the opposing licensee consents or the judge, justice of the peace, or adjudicator allows it. A paralegal's duties under Rule 4.03 will be further examined throughout Chapters 11, 12, and 13.

Finally, a paralegal representing a client in a criminal or quasi-criminal proceeding has special duties before entering into an agreement about a **guilty plea** on behalf of his or her client. A paralegal cannot simply do what a client says with respect to negotiating a guilty plea. The paralegal is required under the rules to take steps to ensure that the client is informed about the consequences and implications of a guilty plea and that the necessary admissions required for the offence charged are voluntary. Before entering into an agreement with a prosecutor about a guilty plea, Rule 4.01(9) requires the paralegal to

1. advise the client about the prospects for an acquittal or finding of guilt;
2. advise the client of the implications and possible consequences of a guilty plea and particularly of the sentencing authority and discretion of the court, including the fact that the court is not bound by any agreement about a guilty plea;

guilty plea: a voluntary admission, by a defendant in a criminal or quasi-criminal case, of the essential factual and mental elements of an offence, thereby giving up the right to a trial

3. be satisfied that the client is prepared voluntarily to admit the necessary factual and mental elements of the offence charged; and

4. be satisfied that the client has voluntarily instructed the paralegal to enter into an agreement as to a guilty plea.

The Paralegal as Witness

A paralegal who appears as an advocate before a court or tribunal should avoid making statements about his or her personal opinions or beliefs. This includes stating facts that have not been presented in evidence (either by way of affidavit or oral testimony) in the proceeding. Facts relied upon in a legal proceeding should be subject to legal proof by way of cross-examination.

In addition, according to Rule 4.04, a paralegal who appears as an advocate in a proceeding before a tribunal must not testify or submit his or her own affidavit evidence before the tribunal except where

1. the paralegal is permitted by law to do so;
2. the paralegal is permitted by the tribunal to do so;
3. the paralegal is permitted to do so by the rules of procedure of the court or tribunal before which the paralegal appears; or
4. the matter on which the paralegal appears is purely formal or uncontested.

It is considered unacceptable practice for a paralegal to submit his or her own affidavit to a tribunal in a contentious or contested matter because it requires the paralegal to undertake two different roles in the same proceeding—that of an advocate and that of a witness who may be subject to cross-examination (see Guideline 12). A paralegal should strive to obtain evidence from a witness with direct and actual knowledge of the facts being relied upon, usually the client, who will have first-hand knowledge of the events that have led up to the particular proceeding.

Dealing with Unrepresented and Represented Persons

As an advocate, a paralegal will likely deal on a client's behalf with a party who does not have legal representation. For example, an opposing party in a Small Claims Court proceeding may not be represented by a paralegal or a lawyer. In such a case, the paralegal will have to deal directly with the unrepresented opposing party regarding all matters relating to the proceeding, including the scheduling of dates and engaging in settlement negotiations. A paralegal who represents a client in a matter has special duties toward **unrepresented persons**. Rule 4.05 requires a paralegal to do the following when dealing with an unrepresented person:

1. Take care to see that the unrepresented person is not proceeding under the impression that his or her interests will be protected by the paralegal.

---

unrepresented persons: individuals involved in a legal proceeding without legal representation by a lawyer or paralegal

2. Make clear to the unrepresented person that the paralegal is acting exclusively in the interests of the client and, accordingly, the paralegal's comments may be partisan.

If the opposite party does have legal representation, Rule 7.02 requires the paralegal to deal with the legal representative and not to approach or communicate or deal with the party directly on the matter (unless the legal representative consents).

NOTES

1   Law Society of Upper Canada, "By-Laws," online: <http://www.lsuc.on.ca/by-laws>.

2   Law Society of Upper Canada, *Paralegal Rules of Conduct* (Toronto: LSUC, 2007), online: <http://www.lsuc.on.ca/paralegal-conduct-rules>.

3   *Law Society Act*, RSO 1990, c L.8.

4   Law Society of Upper Canada Priority Planning Committee, "Report to Convocation" (4 December 2015).

5   Law Society of Upper Canada, *Paralegal Professional Conduct Guidelines* (Toronto: LSUC, 2008), online: <http://www.lsuc.on.ca/paralegal-conduct-guidelines>.

KEY TERMS

guilty plea, 17
Law Society of Upper Canada, 12
Paralegal Professional Conduct Guidelines, 13
Paralegal Rules of Conduct, 13
permitted scope of practice for licensed paralegals, 13
unrepresented persons, 18

REVIEW QUESTIONS

1. What must an applicant for a paralegal licence do in order to qualify for admission to the Law Society of Upper Canada as a licensed paralegal?

2. What is the permitted scope of practice for licensed paralegals?

DISCUSSION QUESTIONS

1. Licensed paralegal Harry Hothman is appearing before the Landlord and Tenant Board on behalf of a tenant. The adjudicator renders her decision against Harry's client. Harry slams his hand down on the table, shouts, "What a load of garbage!" and storms out of the hearing room. What has Harry done wrong? Explain your answer with reference to the *Paralegal Rules of Conduct*.

2. Licensed paralegal Saher Henry represents the defendant, Lionel Lee, in Small Claims Court. The trial was held recently, and a judgment was made by Deputy Judge LaSalle in favour of the plaintiff. Saher now brings a motion for a new trial following the judgment on the basis that the plaintiff failed to produce a certain document and that the defendant could not have discovered this new document prior to the trial. The plaintiff opposes the motion. Saher prepares an affidavit in her own name that attests to Lionel's discovery of the document after trial and the circumstances surrounding Lionel's discovery, as told to her by Lionel. The affidavit is commissioned by Saher's associate and is served on the plaintiff and then filed

with the court. Saher appears before the court to argue the motion, and she relies upon her own affidavit in support of the motion.

   a. What, if anything, has Saher done wrong? Explain your answer with reference to the *Paralegal Rules of Conduct*.

   b. If Saher has done something wrong, what could she have done in order to avoid it?

3. Licensed paralegal Wilma Henderson is appearing before the Ontario Court of Justice on behalf of her client who has been charged with an offence under the *Highway Traffic Act*. The client authorized Wilma to resolve the case for him, in his absence, at the trial. It is the morning of the trial and Wilma arrives at the Ontario Court of Justice. She checks in with the prosecutor to advise that she is ready to proceed with the trial. The prosecutor and Wilma enter into a plea negotiation in an attempt to resolve the case without a trial. The proposed plea deal would involve Wilma's client pleading guilty to a different offence under the *Highway Traffic Act*. Wilma accepts the deal on behalf of her client without consulting with him.

   a. What, if anything, has Wilma done wrong? Explain your answer with reference to the *Paralegal Rules of Conduct*.

   b. If Wilma has done something wrong, what should she have done in this situation?

4. Licensed paralegal Lynette Vu is representing her client, a landlord, at the Landlord and Tenant Board. There is a hearing scheduled for today; however, Lynette realizes she double-booked herself and decides instead to speak at a conference in downtown Toronto. Lynette calls the Landlord and Tenant Board to advise the board that she is stuck in traffic and unable to arrive on time for the hearing. The hearing is adjourned for two weeks. On the morning of the hearing two weeks later, Lynette realizes she has client meetings booked all day. She calls the Landlord and Tenant Board to advise that she is out of the country and will not be returning until tomorrow. What, if anything, has Lynette done wrong? Explain your answer with reference to the *Paralegal Rules of Conduct*.

PART II

Overview of the Litigation Process

CHAPTER 3

Steps in the Litigation Process

The focus of this book is advocacy at a trial or hearing, but the foundation for good advocacy starts at the earliest stages of the dispute. It is therefore necessary to understand the steps that take place in the litigation process, both before and during the actual trial or hearing.

This chapter provides an overview of the pre-trial procedures of the Ontario Small Claims Court, the Provincial Offences Court, and one administrative tribunal—the Landlord and Tenant Board.

The Civil Litigation Process: Small Claims Court

Paralegals may appear on civil trials before the Ontario Small Claims Court. The Small Claims Court handles civil disputes involving money or personal property to a maximum of $25,000. The forms and procedures of the Small Claims Court are simplified to allow parties to represent themselves, but parties often choose to retain a paralegal or lawyer, especially for more complicated disputes.

The parties to a Small Claims Court action are the **plaintiff** and the **defendant**. A Small Claims Court action is started when the plaintiff prepares and files a **claim** with the court (in person, by mail, or online), setting out the nature of the plaintiff's case against the defendant, together with any documents that support the claim, such as an invoice, a contract, or a letter. The plaintiff pays a filing fee to the court, and the court issues the plaintiff's claim by assigning a court file number and stamping the original claim form. The plaintiff must then **serve** the defendant with the

---

plaintiff: person who brings a civil action against another

defendant: person against whom relief is sought in an action

claim: a document in prescribed form setting out the facts that the plaintiff intends to rely on to prove his or her case

serve: provide a copy of a party's court or tribunal documents to the opposite party

claim and supporting documents by providing him or her with a copy. A defendant who wishes to dispute the plaintiff's claim has 20 days in which to serve the plaintiff with a **defence**, setting out the nature of the defendant's defence against the plaintiff's claim, together with any documents that support the defence, and file it with the court. The plaintiff's claim and the defence documents are referred to as the **pleadings** in the case. Pleadings are court documents that set out the facts on which each party relies in support of the claim or defence, and are designed to provide the opposing side with notice of the claim or defence.

In some cases, a party may make a **motion** to ask the court to make an order to resolve an issue in the case or get directions on how to proceed in the case. For example, a defendant may bring a motion to strike out the plaintiff's claim because it discloses no reasonable cause of action. Likewise, a plaintiff may bring a motion to strike out a defendant's defence on the basis that it discloses no reasonable defence.

A **settlement conference** is held in every defended action in the Small Claims Court before a judge (who will not be the judge at trial), a referee, or another court-appointed person. The settlement conference, which is scheduled by the court, is an informal and confidential meeting during which the parties try to resolve or simplify the issues that are in dispute. As stated in Rule 13.03(1) of the *Rules of the Small Claims Court*, the purposes of a settlement conference are

- to resolve or narrow the issues in the action,
- to expedite the disposition of the action,
- to encourage settlement of the action,
- to assist the parties in effective preparation for trial, and
- to provide full disclosure between the parties of the relevant facts and evidence.

At the conference, the parties are required to disclose all the important facts and evidence about the case, and must therefore bring all relevant documents that relate to the case, such as receipts, estimates, contracts, letters, and photographs. At the conference, the judge or referee will comment on the strengths and weaknesses of each party's case and encourage the parties to consider settling all or some of the issues. The parties must attend the settlement conference, but the witnesses do not attend. If either of the parties is represented by a lawyer or agent, the lawyer or agent may also attend, but the parties must still be there.

---

defence: a document in prescribed form setting out the facts that the defendant intends to rely on to prove his or her defence

pleadings: court documents setting out the nature of the plaintiff's and defendant's cases

motion: an interim step in a proceeding in which a party makes a request to the court for an order or directions

settlement conference: informal and confidential meeting during which the parties try to resolve or simplify issues in dispute

If the claim is for under $2,500, both parties can file a consent before the conference starts, stating that they wish the judge to make a final judgment at the conference if the parties do not arrive at a settlement. In all other cases, if the parties cannot resolve the dispute at the settlement conference, they should request that the court set a date for trial.

The parties can continue to discuss the possibility of settlement after the settlement conference, right up to the trial. In addition, either party can serve an **offer to settle**, a formal written offer, on the other party at any time until the judge disposes of the case at trial. If the matter is not settled by the date set for trial, the trial will proceed.

The Provincial Offence Litigation Process: Provincial Offences Court

The Provincial Offences Court deals with charges under the *Provincial Offences Act*. **Provincial offences** are non-criminal offences arising under provincial statutes, such as the *Highway Traffic Act*. The most common of these are driving-related offences, such as speeding, careless driving, driving without insurance, driving while suspended, and failing to stop at a red light. Provincial Offences Court is relatively informal, and some defendants represent themselves. However, the penalties for traffic offences can include fines, demerit points, and licence suspension. In addition, a conviction can result in higher insurance premiums. For these reasons, many people choose to retain a lawyer or a paralegal to represent them.

The parties in a provincial offence matter are Her Majesty the Queen (or the Crown) and the defendant. The provincial offence process (for an offence under part I of the *Provincial Offences Act*) starts with the issuance of an **offence notice** or **summons**, depending on the nature of the offence. A defendant who wishes to dispute the charge must schedule a trial. In some municipalities this can be done by mail; in others, it is necessary to file a **notice of intention to appear** form with the appropriate provincial offences office. In certain cases, the defendant is given the option of requesting a meeting with a prosecutor to discuss the possible resolution of the charge.

---

offer to settle: formal written offer made by one party to another, outlining the terms by which the party making the offer agrees to settle an issue or all issues in the proceeding

provincial offences: non-criminal offences arising under provincial statutes

offence notice: document that starts some types of provincial offence processes

summons: document that initiates some types of provincial offence processes

notice of intention to appear: form to be filed by the defendant with the provincial offences office notifying the court of the defendant's intention to dispute the charge

The defendant is entitled to receive, free of charge, disclosure of all the information in the Crown's possession or control that is relevant to the charge. The defendant requests disclosure by mail or fax to the Crown prosecutor handling the matter. The prosecutor should provide all relevant information, such as documents relied on, witness statements, and police officers' notes. It is possible to request additional disclosure from the prosecutor if important details that are essential for the preparation of the defence are missing from the initial disclosure.

In some cases, the defendant may make a motion for certain relief, for example, to quash the information for a defect apparent on its face, or to change the location of the hearing.

Administrative Tribunal Process: The Landlord and Tenant Board

An **administrative tribunal** is a quasi-judicial body created by statute law to deal with matters arising under specific statutes. For example, the Landlord and Tenant Board is created by the *Residential Tenancies Act, 2006* to administer the statute and to deal with disputes between residential landlords and tenants. Other administrative tribunals in Ontario are the Social Benefits Tribunal, the Financial Services Commission, the Assessment Review Board, and the Ontario Municipal Board. We use the Landlord and Tenant Board to illustrate the pre-hearing and hearing process before an administrative tribunal.

At the Landlord and Tenant Board ("the board"), either the landlord or the tenant may make an application to the board, and a hearing will be scheduled before a board member. In a proceeding before the board, the party who files the application is called the **applicant** and the other party is called the **respondent**.

The applicant files an **application** with the board. The board will issue a **notice of hearing**, which must be served on the respondent together with the application. A respondent who wishes to defend an application may simply appear at the hearing and does not have to serve and file any form of dispute. Landlord and Tenant Board mediators are available at most hearing locations. If both parties are willing, a mediator will meet with the parties to discuss the possibility of settlement.

---

administrative tribunal: quasi-judicial body dealing with matters under a specific statute

applicant: party who files an application with a tribunal

respondent: party against whom an applicant files an application with a tribunal

application: document filed by an applicant that starts a proceeding at a tribunal

notice of hearing: tribunal document served on a respondent along with an application

KEY TERMS

REVIEW QUESTIONS

1. What is the monetary jurisdiction of the Ontario Small Claims Court?

2. Who are the parties to a Small Claims Court action?

3. How is a Small Claims Court action started?

4. What must a defendant do to dispute the plaintiff's claim?

5. What are pleadings?

6. What is a Small Claims Court settlement conference, and what is its purpose?

7. What matters are dealt with by the Provincial Offences Court?

8. What are provincial offences? Provide some examples.

9. Who are the parties in a provincial offence matter?

10. How is the provincial offence process started for an offence under part I of the *Provincial Offences Act*?

11. What must a defendant do if he or she wishes to dispute a charge under the *Provincial Offences Act*?

12. How does a defendant request disclosure of the evidence on which the Crown will be relying at trial?

13. What is an administrative tribunal?

14. Provide some examples of administrative tribunals.

15. Who are the parties to a proceeding before the Landlord and Tenant Board?

16. Briefly describe the process by which a matter is brought before the Landlord and Tenant Board.

The Courtroom Experience

LEARNING OUTCOMES

After reading this chapter, you should be able to summarize

- the general structure of a trial or hearing
- the in-court procedure of the Small Claims Court
- the in-court procedure of the Provincial Offences Court
- the in-hearing procedure of the Landlord and Tenant Board

The trial or hearing is the last step in the litigation process. Appearing at a trial or hearing can be a daunting prospect for a new and inexperienced advocate. Even an experienced advocate may feel intimidated when appearing before a particular court or tribunal for the first time. It is very helpful to gain some familiarity with the courtroom procedure at the court or tribunal before your first appearance there. The best way to gain that familiarity is to go to the court or tribunal and observe.

This chapter discusses the structure of trials generally, and then focuses on the in-court procedure of Ontario's Small Claims Court, Provincial Offences Court, and Landlord and Tenant Board (as an example of an administrative tribunal).

The Structure of a Trial or Hearing

A trial or hearing has three parts:

1. opening
2. evidence
3. closing.

At the opening of the trial or hearing, each party may be asked by the judge or other decision-maker to summarize the case and the issues that are in dispute.

The parties will then present evidence so that the decision-maker—a judge, justice of the peace, or other adjudicator—can determine the facts of the case; in other words, decide what actually happened between the parties. Evidence is presented by witnesses—the parties to the case and others with direct knowledge relevant to the case.

After all the evidence has been presented to the court, both parties will have the opportunity to make a closing argument in which they summarize the evidence that supports their case, the relevant law, and the reasons the decision-maker should resolve the dispute in that party's favour.

Small Claims Court

As stated in Chapter 3, the Small Claims Court handles civil disputes involving money or personal property up to a maximum of $25,000. Matters are dealt with by a judge, who is addressed as "Your Honour."

Arriving at Court

Small Claims Court trials usually start at 10:00 a.m. In many Small Claims Courts a motions court precedes the trial list, commencing at 9:30 a.m. An Event Activity Report is posted on a bulletin board just outside the courtrooms. This report lists all matters scheduled for the day and sets out the courtrooms in which each matter will take place. Better still, before you go to court, you can check your courtroom and time of trial at <http://www.ontariocourtdates.ca>. If you arrive early and the courtroom is locked, sit in the waiting area until the clerk announces that the courtroom is open.

As you enter the courtroom, the elevated judge's bench is usually directly ahead of you at the front of the courtroom. The court clerk sits at a table in front of the judge's desk facing the courtroom. Usually, the witness box is to the judge's left (on your right as you face the judge). There are also two counsel tables, one on each side, facing the judge. Usually, the table on the right as you face the judge is for the plaintiff, and the one on the left is for the defendant. (See Figure 4.1.)

FIGURE 4.1   **Standard Small Claims Court Courtroom Layout**

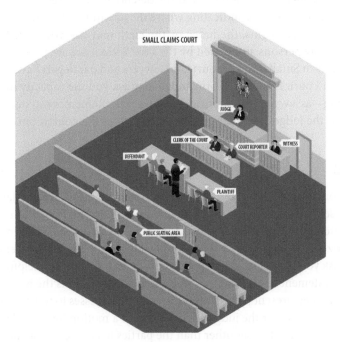

Source: Fairbridges Wertheim Becker—Attorneys, "What Is the Small Claims Court?", online: <http://www.fwb attorneys.co.za/what-is-the-small-claims-court/>.

After you enter the courtroom, go up to the clerk. The clerk will ask you to identify yourself and the case on which you are appearing, how many witnesses you intend to call during the trial, and the estimated length of time your case will take. After speaking to the clerk you should sit in the gallery, the seating area at the back of the courtroom, until your case is called. If court is already in session when you arrive, enter the courtroom quietly and sit down in the gallery. If there is a break in the proceedings, you can identify yourself and your case to the clerk. Otherwise, wait until your case is called.

At 10:00, the clerk will leave the courtroom to go and get the judge. The clerk will return and tell everyone to stand up, and the judge will enter the courtroom. The judge sits and will tell everyone to be seated. The judge will then go through the list of scheduled matters to determine who is present for each matter. Judges typically deal with consent matters, adjournments, and assessments or damages before dealing with trials. If a party to a case is not in the courtroom, the judge may hold the matter down for half an hour, after which time the judge will proceed with the trial in the party's absence.

Under Rule 3.02(11) of the *Paralegal Rules of Conduct*, a paralegal has a duty to advise and encourage a client to compromise or settle a dispute whenever possible. So, while you are waiting for your case to be called, and subject to your client's instructions, you should talk to the party on the other side about the possibilities of settlement. Most Small Claims Courts have a mediation room that the parties may use to talk.

When your case is called, walk to the counsel table at the front of the courtroom. As stated previously, the plaintiff's counsel table is usually on the right side of the courtroom (when facing the judge), and the defendant's counsel table is on the left. The tables usually have signs indicating where the plaintiff and the defendant should sit. Before your case begins, the judge or the clerk may ask you to state and spell your name. Only persons authorized by the *Law Society Act* are permitted to act as representatives in Small Claims Court, and lawyers and paralegals have equal standing before the court. Nonetheless, the judge may ask you the capacity in which you are appearing—as lawyer, paralegal, or student-at-law. Remember to stand whenever you speak to the judge and whenever the judge leaves the courtroom.

The Trial

Although formal opening statements are not mandatory in Small Claims Court, many representatives choose to make an opening statement. If you do not make an opening statement and the judge is unclear about the issues, he or she may ask you to summarize what your case is about and to identify the issues. For example, the judge may ask you, "What exactly is your claim/defence?" It is very helpful to prepare an opening statement so that you can respond to any questions the judge may have.

The parties then present their evidence by calling witnesses to testify as to the facts of the case. Either side or the judge will likely make a motion for an order excluding from the courtroom witnesses other than the parties to ensure that witnesses are not influenced by hearing the testimony of other witnesses before they testify. The clerk records the testimony of each witness. The plaintiff's representative presents the plaintiff's evidence first. The judge asks the representative to call the plaintiff's first witness, and the witness proceeds to the witness box. The clerk will ask the witness to state his or her name and spell it for the record. The clerk will then ask the witness to indicate a preference for either swearing on a holy book or solemnly affirming, and will ask, "Do you solemnly promise to tell the truth in this proceeding?"

Once the witness is sworn in or affirmed, the plaintiff's representative conducts a **direct examination** of the witness by asking questions of that witness. The defendant's representative then conducts a **cross-examination** of the witness. At the end of the cross-examination, the plaintiff's advocate is given an opportunity to conduct a **re-examination** of the witness, limited to questions about new issues raised in the cross-examination. The judge may then have some questions for the witness. At the end of the questioning, the witness is excused and may be seated in the courtroom. If the witness had been excluded from the courtroom prior to testifying, he or she may now stay in the courtroom and observe. This process is repeated for each of the plaintiff's witnesses.

At the end of the plaintiff's evidence, the defendant's advocate presents the defendant's evidence. Each of the defendant's witnesses is sworn in, after which the defendant's advocate conducts a direct examination, followed by cross-examination by the plaintiff's advocate, re-examination by the defendant's advocate, and possibly, questioning by the judge.

At the end of the defendant's evidence, the plaintiff's advocate is given the opportunity to present **reply evidence** to respond to new matters raised by the defendant during the case.

At the end of the evidence, the judge will usually ask both parties' advocates to make a **closing argument** summarizing their case and discussing the relevant law. The plaintiff's advocate gives his or her closing argument first, followed by the defendant's advocate. After the defendant's closing argument, the plaintiff is given an opportunity to reply.

Once the closing arguments are completed, it is up to the judge to make a decision and render judgment. The judge may deliver judgment immediately or after a brief recess. Occasionally, the judge will reserve decision until a later date. The judge will **endorse** the decision on the court record. The judge may then ask for submissions on costs. If there is a photocopier in the courtroom, the clerk will make a copy of the judge's endorsement and give it to the parties to take with them.

---

direct examination: questioning of a witness by the advocate of the party who called that witness

cross-examination: questioning of a witness by the advocate of the opposing party

re-examination: questioning of a witness by the advocate of the party who called the witness after the opposing advocate has cross-examined

reply evidence: plaintiff's opportunity to introduce new evidence to respond to new matters raised by the defendant

closing argument: summary of a party's case, including a discussion of the relevant law

endorse: make note of a decision

Provincial Offences Court

As stated in Chapter 3, the Provincial Offences Court deals with charges under the *Provincial Offences Act*. Matters are dealt with by a justice of the peace (JP), not a judge, who is addressed as "Your Worship."

Arriving at Court

When you arrive at the court, you will be required to go through security screening by court personnel. No weapons are permitted in court, including pocket or miniature knives.[1]

There are lists posted outside the courtrooms setting out the matters scheduled for the day. There are four "tiers"—9:00 a.m., 10:30 a.m., 1:30 p.m., and 3:00 p.m. The notice of trial will state the time of your trial and the courtroom number.

Approximately 15 minutes before court opens, there will be an announcement advising people who have a matter in the courtroom to enter. When you enter the courtroom, the elevated bench for the justice of the peace will usually be directly ahead of you at the front of the courtroom. The court clerk will sit at a table in front of the JP's desk, facing the courtroom. Usually, the witness box will be to the JP's left (on your right as you face the JP). There will also be two counsel tables, one on each side, facing the JP. The Crown (prosecutor) usually sits at the table on the right as you face the JP. The table on the left is usually for the defendant. (See Figure 4.2.)

FIGURE 4.2   Standard Provincial Offences Court Courtroom Layout

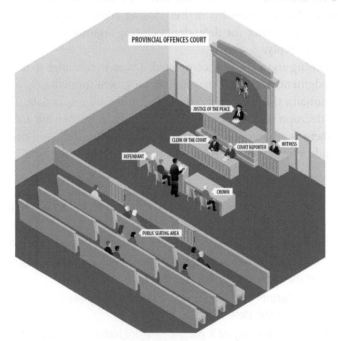

Source: Adapted from Fairbridges Wertheim Becker—Attorneys, "What Is the Small Claims Court?", online: <http://www.fwbattorneys.co.za/what-is-the-small-claims-court/>.

When you enter the courtroom, go up to the clerk, who will ask you to identify yourself and the case on which you are appearing. If you have not been able to meet with the prosecutor before, you may wish to speak to the Crown about your case to negotiate or **plea bargain**.[2] After speaking to the clerk and Crown, sit in the counsel section of the courtroom, if there is room, until your case is called. If there is no room, sit in the gallery, the seating area at the back of the courtroom. There is also a seating area outside the courtroom where you can wait. You will be paged when the court reaches your case.

Stand when the JP arrives in the courtroom. The JP will sit and tell everyone to be seated. The JP will deal with unopposed matters first, and then hear the trials.

The Trial

When your case is called, approach the counsel table and identify yourself. The JP may ask you the capacity in which you are appearing—as lawyer, paralegal, or student-at-law. The clerk will read the charge and ask how your client pleads. If your client pleads not guilty, the trial will begin.

The Crown presents its case first, by calling witnesses to give evidence. The clerk asks each witness to state and spell his or her full name and to either swear on the Bible or affirm that the evidence to be given will be the truth. Witnesses may sit while giving evidence. Once the witness is sworn in, the Crown conducts a direct examination by asking questions of that witness. The defendant's representative then conducts a cross-examination of the witness. At the end of the cross-examination, the Crown is given an opportunity to conduct a re-examination of the witness, limited to questions about new issues raised in the cross-examination. The JP may then have some questions for the witness. At the end of the questioning, the witness is excused and may be seated in the courtroom. This process is repeated for each of the Crown's witnesses.

At the end of the Crown's evidence, the defendant's representative presents the defendant's evidence, if any. Each of the defendant's witnesses is sworn in, after which the defendant's representative conducts a direct examination, followed by cross-examination by the Crown, re-examination by the defendant's advocate, and possibly, questioning by the JP.

After all the evidence has been given, the JP will ask both the defence and the prosecution to make closing arguments summarizing their cases and discussing the relevant law. The defendant's representative speaks first. After the closing arguments, the JP makes a decision to convict or acquit, and gives reasons for that decision.

A defendant who is acquitted is free to leave the court. If the defendant is convicted, the JP may ask for submissions regarding the appropriate sentence to be given.

---

plea bargain: negotiate a resolution to a criminal or provincial offence matter

Landlord and Tenant Board

As stated in Chapter 3, the Landlord and Tenant Board ("the board") deals with disputes between residential landlords and tenants. Matters are dealt with by a member of the board sitting as an adjudicator, who is addressed as either Mr. or Madam Adjudicator, Mr. or Madam Member, or Mr. or Ms. (last name).

Arriving at the Board

Your hearing will be scheduled for either the morning or the afternoon. Many hearings are scheduled for the same day and time, and everyone is required to arrive at the same time. The board member decides the order in which to hear cases. It is possible that your case may not be called until much later than the time listed on your notice of hearing.

When you arrive at the tribunal on the day of your hearing, sign in with the clerk. There is also a mediation sign-up sheet for parties who agree to meet with a Landlord and Tenant Board mediator. There may be an electronic screen setting out the hearings, hearing rooms, and times. If not, ask the clerk, and then proceed to the appropriate hearing room. The hearing room is less formal than a courtroom. The adjudicator sits at the front of the room, and there are two counsel tables in front of him or her. Usually, the applicant's advocate sits at the table on the right (when facing the adjudicator), and the respondent's advocate sits at the one on the left. There is no clerk. Witnesses sit to the adjudicator's left. (See Figure 4.3.) Sit in the body of the hearing room until your case is called.

FIGURE 4.3   **Standard Landlord and Tenant Board Hearing Room Layout**

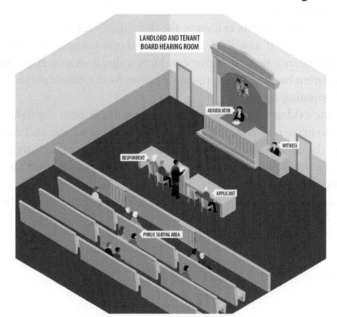

Source: Adapted from Fairbridges Wertheim Becker—Attorneys, "What Is the Small Claims Court?", online: <http://www.fwbattorneys.co.za/what-is-the-small-claims-court/>.

The adjudicator will introduce himself or herself and explain the hearing process. He or she will also discuss the mediation services available and encourage parties to attempt to resolve their dispute with the assistance of a staff mediator.

The adjudicator calls cases by referring to the names of the parties and the street address of the residential property. Short matters, such as consents, withdrawals, adjournments, and unopposed matters, are typically dealt with first. Matters that require a hearing are called next, usually in order of their position on the list. Sometimes, the adjudicator will ask the parties to estimate the expected length of time their case will take (depending on such matters as the complexity of issues and the number of witnesses). The adjudicator may then proceed to deal first with the matters that are expected to take the least amount of time, saving the longer cases for last.

The Hearing

When your case is called, move up to the appropriate counsel table. The adjudicator will ask both representatives to identify themselves and the capacity in which they are representing their clients—as lawyer, paralegal, or student-at-law.

The applicant's representative speaks first and starts by explaining why the applicant has made the application. The representative will then call witnesses to give evidence in support of the applicant's case. Each witness is sworn in by the adjudicator. Once the witness is sworn in, the applicant's representative conducts a direct examination by asking questions of that witness. The respondent's representative then conducts a cross-examination of the witness. At the end of the cross-examination, the applicant's representative may be given an opportunity to conduct a re-examination of the witness, limited to questions about new issues raised in the cross-examination. The adjudicator may then have some questions for the witness. At the end of the questioning, the witness is excused and may be seated in the hearing room. This process is repeated for each of the applicant's witnesses.

After the applicant's case is finished, the respondent's representative will summarize the respondent's side of the story and will then call witnesses in support of the respondent's case. Each of the respondent's witnesses is sworn in, after which the respondent's representative conducts a direct examination, followed by cross-examination by the applicant's representative, re-examination by the respondent's representative, and possibly, questioning by the adjudicator.

After all the evidence has been presented, each party is given the opportunity to make a closing argument. The applicant speaks first. The adjudicator will usually make a decision, or order, immediately at the end of the hearing. Sometimes, the adjudicator may need more time to make a decision, in which case the final order will be mailed to all the parties.

NOTES

1 Since 2012 in Ontario, an exception is made for the kirpan carried by Sikhs.

2 In keeping with your obligations under the *Paralegal Rules of Conduct*, Rule 4.01(9), do not make any agreements with the Crown without specific instructions from your client.

KEY TERMS

closing argument, 37
cross-examination, 37
direct examination, 37
endorse, 37
plea bargain, 39
re-examination, 37
reply evidence, 37

REVIEW QUESTIONS

1. State the three parts of a trial, and briefly describe what happens during each part.

2. Who decides matters in the Small Claims Court, and how should you address that person?

3. What do you speak to the clerk about when you arrive at Small Claims Court?

4. What should you do when the judge enters the courtroom?

5. In what order are Small Claims Court matters generally dealt with?

6. What should you do when your case is called in Small Claims Court?

7. Is there an opening statement in Small Claims Court?

8. How do the parties present their evidence in Small Claims Court?

9. What happens after the evidence of both parties has been presented in Small Claims Court?

10. When and how does the judge make a decision in a Small Claims Court case?

11. Who decides matters in the Provincial Offences Court, and how should you address that person?

12. To whom should you speak when you arrive at Provincial Offences Court, and why?

13. What should you do when the justice of the peace enters the courtroom in Provincial Offences Court?

14. In what order are matters generally dealt with in Provincial Offences Court?

15. What should you do when your case is called in Provincial Offences Court?

16. How do the parties present their evidence in Provincial Offences Court?

17. What happens in Provincial Offences Court after the evidence of both parties has been presented?

18. When and how does the justice of the peace make a decision in a provincial offences case?

19. Who deals with matters at the Landlord and Tenant Board, and how should you address that person?

20. To whom should you speak when you arrive at the Landlord and Tenant Board, and why?

21. In what order are matters generally dealt with at the Landlord and Tenant Board?

22. How do the parties present their evidence at the Landlord and Tenant Board?

23. What happens at the Landlord and Tenant Board after the evidence of both parties has been presented?

24. When and how does the adjudicator make a decision at the Landlord and Tenant Board?

CHAPTER 5

Courtroom Etiquette

LEARNING OUTCOMES

After reading this chapter, you will understand

- what an advocate should do when he or she first arrives at the courthouse or tribunal, and when he or she arrives in the hearing room

- how an advocate should behave during a trial or hearing

- how to educate a client about courtroom etiquette prior to his or her trial or hearing

Courts and tribunals are formal settings steeped in years of legal tradition. An advocate is expected to behave in a polite and respectful manner, and to comply with rules of **courtroom etiquette**. Part of being prepared as an advocate is knowing those rules. This chapter discusses courtroom etiquette—how you and your client and witnesses should behave when appearing in court or before a tribunal—by answering questions commonly asked by paralegals.

What Do I Wear?

You should dress in a way that demonstrates respect for the court or tribunal, and that invites the participants in your trial or hearing to treat you with respect. Dress conservatively—you will look more professional. If your clothing is inappropriate, you will draw negative attention to yourself. Keep in mind that your credibility as an advocate is at stake, and your appearance influences the first impression you create on the judge, justice of the peace, or adjudicator.

Men should wear a suit and tie or dress pants and a sports jacket and tie. Women should wear a suit, or dress pants, or a skirt with a jacket or sweater. Women should avoid wearing sleeveless shirts or dresses. Open-toed shoes may be considered inappropriate; hats are not permitted to be worn in a courtroom or tribunal hearing room. An exception is made in the case of religious head coverings.

What Time Should I Arrive at the Court or Tribunal?

You should plan to arrive about an hour before the time set for your trial or hearing. If your trial is set for 10:00 a.m., make sure you arrive by 9:00 a.m. It is always better to be early, just in case you need to call a witness, use the washroom, or review your case. Also, you will have time to familiarize yourself with the courtroom or hearing

---

courtroom etiquette: a set of customary rules of behaviour for individuals appearing before a judge, justice of the peace, or adjudicator

room and to relax before your case starts. It can be very unnerving to arrive late and be expected to proceed right away. You may also wish to use this time to speak with your client or with opposing counsel or the prosecutor.

What Do I Do When I Arrive at the Court or Tribunal?

When you arrive at the court or tribunal, check the daily hearing list for the room number in which your matter is scheduled to be heard. Once you get to the hearing room, check in with the court registrar or, in some cases, with the prosecutor. Most courts and tribunals have sign-in slips at the front of the hearing room. Always remember to identify yourself as a licensed paralegal.

Where Do I Sit?

Seating varies among the various courts and tribunals. Ideally, you should arrive at the court or tribunal early enough so that you can ask the court officers (if any) or other more experienced advocates where to sit. Make sure to speak to court officers and other advocates politely. Even though the judge is not present, this does not give you licence to be rude or disrespectful.

Usually, you will be required to sit in the gallery or body of the courtroom or tribunal room until your case is called. When your case is called, sit at the counsel table in front of the judge, justice of the peace, or adjudicator. The plaintiff, prosecutor, or applicant usually sits on the right side of the room as you are facing the bench, and the defendant or respondent sits on the left. The seating arrangement may be different at some tribunals. For example, advocates might instead sit opposite each other at a boardroom table.

Where Does My Client Sit?

When your case is called, your client will usually sit beside you at the counsel table. However, proper courtroom etiquette requires that you ask permission from the judge, justice of the peace, or adjudicator for your client to sit at the counsel table.

Where Do My Witnesses Sit?

Your witnesses may sit in the body of the court until they are required to give evidence. However, at the beginning of the trial, the judge or justice of the peace may make an order excluding all witnesses from the courtroom so that those who have not yet given evidence will not be influenced by the testimony of other witnesses. If there is an exclusion order, your witnesses must leave the courtroom until each one is called back to testify. When a witness is called to testify, he or she will proceed to the witness box located next to the judge, justice of the peace, or adjudicator (usually to that person's left). In some courts, the witness is permitted to sit while testifying; in others, the witness must stand. When the witness has finished giving evidence, he or she returns to the body of the court and sits down.

How Do I Address the Judge, Justice of the Peace, or Adjudicator?

Always stand before you speak to the judge, justice of the peace, or adjudicator. You must also stand immediately when the judge, justice of the peace, or adjudicator speaks to you. In Small Claims Court, refer to the judge as "Your Honour." In Provincial Offences Court, refer to the justice of the peace as "Your Worship." At a tribunal, you may address the adjudicator as either Mr. or Madam Adjudicator, Mr. or Madam Member, or Mr. or Ms. (last name). The adjudicator's name may be displayed on the bench and, in opening remarks, the adjudicator may state how he or she prefers to be called (for example, Mr. Smith, Ms. Jones). Always be respectful and polite when speaking to the judge, justice of the peace, or adjudicator.

How Do I Address the Lawyer or Agent for the Other Side?

You may use the term "my friend" to refer to counsel for the other side. However, it is preferable to refer to the other lawyer or agent as "counsel for the plaintiff/defendant" or "agent for the plaintiff/defendant." You may also refer to counsel by name (for example, Mr./Ms. Gentili). Never refer to opposing counsel by first name.

How Do I Address a Party to the Case?

Refer to a party to the case by his or her legal status in the matter—the plaintiff/defendant, or the applicant/respondent. Alternatively, you may refer to a party by his or her status in the case—for example, the landlord/tenant, or the homeowner/contractor. You may also refer to a party simply by name (for example, Mr. Li). Again, never refer to a party by first name.

How Do I Address a Witness?

Refer to witnesses by name (for example, Ms. Schwartz). Again, do not refer to or address a witness by first name.

What Do I Do When My Matter Is Ready to Proceed?

If you represent the plaintiff or applicant, stand and identify yourself as soon as the court registrar, judge, justice of the peace, or adjudicator indicates that your matter is ready to be heard. State the party that you represent in the matter. For example, you might say, "Good morning, Your Honour; my name is [surname], [first initial], a licensed paralegal. I appear for the plaintiff, Ms. Cathy Lee." You should then introduce the other party or the representative of the other party. For example, you might say, "My friend, Mr. Williams, appears for the defendant, Mr. Denis Roberts."

If you represent the defendant or the respondent and have no preliminary issues to raise with the court, then sit quietly until it is your turn to make your submissions. Your adversary may introduce you to the adjudicator or you may introduce yourself, at which time stand briefly and then sit down.

What Do I Do If I Am Late?

You should never be late. Being on time and ready to proceed with the hearing as scheduled is a sign of respect for the court and the court process. As discussed above, you should always plan to arrive early. If for some reason you are late, you should always apologize to the court and offer a brief explanation. For example, perhaps you had trouble finding a parking spot or there was a delay on the subway. Always be honest with the judge, justice of the peace, or adjudicator, and never lie. Honesty can go a long way.

How Do I Speak to the Other Side's Agent or Lawyer During the Trial?

While it may be tempting to speak directly to the opposing side's agent or lawyer, you must never do so while your case is being heard. You must always speak through the judge, justice of the peace, or adjudicator. Doing so shows that you recognize the authority of the judge, justice of the peace, or adjudicator to control proceedings in the courtroom or hearing room. Always use a respectful and civil tone whenever you speak to the opposing side. Never be rude.

How Do I Speak to My Client During the Trial or Hearing?

If you must speak with your client during the trial or hearing, first ask permission of the judge, justice of the peace, or adjudicator. For example, in Small Claims Court, you should stand and say, "Excuse me, Your Honour. May I have a moment to confer with my client?" If the judge, justice of the peace, or adjudicator agrees, speak with your client as quietly and quickly as possible.

What Should I Do If I Need to Use the Washroom During the Case?

If at all possible, try to wait until the judge, justice of the peace, or adjudicator calls a recess. If you cannot wait, stand and politely ask the judge, justice of the peace, or adjudicator for a brief recess.

Miscellaneous, but Important!

- Turn off cellphones and all other technology. If you need to use your cellphone to consult your schedule, or if you would like to use your laptop throughout the hearing, always ask the judge's permission to do so.
- Do not use cameras, video recorders, or other such devices.
- Do not eat, drink, chew gum, or read newspapers in the courtroom.
- Remove sunglasses and hats (except religious coverings).
- Stand whenever the judge or justice of the peace enters or leaves the courtroom.
- Do not make noise, or enter or leave while the judge or justice of the peace is speaking.
- If you arrive while court is in session, bow slightly to the judge or justice of the peace as you enter the courtroom.
- If you leave while court is in session, turn to face the judge or justice of the peace and bow slightly before exiting the courtroom.
- Do not drink water while speaking to the judge, justice of the peace, or adjudicator.
- Never interrupt the judge, justice of the peace, or adjudicator when he or she is speaking.

- Never argue with a judge, justice of the peace, or adjudicator.
- Never show your disappointment with, or disapproval of, an adjudicator's order or decision.

Educate Your Client About Courtroom Etiquette

How your client behaves before the judge, justice of the peace, or adjudicator is a reflection on you as an advocate and as a professional. Educate your clients about how they should behave in the court or hearing room by touching on the points discussed above, as part of your preparation of your clients for the hearing. Keep in mind that a client may never have appeared in court before.

KEY TERMS

courtroom etiquette, 46

REVIEW QUESTIONS

1. What should you wear when appearing in a court or tribunal?

2. What time should you arrive at the court or tribunal?

3. Where should you sit in the court or tribunal?

4. Where should your client sit?

5. Where should your witnesses sit?

6. How should you address the judge, justice of the peace, or adjudicator?

7. How should you address the lawyer or agent for the other side?

8. How should you address a party to the case?

9. How should you address a witness?

10. How should you speak to the other side's agent or lawyer during the trial?

11. How do you speak to your client during the trial or hearing?

12. What should you do if you need to use the washroom during the case?

DISCUSSION QUESTIONS

1. You are a licensed paralegal representing your client, Pauline Frangello, who is the defendant in a Small Claims Court matter. You are appearing in the Small Claims Court for the trial. Court is in session and you are about to cross-examine the plaintiff's first witness. Ms. Frangello is sitting in the gallery of the court chewing gum and scrolling through her smartphone. What is wrong with Ms. Frangello's behaviour? How might this situation have been avoided?

2. You are a licensed paralegal appearing in the Provincial Offences Court on behalf of your client, who was charged with an offence under the *Liquor Licence Act*. Your client is late to the hearing. You are sitting in the body of the courtroom listening to the prosecutor introduce you and your matter to the justice of the peace. The justice of the peace then looks at you and asks where your client is. You remain seated in the gallery and simply respond, "I don't know. I told him to be here." What is wrong with your behaviour? What should you have done?

3. You are a licensed paralegal appearing before the Ontario Court of Justice on a criminal matter. Your matter is before the judge, and the prosecutor is requesting an adjournment. The judge asks you if your client is agreeable to adjourning the hearing for two weeks. You need to obtain instructions from your client. You will

also need to check your own schedule to see if you are available in two weeks; however, your calendar is an application on your smartphone. The judge is waiting for an answer. What should you do?

4. You are a licensed paralegal representing Bianca Trudelle, who has been charged under the *Liquor Licence Act* and is scheduled to appear in Provincial Offences Court tomorrow for trial. You are meeting with Ms. Trudelle today to prepare her for the trial tomorrow. Bianca has never been to court before. What should you tell her about proper courtroom etiquette?

PART III

Preparing for a Trial or Hearing

The Theory of the Case

LEARNING OUTCOMES

After reading this chapter, you will understand

▪ what the theory of the case is

▪ why you need to develop a theory of your case

▪ how to develop a theory of your case

When judges, justices of the peace, or other adjudicators make a decision in a case, they do so by applying the relevant law to the facts of the case. To win a trial or hearing you have to be successful in both the facts and the law—you must present the judge or other decision-maker with a view of the facts and law that supports a decision in favour of your client. In other words, you need a theory of the case.

This chapter discusses the theory of the case—what it is, why it is important, and how to develop one.

Theory of the Case: What It Is and Why You Need One

The *theory of the case*—your theory of your case—is a view of the facts and law that can justify a favourable decision for your client. As the saying goes, there are two sides to every story, and your theory of the case is your side of the story. It explains what happened in your case and why it happened. It also explains how the facts give rise to a valid cause of action if you are representing the plaintiff or applicant, a valid charge if you are the prosecutor, or a valid defence if you are representing the defendant or respondent.

Your theory of the case should include all the facts of the case that are not in dispute and your version of the facts that are in dispute. It must account for all the facts of your case, both favourable and unfavourable, and should explain away as many of the unfavourable facts as possible.

Your opponent will have a theory of the case as well. You want your theory to be the more persuasive one. To be persuasive it must be understandable and not just plausible, but compelling. You want the judge or other decision-maker to think not only that the facts might have happened as your theory suggests, but that it makes sense for them to have happened just that way.

You will not succeed at trial or hearing with merely a compelling and convincing story. The story must also satisfy the requirements of substantive law. In other words, the facts must constitute either a valid cause of action or offence or a valid defence. Your theory of the case must apply the relevant law to the facts of your client's case.

Developing a theory of your case will help you understand and develop the case. It will help you to separate relevant facts from irrelevant ones, and to distinguish between favourable facts and unfavourable ones. At the trial or hearing, your theory of the case will provide a context for the judge or other decision-maker to understand your client's case as well.

Do not wait until you start to prepare for a trial or hearing to develop your theory of the case. It should be your first step in a case, starting with your very first client interview as you sort through the facts of your client's story and make preliminary decisions about potential causes of action, offences, or defences. Your theory will govern how you draft your pleadings, where applicable; the additional information you seek from your client or witnesses; the legal research you do; and the way in which you conduct the trial or hearing.

How to Develop Your Theory of the Case

There are six steps to follow in developing your theory of the case:

1. Gather the facts of the case.
2. Identify the legal issues raised by the facts.
3. Research and find the relevant law.
4. Determine how you will put the relevant facts into evidence.
5. Assess your own case.
6. Assess your opponent's case.

1. Gather the Facts of the Case

The facts are the foundation of your case. They are at the source of your client's legal problem and determine the legal issues involved.

The first step in the fact-gathering process is to conduct a detailed interview of your client. Start by letting the client tell the story in his or her own words. If your client is a plaintiff or applicant, find out why he or she wants to start proceedings. If you are the prosecutor, find out why the charge has been laid. If your client is a defendant or respondent, find out why he or she has been sued or what offence he or she has been charged with. As you develop a sense of the area of law involved, you can start to focus on the relevant facts and weed out irrelevant facts. Ask your client for any documentary evidence, such as letters, contracts, or photographs, making sure to protect and preserve any physical evidence you obtain.

Depending on the complexity of the case, consider interviewing potential witnesses and obtaining documents from third parties. Memories fade over time, so contact witnesses sooner rather than later. Prepare a summary of each witness's statement and, if possible, have the witness sign it. There is a more complete discussion of witness interviews in Chapter 7.

Objective facts are the most valuable—for example, the fact that the tenant signed a written lease, or the fact that it was snowing at the time of a motor vehicle accident. The more objective facts you have, the stronger your case will be. Conversely, the more objective facts you face, the more difficult your case will be.

2. Identify the Legal Issues Raised by the Facts

Identify the client's problem—why the client is retaining you or, if you are the prosecutor, the charge that has been laid. Then identify the legal issues raised by the facts.

Start with what the client wants. For example, the client may want to terminate a lease or may wish to avoid having to pay damages for breach of contract.

Next, determine the area of law involved. Start by identifying the problem by general area—for example, landlord and tenant law, contract law, tort law, or highway traffic law. Then, identify the specific area of law involved: if the general area of law is landlord and tenant law, is the specific area assignment of tenancy or termination of tenancy? Narrow the area of law as much as possible: if the specific area of law is termination of tenancy, is the narrower area non-payment of rent or damage to the premises? The more specific the area of law that you investigate, the more quickly and easily you will find answers. You may have to do some preliminary research to educate yourself on a particular area of law before you can narrow the area of law.

Finally, formulate the issues. Write down each issue you identify, starting with the word "whether"—for example, "whether a landlord has the right to terminate a tenancy because of damage caused by the tenant."

3. Research and Find the Relevant Law

Substantive law defines the elements of a civil cause of action or a defence to a civil action, and defines the elements of a criminal or provincial offence and the defences available to that offence. Substantive law also determines the facts you must establish to constitute your claim, charge, or defence. In other words, the law provides a context for the facts you have gathered. Your research helps you to determine which facts are relevant and often requires you to find additional facts.

Start your legal research with secondary sources, such as textbooks, encyclopedias, and digests that provide a general overview of the subject area, and use these to find the primary sources of law (cases, statutes, and regulations) that are relevant to your client's issues. Once you have looked at the law, you may find that the issues you identified on a preliminary basis are not correct; you may also find that you need more information from your client or other witnesses. If your preliminary identification of the issues was faulty, or if you receive new information, you may have to do further research on the subject.

4. Determine How You Will Put the Relevant Facts into Evidence

Substantive law tells you which facts you need to prove. You must then consider *how* you will prove these facts.

Make a list of each fact you must prove. For each fact, ask yourself what evidence is required to prove that fact and how that evidence will be produced at a trial or hearing. Will a particular fact be proved by the testimony of a witness, and if so, which witness? Do you have documentary evidence to support a particular fact, and if so, which witness can prove and explain the particular document?

5. Assess Your Own Case

Once you have completed steps 1 through 4, you must take a critical look at your theory to identify the strengths and weaknesses of your own case. Your theory should have a firm foundation in strong facts, and the inferences drawn from those facts must be reasonable. Your theory should also explain away, in a plausible manner, as many unfavourable facts as possible. Finally, your theory must make sense—it cannot be based on wishful thinking!

6. Assess Your Opponent's Case

Developing your theory of the case involves not only preparation of *your* case but also preparation for *your opponent's* case. Your opponent will also have a theory of the case. You must anticipate what that theory of the case is likely to be and prepare for it. Your opponent will most likely know about any facts that are unfavourable to your case. Consider whether there is some point of law that can defend you against that fact. If not, consider a way to explain the fact away in a reasonable fashion. It is far better to admit an unfavourable fact and explain it on your own terms than to allow the fact to be drawn out by your opponent. For example, your client may have signed the contract, but you can argue that it was signed under duress or as a result of undue influence.

Be honest in your assessment of the relative strengths and weaknesses of your case and your opponent's case. It may be in your client's best interests to settle rather than to proceed to a trial or hearing.

Developing the Theory of the Kitchen Renovation Small Claims Court Case

In Chapter 1, Fact Situation 1 set out the basic facts of a Small Claims Court dispute involving a kitchen renovation contract. In the sections below, we apply the six steps for constructing a theory of the case to the Kitchen Renovation Case, for both the plaintiff and the defendants.

Theory of the Plaintiff's Case

Step 1: Gather the Facts of the Case

Box 6.1 contains the witness statements prepared from the interview notes of Alec Baldwin and Stephen Baldwin, the principals of the plaintiff corporation Baldwin Brothers Construction in the Kitchen Renovation Case.

BOX 6.1

Baldwin Brothers Witness Statements in the Kitchen Renovation Case

Alec Baldwin's Witness Statement

My brother Stephen and I are the owners of a contracting company called Baldwin Brothers Construction. We're licensed contractors and have been in business for ten years, and do general contracting work, specializing in small renovation projects. Six months ago, Tina Fey called me to discuss a renovation of her kitchen. She found out about my company because we were doing some work in the neighbourhood. I went to her house to discuss the work she wanted to have done. She told me that she wanted to have her kitchen cabinets painted white and to have new hardware installed on the doors. She also wanted a new countertop, and to replace the existing lighting with pot lights. She also wanted to have the walls and ceiling painted.

We talked about how many pot lights she would need to make her kitchen bright. I told her that pot lights normally cost $250 each installed, and that five would be the right number for her kitchen. She asked what would happen if she wanted more light, and I said, "Then we can install more" even though I was sure five would be enough. Based on our discussions I gave her a price of $7,500 for all the work, and she agreed.

My brother Stephen and I came a week later to start the work, and Tina paid me a deposit of $2,500. After the kitchen counter was installed, I left to work on another job, and Stephen did the rest of the work himself.

The job was finished within a week. We did a good job, and the Feys seemed happy with our work. Everything was fine until Stephen gave Tommy Fey the bill for the work. The bill was for $8,250—the original contract price of $7,500 plus $750 for supplying and installing the three additional pot lights.

Stephen Baldwin's Witness Statement

My brother Alec and I are owners of a contracting company called Baldwin Brothers Construction. Six months ago, we were hired by Tommy and Tina Fey to renovate their kitchen. We were hired to paint the kitchen and the cabinets, install a new countertop, and install pot lights. Alec negotiated the contract with the Feys.

My brother and I came a week later to start the work. Tommy Fey was at home during the renovation. When it was time to install the pot lights, I checked with Tommy about the location of the five lights I was planning to install. Tommy told me he didn't think that five lights would provide enough light. I told him that I could install more and to tell me how many he wanted. He said he wanted three more, and I said fine. He never asked me what it would cost, so we never discussed money.

The job was finished within a week, and the Feys seemed happy with our work. Everything was fine until I gave Tommy the bill, which was for $8,250—the original contract price of $7,500 plus $750 for supplying and installing three additional pot lights. He asked what the extra $750 was for, and I said it was for three extra pot lights at $250 each, over and above the five lights that were included in the contract. He said the contract included "all necessary lights" and he wouldn't pay any more than the $7,500 originally agreed to. He gave me a cheque for $5,000.

After completing the interviews, the plaintiff's advocate will prepare a summary of the facts, as follows:

- The defendants hired the plaintiff to do some renovations to their kitchen.
- The plaintiff agreed to install a new countertop, paint the kitchen cabinets and install new hardware on the doors, paint the walls and ceiling, and install five pot lights.
- The contract price was $7,500.
- The defendants gave the plaintiff a deposit in the amount of $2,500.
- At the request of the defendants, the plaintiff installed three additional pot lights at a cost of $250 each.
- The plaintiff completed all the work required and gave the defendants an invoice for $8,250 (the original contract price of $7,500 plus $750 for the installation of three additional pot lights).
- The defendants paid $5,000.
- The defendants owe $750.

Step 2: Identify the Legal Issues Raised by the Facts

The primary legal issue in this case is whether the Feys breached the contract by failing to pay the entire amount billed. The issue turns on a determination of the terms of the agreement between the parties, specifically whether the contract price included the installation of only five pot lights or of all necessary lights, and, if the latter, what the meaning of "all necessary lights" is.

The area of law involved is contract law, and in particular contract interpretation.

Step 3: Research and Find the Relevant Law

Common law principles of contract law apply to this case. There is clearly a contract between the parties. The only issue is one of interpretation. In interpreting contracts, the courts try to give effect to the intention of the parties on the basis of the clear meaning of the words they use. Each party must persuade the court that his or her interpretation of the contract is the correct one.

Step 4: Determine How You Will Put the Relevant Facts into Evidence

There is only one document in this case—the Baldwin Brothers' invoice. The contract was oral.

Alec will testify about the negotiation of the original contract, including the number and cost of the pot lights, and the payment of the deposit. He can also testify that only five pot lights were needed to make the kitchen bright.

Stephen will testify about the completion of the work, Tommy Fey's request for additional pot lights, the delivery of the invoice, and the fact that full payment was not received upon completion.

Step 5: Assess Your Own Case

Alec will give evidence that the contract provided for five pot lights only, not for "all necessary lights." A judge should be willing to accept Alec's version of the facts because it is not likely that a contractor would agree to provide an undefined number of lights. Even if the judge agrees that the contract was for "all necessary lights," the plaintiff maintains that five pot lights were all that was necessary.

Step 6: Assess Your Opponent's Case

It is possible that the defendants will persuade the judge to accept their version of the terms of the contract, and that eight pot lights were necessary to make the kitchen bright.

Theory of the Defendants' Case

Step 1: Gather the Facts of the Case

Box 6.2 contains the witness statements prepared from the interview notes of the defendants, Tina Fey and Tommy Fey, in the Kitchen Renovation Case.

BOX 6.2

Tina and Tommy Fey's Witness Statements in the Kitchen Renovation Case

Tina Fey's Witness Statement

Six months ago, I met with Alec Baldwin of Baldwin Brothers Construction about renovating my kitchen. I found out about the company because they had done some work in the neighbourhood. Alec came to my house to discuss with me the work I wanted to have done. I told him that I wanted to have my kitchen cabinets painted white and to have new hardware installed on the doors. I also wanted a new countertop, and to replace the existing lighting with pot lights. I further wanted to have the walls and ceiling painted.

When we talked about the pot lights, he mentioned that pot lights cost about $250 each. I told him that I wanted the kitchen to be bright, and he assured me that he would install the necessary number of pot lights as part of the contract price. I asked him how many that would be, and he said five. I asked what would happen if I needed more lights, and he said, "Then we can install more."

Alec and his brother Stephen came a week later to start the work, and I gave them a deposit of $2,500. My husband took some time off work so that he could be home to supervise. The job was finished within a week. The work was excellent, and everything looked great. Everything was fine until Stephen gave my husband the bill for the work. Instead of $7,500, as we had agreed, the bill was for $8,250. My husband dealt with the bill.

Tommy Fey's Witness Statement

Six months ago, my wife and I hired Baldwin Brothers Construction to renovate our kitchen. They were going to paint the kitchen and the cabinets, install a new countertop, and install pot lights. My wife negotiated the contract with the company.

Alec and his brother Stephen came a week later to start the work. I took some time off work to stay home to supervise. When it was time to install the pot lights, Stephen checked with me about the number and location of the lights. He said he was planning to install five lights and showed me where. I told him I didn't think that would provide enough light. Stephen said, "Tell me what you want. I can install more." I told him three more, and he said fine. We never discussed money.

The job was finished within a week, and we were happy with the work. Everything was fine until Stephen gave me the bill. Instead of $7,500, as we had agreed, the bill was for $8,250. I asked what the extra $750 was for, and Stephen said it was for three extra pot lights. I told him that all lighting was included in the original price and that I wouldn't pay any more than $7,500. I gave him a cheque for $5,000.

After completing the interviews, the defendants' advocate will prepare a summary of the facts, as follows:

- The defendants hired the plaintiff to make some renovations in their kitchen.
- The plaintiff agreed to install a new countertop, paint the kitchen cabinets and install new hardware on the doors, paint the walls and ceiling, and install all necessary pot lights to make the kitchen bright.
- The contract price was $7,500.
- The defendants gave the plaintiff a deposit in the amount of $2,500.
- While the work was being done, Tommy Fey and Stephen Baldwin discussed the number and placement of the pot lights and settled on eight lights.
- The plaintiff completed all the work required and gave the defendants an invoice for $8,250 ($750 more than the contract price).
- The defendants paid $5,000, which covered the contract in full. The plaintiff is not entitled to any additional payment.

Step 2: Identify the Legal Issues Raised by the Facts

The primary legal issue in this case is whether the defendants are contractually obligated to pay $750 above the original contract price. The issue turns on a determination of the terms of the agreement between the parties, specifically whether the contract price included the installation of only five pot lights or of all necessary lights, and, if the latter, what the meaning of "all necessary lights" is.

The area of law involved is contract law, and in particular contract interpretation.

Step 3: Research and Find the Relevant Law

Common law principles of contract law apply to this case. There is clearly a contract between the parties. The only issue is one of interpretation. In interpreting contracts, the courts try to give effect to the intention of the parties on the basis of the clear meaning of the words they use. Each party must persuade the court that his or her interpretation of the contract is the correct one.

Step 4: Determine How You Will Put the Relevant Facts into Evidence

There is only one document in this case—the Baldwin Brother' invoice. The contract was oral.

Tina will testify about the negotiation of the original contract, including the number and cost of the pot lights, and the payment of the deposit. She will testify that Baldwin Brothers agreed to provide all necessary pot lights as part of the contract price. She can also testify that eight pot lights were needed to make the kitchen bright.

Tommy will testify about the completion of the work and his discussion with Stephen about the number and location of the pot lights. He will testify that eight pot lights were needed to make the kitchen bright. He will also testify that he paid the contract price in full.

Step 5: Assess Your Own Case

Tina will give evidence that the contract provided for "all necessary lights" and that Alec merely suggested that five lights would be enough. Both Tina and Tommy will testify that eight lights were necessary to make the kitchen bright. Tina's evidence will make it clear that her main concern was the brightness of the kitchen, not the actual number of lights.

Step 6: Assess Your Opponent's Case

A judge may be willing to accept Alec's version of the facts because it is not likely that a contractor would agree to provide an undefined number of lights. Even if the judge agrees that the contract was for "all necessary lights," the judge may not be persuaded that eight lights were in fact necessary.

Developing the Theory of the Liquor Licence Case

In Chapter 1, Fact Situation 2 set out the basic facts of a Provincial Offences Court case involving a charge under the *Liquor Licence Act*. In the sections below, we apply the six steps for constructing a theory of the case to the Liquor Licence Case for both the prosecution and the defendants.

Theory of the Prosecution's Case

Step 1: Gather the Facts of the Case

Box 6.3 contains the witness statements prepared from the interview notes of Patrick Elder and Police Constable Matthew Lee, the prosecution's witnesses in the Liquor Licence Case.

BOX 6.3

Patrick Elder's and Police Constable Matthew Lee's Witness Statements in the Liquor Licence Case

Patrick Elder's Witness Statement

I live in the apartment building at 1310 Olde Street in Toronto, next to the Simpson Academy campus. My apartment is on the fifth floor and my balcony overlooks the outdoor patio of the Simpson Academy student lounge and the adjoining lawn.

I was home during the evening of May 16, 2016. Starting at around 7:00 or 7:30 p.m., I could hear that there was some kind of event taking place at the Simpson Academy. At first it was just the usual sound of people outside talking and laughing, but as the evening wore on, the voices got louder and louder. By about 11:00 p.m. the party was so loud that I couldn't get to sleep. I looked out over my balcony and saw at least 20 people on the patio and the grass. So I called the police to complain.

Constable Matthew Lee's Witness Statement

I am a police constable with the Toronto Police Service. On May 16, 2016 I was dispatched to the Simpson Academy campus to investigate a noise complaint involving an outdoor event at the student lounge.

I arrived at the Simpson Academy campus at about 11:30 p.m. I made my way to the student lounge, where some sort of a party was taking place. I observed that the lounge included both an indoor bar and a fenced outdoor patio area. I noted that a liquor sales licence and catering notification form were posted over the bar in the name of Treetop Catering Inc. The catering notification form stated that the approximate hours of the event were 7:00 p.m. to midnight, and also contained a statement to the effect that the boundaries of the event premises were the student lounge and outdoor fenced patio at 1292 Olde Street in the City of Toronto. There was a bartender behind the bar. I asked him to direct me to the person in charge, and he introduced me to a woman who identified herself as Victoria Levens. She told me that she was the owner of Treetop Catering Inc., the organizer of the event. I advised Ms. Levens that there had been a noise complaint. By this time it was close to midnight, so Ms. Levens said that she would advise the guests that the party was over. I suggested that she start with the guests on the patio, since they were the source of the noise complaint.

I followed Ms. Levens out to the patio and noted that it was enclosed by a low fence, with a gate opening to a grassy area beyond. I noticed that there was a sign posted at the door leading out to the patio stating, "No alcoholic beverages permitted outside the patio." There was an identical sign on the gate leading out of the patio to the grassy area. I observed as Ms. Levens spoke to a rather large gentleman wearing a black T-shirt with the word "Security" across the front. He immediately started to direct the guests to leave. While there were no guests on the grass at this time, I did observe empty beer bottles and plastic wine glasses on the grassy area just beyond the fence. I walked over to inspect them. They looked like the same type of clear plastic wine glasses and beer bottles that I observed behind the bar earlier. I could also smell alcohol coming from them.

As a result, I advised Ms. Levens that I would be charging her and Treetop Catering Inc. with the offence of permitting the removal of alcohol from the premises.

I subsequently appeared before a justice of the peace and swore the following informations:

Information No. 9211

Victoria Levens of Brampton, Ontario stands charged that on or about the 16th day of May 2016, at the City of Toronto, in the Province of Ontario, she did permit the removal of alcohol from the premises situated at 1292 Olde Street in the City of Toronto, Province of Ontario, as stated in section 34 of the Ontario Licences to Sell Liquor Regulation, RRO 1990, regulation 719, contrary to section 61(1)(c) of the *Liquor Licence Act*, RSO 1990, chapter L.19.

Information No. 9212

Treetop Catering Inc. stands charged that on or about the 16th day of May 2016, at the City of Toronto, in the Province of Ontario, it did permit the removal of alcohol from the premises situated at 1292 Olde Street in the City of Toronto, Province of Ontario, as stated in section 34 of the Ontario Licences to Sell Liquor Regulation, RRO 1990, regulation 719, contrary to section 61(1)(c) of the *Liquor Licence Act*, RSO 1990, chapter L.19.

Summonses were issued requiring both defendants to appear in court to answer the charges.

After completing the interviews, the prosecution's advocate will prepare a summary of the facts, as follows:

- On May 16, 2016, in response to a noise complaint made to the Toronto police, Constable Matthew Lee was dispatched to Simpson Academy, arriving at the student lounge at approximately 11:30 p.m. where a party was in progress.

- A liquor sales licence and catering notification form were posted over the bar in the name of Treetop Catering Inc. The hours of the event were stated to be from 7:00 p.m. to midnight, and the boundaries of the event premises were stated to be the student lounge and outdoor fenced area.
- Victoria Levens identified herself as the owner of Treetop Catering Inc. and the organizer of the event.
- Constable Lee advised Ms. Levens of the noise complaint, and she agreed to advise the guests that the party was over.
- Constable Lee and Ms. Levens went out to the patio. The patio was fenced, with a gate opening to a grassy area beyond. There was a sign posted at the door leading out to the patio stating, "No alcoholic beverages permitted outside the patio." There was an identical sign on the gate leading out of the patio to the grassy area.
- There was a security guard on the patio. On Ms. Levens's instructions, the security guard directed the guests to leave.
- Constable Lee observed empty beer bottles and plastic wine glasses on the grassy area just beyond the fence. There were no guests on the grass.

Step 2: Identify the Legal Issues Raised by the Facts

The legal issue in this case is whether the defendants, Treetop Catering and Victoria Levens, committed an offence under the *Liquor Licence Act* by permitting the removal of alcohol from the premises.

The area of law involved is provincial offences, in particular, offences under the *Liquor Licence Act*.

Step 3: Research and Find the Relevant Law

This situation is governed by the *Liquor Licence Act*, RSO 1990, chapter L.19. Section 61(1)(c) provides as follows:

61(1) A person is guilty of an offence if the person, ...
    (c) contravenes any provision of this Act or the regulations.

The applicable regulation is RRO 1990, regulation 719: *Licences to Sell Liquor*. The relevant sections are as follows:

8(1) The following classes of licences to sell liquor are established:
    1. A liquor sales licence authorizing the sale and service of liquor for consumption on the premises to which the licence applies.
    (2) The following endorsements to liquor sales licences are established: ...
    3. A caterer's endorsement authorizing the applicant to sell and serve liquor for an event held on premises other than the premises to which the liquor sales licence applies.

34(1) The licence holder shall not permit a patron to remove liquor from the premises to which the licence applies.

63.1(1) At least 10 days before a catered event begins, a holder of a liquor sales licence with a caterer's endorsement shall provide to the Registrar and the local police, fire, health and building departments details concerning,

    (a) the nature of the event and the name of the sponsor;

    (b) the address at which the event will be held;

    (c) the dates on which and the hours during which the event will be held;

    (d) the estimated attendance for the event; and

    (e) the boundaries of the area within which liquor will be sold and served and the location of any tiered seating in the area.

According to the case of *R v Sault Ste Marie*, [1978] 2 SCR 1299, in order to secure a conviction, the prosecution must prove beyond a reasonable doubt that the defendants committed the *actus reus* of the offence, namely, permitting the removal of alcohol from the licensed area of the premises. If the prosecution succeeds in doing so, it will be up to the defendants to prove, on a balance of probabilities, that they had taken all reasonable steps in the circumstances to comply with the law.

Step 4: Determine How You Will Put the Relevant Facts into Evidence

The prosecution's evidence will consist of witness testimony and documents.

Patrick Elder can testify that he saw and heard people on the patio of the student lounge and the grassy area beyond the patio.

Constable Lee can testify that a party was taking place at the Simpson Academy student lounge and that Victoria Levens identified herself as the owner of Treetop Catering Inc., stating that she was the organizer of the event. He can also testify about the contents of the catering notification form posted over the bar and introduce it into evidence. In particular, he can point out that the boundaries of the event were stated to be the student lounge and the outdoor fenced patio. In addition, he can testify that while he did not observe any guests on the grass, he did observe empty beer bottles and plastic wine glasses on the grass just beyond the fence.

Step 5: Assess Your Own Case

Neither prosecution witness observed guests holding alcoholic beverages while standing on the grass beyond the patio. However, Mr. Elder observed guests on the grass, and Constable Lee observed beer bottles and wine glasses on the grass. The justice of the peace should be willing to conclude that guests removed alcohol beyond the licensed premises.

Step 6: Assess Your Opponent's Case

Given that neither prosecution witness observed guests beyond the licensed premises actually carrying alcoholic beverages, the justice of the peace may conclude that there is a reasonable doubt that guests went beyond the patio while carrying alcoholic beverages. Even if the justice of the peace is satisfied as to this point, because of the signs and the security guard, the justice of the peace may conclude that the defendants took all reasonable steps in the circumstances to comply with the law.

Theory of the Defendants' Case

Step 1: Gather the Facts of the Case

Box 6.4 contains the witness statements prepared from the interview notes of Victoria Levens, one of the defendants, and Calvin Hobbs, the defendant's witness in the Liquor Licence Case.

BOX 6.4

Victoria Levens's and Calvin Hobbs's Witness Statements in the Liquor Licence Case

Victoria Levens's Witness Statement

I am the sole director, officer, and shareholder of Treetop Catering Inc. I have been in business for five years.

I was hired by the Simpson Advocacy Club to organize and manage a party for its members to be held at the Simpson Academy student lounge at 1292 Olde Street, Toronto, on May 16, 2016 from 7:00 p.m. to midnight. By the terms of our agreement, I was to provide a light buffet, beer, wine, and soft drinks for 40 guests. I made a site visit to the lounge on May 1st to see what the facilities were like. I saw that the lounge included an indoor bar and a fenced outdoor patio, with a gate opening onto a grassy area. I noticed that there was a sign posted at the door leading out to the patio stating, "No alcoholic beverages permitted outside the patio." There was an identical sign on the gate leading out of the patio to the grassy area. In addition to my usual wait staff and a bartender, I hired a security guard for the event to make sure that guests did not take alcohol outside of the patio.

Treetop Catering holds a liquor sales licence. I applied for and was granted a caterer's endorsement authorizing Treetop Catering to sell and serve liquor at the Simpson Academy student lounge for the event. On May 2nd I provided the Registrar of Alcohol and Gaming and the local police, fire, health, and building departments details concerning

- the nature of the event and the name of the sponsor;

- the address of the Simpson Academy student lounge;
- the date and hours of the event;
- the estimated attendance for the event; and
- the boundaries of the area within which liquor would be sold and served at the event—namely, the indoor lounge and the outdoor fenced patio area.

My staff and I arrived at the venue at about 5:00 p.m. to set up for the evening. Guests started to arrive at about 7:00 p.m. I stayed inside the venue during the event helping to staff the buffet. I noticed that guests were on the patio, but did not go out there because I was too busy with the buffet.

Some time after 11:30 p.m., a police officer arrived at the venue. He advised me that there had been a noise complaint. By this time it was close to midnight, so I said that I would advise the guests that the party was over. The police officer suggested that I start with the guests on the patio, since they were the source of the noise complaint.

I went out to the patio and told my security guard, Calvin Hobbs, to advise the guests that the party was over. He immediately started to direct the guests to leave. There were no guests on the grass at this time. However, the police officer stated that he had observed empty beer bottles and plastic wine glasses on the grassy area, and that my company and I would be charged with the offence of permitting the removal of alcohol from the premises.

I was subsequently served with two summonses charging that we permitted the removal of alcohol from the premises situated at 1292 Olde Street in the City of Toronto, Province of Ontario, as stated in section 34 of the Ontario Licences to Sell Liquor Regulation, RRO 1990, regulation 719, contrary to section 61(1)(c) of the *Liquor Licence Act*, RSO 1990, chapter L.19.

Calvin Hobbs's Witness Statement

I have worked as a security guard for three years.

I was hired by Treetop Catering Inc. to work security at an event to be held at the Simpson Academy student lounge on May 16, 2016 from 7:00 p.m. to midnight.

I arrived at the venue at 6:30 p.m. Victoria Levens, the owner of Treetop Catering, instructed me to position myself on the outside patio at the gate leading out of the patio to the grass, and to make sure that guests did not take any alcoholic beverages outside of the patio. During the course of the event, a number of guests left the patio to stand on the grass beyond the fence, usually to have a smoke. I advised every guest who left the patio that alcoholic beverages were not permitted to leave the patio area, and I did not see anyone carrying alcoholic drinks as they left the patio.

Close to midnight, Ms. Levens came out onto the patio with a police officer. Ms. Levens told me that there had been a noise complaint, and that I was to tell the guests that the party was over and direct them to leave. I did as I was told. As the guests were leaving the patio, I looked to make sure that there were no guests on the grass beyond the patio. While there were no guests on the grass, I did notice a few empty beer bottles and plastic wine glasses on the grass. This was the first time that I saw any bottles or glasses on the grass, and I don't know how they got there.

After completing the interviews, the defendant's advocate will prepare a summary of the facts, as follows:

- Victoria Levens is the sole director, officer, and shareholder of Treetop Catering Inc.
- Treetop Catering Inc. was hired by the Simpson Advocacy Club to organize and manage a party for its members on May 16, 2016 in the Simpson Academy student lounge.
- The lounge included an indoor bar and a fenced outdoor patio, with a gate opening to a grassy area.
- Treetop Catering holds a liquor sales licence and applied for and was granted a caterer's endorsement authorizing it to sell and serve liquor at the event in the indoor lounge and outdoor patio.
- There was a sign posted at the door leading out to the patio stating, "No alcoholic beverages permitted outside the patio." There was an identical sign on the gate leading out of the patio to the grassy area.
- Treetop Catering hired a security guard for the event to make sure that guests did not take alcohol outside of the patio.
- During the course of the event, a number of guests left the patio to stand on the grass beyond the fence, typically in order to smoke. The security guard advised every guest who left the patio that alcoholic beverages were not permitted to leave the patio area.
- The security guard did not see anyone carrying alcoholic drinks as they left the patio.

Step 2: Identify the Legal Issues Raised by the Facts

The legal issue in this case is whether the defendants, Treetop Catering and Victoria Levens, committed an offence under the *Liquor Licence Act* by permitting the removal of alcohol from the premises.

The area of law involved is provincial offences, in particular, offences under the *Liquor Licence Act*.

Step 3: Research and Find the Relevant Law

This situation is governed by the *Liquor Licence Act*, RSO 1990, chapter L.19. Section 61(1)(c) provides as follows:

> 61(1) A person is guilty of an offence if the person, …
>   (c) contravenes any provision of this Act or the regulations.

The applicable regulation is RRO 1990, regulation 719: *Licences to Sell Liquor*. The relevant sections are as follows:

8(1) The following classes of licences to sell liquor are established:

1. A liquor sales licence authorizing the sale and service of liquor for consumption on the premises to which the licence applies.

(2) The following endorsements to liquor sales licences are established: …

3. A caterer's endorsement authorizing the applicant to sell and serve liquor for an event held on premises other than the premises to which the liquor sales licence applies.

34(1) The licence holder shall not permit a patron to remove liquor from the premises to which the licence applies.

63.1(1) At least 10 days before a catered event begins, a holder of a liquor sales licence with a caterer's endorsement shall provide to the Registrar and the local police, fire, health and building departments details concerning,

    (a) the nature of the event and the name of the sponsor;

    (b) the address at which the event will be held;

    (c) the dates on which and the hours during which the event will be held;

    (d) the estimated attendance for the event; and

    (e) the boundaries of the area within which liquor will be sold and served and the location of any tiered seating in the area.

According to the case of *R v Sault Ste Marie*, [1978] 2 SCR 1299, in order to secure a conviction, the prosecution must prove beyond a reasonable doubt that the defendants committed the *actus reus* of the offence, namely, permitting the removal of alcohol from the licensed area of the premises. If the prosecution succeeds in doing so, it will be up to the defendants to prove, on a balance of probabilities, that they had taken all reasonable steps in the circumstances to comply with the law.

Step 4: Determine How You Will Put the Relevant Facts into Evidence

The defendants' evidence will consist of witness testimony and documents.

Victoria Levens can testify that she is the sole director, officer, and shareholder of Treetop Catering and that her company was hired by the Simpson Advocacy Club to organize and manage a party for its members to be held at the Simpson Academy student lounge at 1292 Olde Street, Toronto, on May 16, 2016. She can testify that her company holds a liquor sales licence and applied for and was granted a caterer's endorsement authorizing Treetop Catering to sell and serve liquor at the Simpson Academy student lounge for the event, and can introduce the catering notification form into evidence. She can also testify about the layout of the student lounge and patio and can introduce a diagram she created of the premises. In addition, she can testify that there was a sign posted at the door leading out to the patio stating, "No alcoholic beverages permitted outside the patio," and that there was an identical sign on the gate leading out of the patio to the grassy area. Also, she can testify that she hired a security guard to make sure that guests did not take alcohol outside of the patio.

Calvin Hobbs can testify that he was hired as a security guard by Treetop Catering for the event at the Simpson Academy student lounge on May 16, 2016, and that he was directed to ensure that guests did not take any alcoholic beverages outside of the patio. He can testify that he advised every guest who left the patio that alcoholic beverages were not permitted to leave the patio area, and that, even though there were empty beer bottles and wine glasses on the grass, he did not see anyone carrying alcoholic drinks as they left the patio.

Step 5: Assess Your Own Case

Given that neither prosecution witness observed guests beyond the licensed premises actually carrying alcoholic beverages, the justice of the peace may conclude that there is a reasonable doubt that guests went beyond the patio while carrying alcoholic beverages. Even if the justice of the peace is satisfied as to this point, the justice of the peace may conclude that the defendants took all reasonable steps in the circumstances to comply with the law because of the signs and the security guard.

Step 6: Assess Your Opponent's Case

There were beer bottles and wine glasses on the grass. The justice of the peace may be willing to conclude that they got there because guests removed alcohol beyond the licensed premises, and the justice of the peace may not conclude that the defendants took all reasonable steps to comply with the law.

Developing the Theory of the Landlord and Tenant Tribunal Dispute

In Chapter 1, Fact Situation 3 set out the basic facts of a tribunal case involving a landlord and tenant dispute. In the sections below, we apply the six steps for constructing a theory of the case to the Landlord and Tenant Dispute, for both the landlord and the tenant.

Theory of the Tenant's Case

Step 1: Gather the Facts of the Case

Box 6.5 contains the witness statements prepared from the interview notes of Alice Guthrie and Arlo Guthrie, the tenants in the Landlord and Tenant Dispute.

Alice and Arlo Guthrie's Witness Statements in the Landlord and Tenant Dispute

Alice Guthrie's Witness Statement

My husband Arlo and I rented a one-bedroom apartment from Jim Croce at 234 Sycamore Street in Toronto. Our one-year lease would begin on May 1, 2015 and end on April 30, 2016 at a monthly rent of $1,250. The building had two units, and Jim and his wife Julia lived in the other unit. We were happy in the apartment, paid our rent on time, and never had any problems with the landlords.

On March 1, 2016 Jim knocked on our door and handed me a form N12 "Notice to End Your Tenancy Because the Landlord, a Purchaser or a Family Member Requires the Rental Unit," saying we had to move out by April 30, 2016. Jim told me that his daughter Cynthia was finishing her studies at the University of Ottawa and was moving back to Toronto.

Arlo and I began to hunt for another apartment the next day in the same neighbourhood. We searched online, checked newspaper ads, walked the neighbourhood looking for "For Rent" signs, and asked our friends. We weren't able to find a similar apartment for the same rent, but, after almost two weeks, managed to find a suitable apartment in the same neighbourhood for a bit more money, $1,350 per month, available on April 1, 2016. We signed a one-year lease. On March 15th, Arlo and I prepared and signed a form N9 "Tenant's Notice to End the Tenancy," terminating our tenancy as of March 31, 2016. Arlo handed the notice to Jim on March 16, 2016.

We moved out of Jim's apartment on March 31st. We hired Two Guys Moving to move our belongings to the new apartment. Their bill was $750, which Arlo paid.

On April 15th, Arlo told me that our old apartment was for rent for $1,375 per month. Arlo and I think that Jim never intended to have his daughter move into the apartment. We think that he intended all along to re-rent to a new tenant for a higher rent.

Arlo Guthrie's Witness Statement

My wife Alice and I rented a one-bedroom apartment from Jim Croce at 234 Sycamore Street in Toronto. We signed a one-year lease starting on May 1, 2015 and ending on April 30, 2016 at a monthly rent of $1,250. Jim and his wife Julia lived in the only other unit of the building. The apartment was a great place to live, and we got along well with Jim and Julia.

When I arrived home from work on March 1, 2016, Alice showed me a form that Jim had given her earlier in the day. It was a form N12 "Notice to End Your Tenancy Because the Landlord, a Purchaser or a Family Member Requires the Rental Unit," saying we had to move out by April 30, 2016. According to the form, Jim's daughter intended to move into the rental unit.

Alice and I wanted another one-bedroom apartment in the same neighbour-hood, but we weren't able to find one for the same rent. About two weeks later we managed to find a nice apartment in the same neighbourhood for $1,350 per month available on April 1, 2016. We signed a one-year lease on the new apart-ment. On March 15th, Alice and I prepared and signed a form N9 "Tenant's Notice to End the Tenancy," terminating our tenancy as of March 31, 2016. I handed the notice to Jim at his apartment on March 16, 2016.

Alice and I moved out of Jim's apartment on March 31st. We hired Two Guys Moving to move our stuff to the new apartment. Their bill was $750. I paid the bill.

On April 15, 2016, I took a walk past the Sycamore Street apartment and saw a sign on the front lawn advertising a one-bedroom apartment for rent for $1,375 per month available May 1, 2016. I also saw Jim, who was working in the front garden. I asked Jim about the sign, and he told me that his daughter had decided not to move back to Toronto after all because she got a job in Ottawa.

Alice and I did not believe Jim. We think that he terminated our tenancy in bad faith, intending all along to re-rent to a new tenant for a higher rent. Alice and I pre-pared and signed a form T5 "Landlord Gave a Notice of Termination in Bad Faith," asking for an order that Jim pay our increased rent for one year ($100 per month × 12 = $1,200) plus our moving costs of $750 for a total of $1,950. I handed the form to Jim on April 22, 2016.

After completing the interviews, the tenant's advocate will prepare a summary of the facts, as follows:

- The tenants were tenants of the landlord under a one-year lease ending April 30, 2016 at a monthly rent of $1,250.

- On March 1, 2016 the landlord served the tenants with a form N12, ter-minating the tenancy as of April 30, 2016 on the basis that the landlord's daughter would be moving into the unit.

- The tenants were unable to find an equivalent apartment in the same neigh-bourhood at the same rent. They found another apartment at a rental of $1,350 per month.

- The tenants moved out of the unit on March 31, 2016. They incurred moving expenses of $750.

- The landlord's daughter did not move into the unit.

- The landlord instead re-rented the apartment at a monthly rent of $1,375.

Step 2: Identify the Legal Issues Raised by the Facts

The primary legal issue in this case is whether the landlord gave the notice of ter-mination in bad faith. The issue turns on whether the landlord's daughter had a real intention to live in the unit at the time the notice was given.

The area of law involved is residential tenancy law, and in particular termination of a tenancy by a landlord at the end of a term.

Step 3: Research and Find the Relevant Law

This situation is governed by the *Residential Tenancies Act, 2006*, SO 2006, chapter 17. Section 48(1)(c) provides as follows:

> 48(1) A landlord may, by notice, terminate a tenancy if the landlord in good faith requires possession of the rental unit for the purpose of residential occupation by, ...
>
> > (c) a child or parent of the landlord or the landlord's spouse.

However, under section 57(1)(a), a former tenant may apply to the Landlord and Tenant Board if

> the landlord gave a notice of termination under section 48 in bad faith, the former tenant vacated the rental unit as a result of the notice ... and no person referred to in clause 48 (1) ... (d) occupied the rental unit within a reasonable time after the former tenant vacated the rental unit.

In such a case, the Landlord and Tenant Board may, under section 57(3), order that the landlord pay a specified sum to the former tenant for

> i. all or any portion of any increased rent that the former tenant has incurred or will incur for a one-year period after vacating the rental unit, and
> ii. reasonable out-of-pocket moving, storage and other like expenses that the former tenant has incurred or will incur.

In addition, Interpretation Guideline G12 of the Landlord and Tenant Board, *Eviction for Personal Use*, deals with interpretation questions respecting eviction applications under section 48. Under the heading "Requirement of good faith," it states, "The issue that arises in some cases is whether the landlord or a family member has a real intention to reside in the rental unit." Under the heading "The landlord requires the unit—test to be applied," it provides as follows:

> The burden of proof is on the landlord. It is relevant to the good faith of the landlord's intention to occupy the unit to determine the likelihood that the intended person will move into it.

The issue here is whether the notice of termination was given in good faith. The tenants must persuade the tribunal that the notice was given in bad faith, while the landlord must persuade the tribunal that the notice was given in good faith.

Step 4: Determine How You Will Put the Relevant Facts into Evidence

The tenants' evidence will consist of witness testimony and documents.

Either Alice or Arlo can testify about the terms of the lease with the landlord and can introduce the written lease into evidence.

Alice can testify about receiving the form N12 notice of termination from the landlord and can introduce the notice into evidence.

Either Alice or Arlo can testify about their attempts to find another apartment and the terms of their new lease, and can introduce the new lease into evidence.

Arlo can testify about the cost of the move and can introduce the moving company's invoice into evidence. He can also testify about his discovery that the apartment was being offered for rent at a higher cost.

Step 5: Assess Your Own Case

There is no dispute that the landlord's daughter did not move into the apartment and that the landlord instead re-rented it at a higher rent than the tenants were paying. The adjudicator should be willing to infer that the notice of termination was given in bad faith.

Step 6: Assess Your Opponent's Case

It is possible that the landlord will persuade the adjudicator that, even though his daughter did not move into the apartment, he reasonably believed that she would be doing so at the time the notice of termination was given.

Theory of the Landlord's Case

Step 1: Gather the Facts of the Case

Box 6.6 contains the witness statements prepared from the interview notes of Jim Croce and Cynthia Croce, the landlord in the Landlord and Tenant Dispute and his daughter.

BOX 6.6

Jim and Cynthia Croce's Witness Statements in the Landlord and Tenant Dispute

Jim Croce's Witness Statement

I have owned 234 Sycamore Street in Toronto since 2002. It's a two-unit building. My family and I have always lived in the downstairs two-bedroom unit and rented out the upstairs one-bedroom unit. My daughter Cynthia lived with us until she graduated high school in 2012 and moved to Ottawa to attend the University of Ottawa. It was always our intention that Cynthia would move back to Toronto and into the one-bedroom apartment when she graduated from university.

In 2015, we rented the upstairs unit to Alice and Arlo Guthrie. They signed a one-year lease starting on May 1, 2015 and ending on April 30, 2016 at a monthly rent of $1,250. Alice and Arlo were good tenants. They paid their rent on time and never caused any problems.

In February 2016, Cynthia told my wife and me that she was on track to graduate that spring and would probably be moving back to Toronto. I prepared a form N12 "Notice to End Your Tenancy Because the Landlord, a Purchaser or a Family Member Requires the Rental Unit," saying that Arlo and Alice had to move out by April 30, 2016. I gave the form to Alice at the apartment on March 1, 2016. I told Alice that my daughter Cynthia was finishing her studies at the University of Ottawa and was moving back to Toronto.

On March 15th, Arlo knocked on my door and handed me a form N9 "Tenant's Notice to End the Tenancy," terminating our tenancy as of March 31, 2016. Alice and Arlo moved out of the apartment on March 31, 2016.

On April 8, 2016 Cynthia called home and told me that she had just gotten a job in Ottawa and would not be returning to Toronto after all. I realized that I had to find a new tenant for the apartment, and figured that I could try to get a higher rent than Arlo and Alice had been paying. I made up a sign advertising the apartment for rent for $1,375 per month starting May 1, 2016.

I was working in the garden about a week later when Arlo happened to walk by the house and see the sign. He asked me about it, and I told him that Cynthia had decided not to move back to Toronto after all, because she got a job in Ottawa. On April 22, 2016 Arlo handed me a form T5 "Landlord Gave a Notice of Termination in Bad Faith."

Cynthia Croce's Witness Statement

My father, Jim Croce, has owned 234 Sycamore Street in Toronto since 2002. It's a two-unit building. Our family lived in the downstairs two-bedroom apartment and rented out the upstairs one-bedroom apartment. I lived at home with my parents until I graduated from high school in 2012 and moved to Ottawa to attend the University of Ottawa. I always planned to move back to Toronto after graduating. My parents promised me that I could then move into the one-bedroom apartment.

In February 2016 I told my parents that I would be graduating that spring and would probably be moving back to Toronto. The University of Ottawa held a job fair in March 2016, and I went hoping to find a job, preferably in Toronto. I spoke to a number of potential employers. During the first week in April, I was offered a job as a human resources assistant with a small manufacturer in Ottawa. On April 8, 2016 I told my parents that I had just gotten a job in Ottawa and wouldn't be returning to Toronto after all.

After completing the interviews, the landlord's advocate will prepare a summary of the facts, as follows:

- The tenants were tenants of the landlord under a one-year lease ending April 30, 2016 at a monthly rent of $1,250.
- The landlord always intended for his daughter to move into the apartment when she graduated from university. In February 2016 the landlord's daughter told him that she would be graduating and would likely be moving back to Toronto.

- On March 1, 2016 the landlord served the tenants with a form N12, terminating their tenancy as of April 30, 2016 on the basis that his daughter would be moving into the unit.
- The tenants moved out of the unit on March 31, 2016.
- On April 8, 2016 the landlord's daughter advised him that she would not be returning to Toronto.
- The landlord instead re-rented the apartment at a monthly rent of $1,375.

Step 2: Identify the Legal Issues Raised by the Facts

The primary legal issue in this case is whether the landlord gave the notice of termination in bad faith. The issue turns on whether the landlord's daughter had a real intention to live in the unit at the time the notice was given. If the landlord is found to have given the notice of termination in bad faith, a secondary legal issue is the reasonableness of the tenants' damages.

The area of law involved is residential tenancy law, and in particular termination of a tenancy by a landlord at the end of a term.

Step 3: Research and Find the Relevant Law

This situation is governed by the *Residential Tenancies Act, 2006*, SO 2006, chapter 17. Section 48(1)(c) provides as follows:

> 48(1) A landlord may, by notice, terminate a tenancy if the landlord in good faith requires possession of the rental unit for the purpose of residential occupation by, …
>
>   (c) a child or parent of the landlord or the landlord's spouse.

However, under section 57(1)(a), a former tenant may apply to the Landlord and Tenant Board if

> the landlord gave a notice of termination under section 48 in bad faith, the former tenant vacated the rental unit as a result of the notice … and no person referred to in clause 48 (1) … (d) occupied the rental unit within a reasonable time after the former tenant vacated the rental unit.

In such a case, the Landlord and Tenant Board may, under section 57(3), order that the landlord pay a specified sum to the former tenant for

> i. all or any portion of any increased rent that the former tenant has incurred or will incur for a one-year period after vacating the rental unit, and
> ii. reasonable out-of-pocket moving, storage and other like expenses that the former tenant has incurred or will incur.

In addition, Interpretation Guideline G12 of the Landlord and Tenant Board, *Eviction for Personal Use*, deals with interpretation questions respecting eviction applications under section 48. Under the heading "Requirement of good faith," it states, "The issue that arises in some cases is whether the landlord or a family member has a real intention to reside in the rental unit." Under the heading "The landlord requires the unit—test to be applied," it provides as follows:

> The burden of proof is on the landlord. It is relevant to the good faith of the landlord's intention to occupy the unit to determine the likelihood that the intended person will move into it.

> The issue here is whether the notice of termination was given in good faith. The tenants must persuade the tribunal that the notice was given in bad faith, while the landlord must persuade the tribunal that the notice was given in good faith.

Step 4: Determine How You Will Put the Relevant Facts into Evidence

The landlord's evidence will consist of witness testimony and documents.

Jim can testify about the terms of the lease with the tenants and can introduce the written lease into evidence. He can also testify about the family's intention for Cynthia to live in the apartment upon graduation from university, Cynthia's statement in February that she would likely be moving back to Toronto, and service of the form N12 notice of termination, which he can introduce into evidence. In addition, Jim can testify that he learned Cynthia would not be returning to Toronto only after the tenants had moved out, and that he then decided to try to re-rent the apartment at a higher rent.

Cynthia can testify about the family's intention for her to live in the apartment upon graduation from university, and her having told her father in February 2016 that she would likely be doing so. She can also testify that in April she decided to take a job in Ottawa rather than return to Toronto.

Step 5: Assess Your Own Case

Even though the landlord's daughter did not move into the apartment and the landlord instead re-rented it at a higher rent than the tenants were paying, the adjudicator should be willing to conclude that the landlord reasonably believed that his daughter would be moving in at the time the notice of termination was given. If the adjudicator concludes that the landlord gave the notice of termination in bad faith, the adjudicator may be persuaded that the amount of the tenants' damages is excessive.

Step 6: Assess Your Opponent's Case

Given that the landlord's daughter did not move into the apartment and that the landlord instead re-rented it at a higher rent than the tenants were paying, the adjudicator may infer that the notice of termination was given in good faith.

REVIEW QUESTIONS

1. What is the theory of the case?

2. What must your theory of the case include?

3. How do you make your theory of the case persuasive?

4. When should you start to develop your theory of the case, and why?

5. What are the six steps to follow in developing a theory of the case?

CHAPTER 7

Interviewing Witnesses

LEARNING OUTCOMES

After reading this chapter, you will understand

■ the preliminary matters to consider before interviewing a witness

■ the key rules of the *Paralegal Rules of Conduct* relating to communicating with witnesses

■ the key rules of the *Paralegal Rules of Conduct* relating to interviewing witnesses

■ the different stages in a witness interview

■ how to conduct an effective witness interview

■ a paralegal's obligations under the *Paralegal Rules of Conduct* with respect to document disclosure

---

In Chapter 6, we introduced the six steps for constructing a theory of the case and applied them to construct a theory for the Kitchen Renovation Case, the Liquor Licence Case, and the Landlord and Tenant Dispute. Those theories are based on Fact Situations 1, 2, and 3 in Chapter 1 and on information obtained from the witness interviews in those cases.

Witness interviews are key in the development of your theory of the case. The goal of a witness interview is to gather facts within a limited amount of time. To be effective as an interviewer, you must be organized, knowledgeable, patient, a good listener, and a good note-taker. Without proper interviewing skills, you are likely to miss material facts that may be helpful to your case and which may adversely affect your ability to provide effective representation of your client.

This chapter discusses the six stages in a witness interview, different types of listening and questioning techniques, and the key *Paralegal Rules of Conduct*[1] relating to witness interviews. Appendixes A and B contain the relevant *Paralegal Rules of Conduct* and *Paralegal Professional Conduct Guidelines*.

Interviewing Witnesses: Preliminary Considerations

Before interviewing a witness, you must consider your obligations under the *Paralegal Rules of Conduct*. The Rules place obligations on licensed paralegals when seeking information from potential witnesses. They also limit a paralegal's ability to communicate with a potential witness when the witness is represented by another licensee.

Rule 4.02 of the *Paralegal Rules of Conduct* permits a paralegal to seek information from any potential witness in the matter. This includes potential witnesses for both sides of the proceeding. However, this ability is restricted by Rule 7.02 when the potential witness is represented by another legal practitioner in respect of the matter for which the paralegal wants to interview the witness. Rule 7.02(1) provides as follows:

> (1) Subject to subrules (2) and (3), if a person is represented by a legal practitioner in respect of a matter, a paralegal shall not, except through or with the consent of the legal practitioner,
>> (a) approach or communicate or deal with the person on the matter, or
>> (b) attempt to negotiate or compromise the matter directly with the person.

Before contacting a potential witness, then, you should determine whether the witness is represented by a lawyer or paralegal. If so, you must contact the witness's legal representative.

If the witness is not represented, you may attempt to contact the witness to obtain information. When you do so, Rule 4.02(1) requires that you disclose your interest in the matter to the witness. If the witness is not your client, this means explicitly telling the witness that you are a paralegal and identifying who your client is and your client's status in the proceeding (for example, plaintiff, defendant, applicant, respondent). Guideline 12 of the *Paralegal Professional Conduct Guidelines*[2] explains that you must make clear to the witness that you are acting in the best interests of your client only.

In addition, Rule 4.02 requires a paralegal to "take care not to subvert or suppress any evidence or procure the witness to stay out of the way." In other words, throughout your witness interview, you cannot encourage the witness to stay away from the proceeding, to keep quiet, or to hide evidence.

Finally, even if you attempt to obtain information from a potential witness and you have complied with your obligations under the *Paralegal Rules of Conduct* as outlined above, the witness does not have to speak to you. You cannot force a potential witness to meet with you and answer your questions. When a potential witness refuses to speak to you and you think he or she has important information relevant to your case, the rules of the court or tribunal may allow you to issue a summons ordering the individual to attend a hearing as a witness.

If the witness agrees to speak to you and you have considered your obligations under the *Paralegal Rules of Conduct* and complied with Rule 4.02 and Rule 7.02, you can proceed to interview your witness.

Interviewing Witnesses: Six Stages to an Effective Witness Interview

A witness is a person who has personal knowledge of something relevant in a proceeding. This is often your client, but can also be any person who may have knowledge of the facts relating to the case. There are different types of witnesses, such as lay witnesses and expert witnesses. How you conduct a witness interview will depend on a number of factors, including the type of witness you are interviewing and whether the witness is your own client.

Below, we outline the six stages to an effective witness interview, along with different interview techniques. Where possible, we highlight the different considerations that arise when conducting an interview with your own client.

The six stages to an effective witness interview are

1. prepare,
2. introduce,
3. listen,
4. question,
5. conclude, and
6. create a witness statement/take notes.

These six stages are broken down into steps as set out in Table 7.1.

1. Prepare

Before you meet with the witness, you must prepare for the interview. Review all of the pleadings in the case, and familiarize yourself with the legal issues involved. Read over any statements or interview notes from your client and any other witnesses.

Many advocates use checklists to prepare for and facilitate a witness interview, particularly when interviewing their client. A checklist will help you proceed with the interview in a structured manner. It may also help you to identify issues to canvass with the witness and remind you to obtain basic information regarding the matter.

2. Introduce

At the start of a witness interview, greet your witness, introduce yourself, and make the witness feel comfortable. Greeting your witness by name in the reception area of your office, for example, rather than having your assistant escort him or her to your office, helps develop a rapport with the witness. Developing a personal rapport

TABLE 7.1   **Stages and Steps of a Witness Interview**

Stage	Steps
1. Prepare	a. Review the pleadings b. Familiarize yourself with the legal issues c. Review statements/interview notes from your client and any other witnesses d. Consider preparing or reviewing a checklist
2. Introduce	a. Greet the witness b. Engage in small talk c. Explain the purpose and structure of the interview and approximately how long it will take d. Explain the importance of being open and honest. If the witness is your client, explain duty of confidentiality
3. Listen	a. Elicit the story with opening questions b. Let the witness set out his or her story in the witness's own words c. Demonstrate understanding and sympathy d. If witness is your client, assess needs and wants
4. Question	a. Question on the facts for gaps, depth, background, ambiguities, accuracy, and relevance b. Confirm the witness's qualifications as to competence, credibility, and bias c. Ask for documents relating to the matter (consider your disclosure obligations under the *Paralegal Rules of Conduct*) d. Restate your view of the facts e. Ask whether the witness agrees with your view of the facts; if the witness does not, ask for and make the necessary corrections f. Ask whether there is anything else the witness has not told you that the witness thinks you should know
5. Conclude	a. Get the witness's complete address, telephone number, and other contact information b. Explain next steps to the witness c. End the interview
6. Create a witness statement	Create a witness statement from the notes you have taken throughout the interview

Note-taking

is important because the more comfortable a witness is with you, the more likely he or she will share information with you.

After introducing yourself, consider engaging in small talk in order to help the witness to relax. For many individuals, your interview will be their first contact with a legal professional or their first time in a law office, and they may feel nervous or intimidated. For example, you can ask whether the witness had any problems finding parking, or whether he or she would like something to drink.

Once you are seated and ready to start the interview, do not immediately start asking the witness questions, but continue to make him or her feel comfortable. Tell the witness the purpose and structure of the meeting and approximately how long it will take. Let the witness know that you will be taking notes throughout the meeting. Letting witnesses know what to expect will help them to relax. For example, when meeting with a client for the first time regarding a landlord and tenant matter, you could say something like this:

> Mr. Drew, I understand you are having problems with your landlord. The purpose of our meeting today is to understand what happened so that I can determine what, if anything, should happen next and whether I can assist you. I will start by asking you to tell me what happened from beginning to end. Once you have told me everything you know and can remember, I will start asking you questions. Some questions may be very specific. This is because I am trying to piece together all the details of what happened. Then, I will talk to you about next steps and answer any questions you might have. I expect this meeting to take about 45 minutes to an hour, and I will be taking notes throughout the meeting. Is all this okay with you?

You should also explain to the witness the importance of being open and honest with you. If the witness is your client and you are meeting for the first time, remind him or her of your duty of confidentiality. In order to be open and honest with you, your client needs to trust you. Your client is less likely to misrepresent facts or withhold information from you if he or she feels you are trustworthy. Reassure your client that anything he or she says to you will be kept confidential in accordance with your ethical obligations under the *Paralegal Rules of Conduct*. Inform your client that you can represent him or her to the best of your ability only if you know all the facts, regardless of whether they are favourable or unfavourable.

3. Listen

The next stage of the witness interview involves the preliminary identification of the legal issue and problem through active listening. At the start of the interview, your major role is that of a listener.

Use effective listening skills to encourage the witness to share information with you. Ask a few general, open-ended questions to elicit the witness's story, such as "Tell me what happened" or "Why have you come to see me today?" Open-ended questions let the witness tell the story in his or her own words. Do not worry if the witness's story is overly detailed (you will not know which details are relevant until you hear the entire story) or disorganized (you can organize the story later).

Your goal is to listen in such a way that you

- *show you are paying attention* in order to encourage the witness to speak—for example, by nodding and by saying, "tell me more," "uh huh," and "I see"; and
- *show understanding by*
  - paraphrasing feelings and sympathizing with the witness—for example, "I can see that upset you very much" or "That must have been very difficult for you";
  - paraphrasing or summarizing content—for example, "So if I can just summarize what you've said, it seems that ... Is that correct?"; and
  - clarifying—asking a question to clear up any ambiguity.

If the witness is your client, you must also employ active listening skills and open-ended questions to determine your client's needs and wants. Often, advocates proceed with a case without truly understanding what the client wants to happen. For example, ask the client questions such as "What do you want to see happen?" and "What made you decide to start this action?"

Take notes while the witness is speaking. It shows that you are paying attention. You will also use your notes while asking the witness questions in order to elicit more information and confirm facts. Make sure you maintain eye contact with the witness throughout the interview, including while you are taking notes. Good eye contact shows the witness you care and are paying attention.

4. Question

After the witness has completed his or her story, you can go back and use various questioning techniques to

- fill in gaps in the story,
- obtain further details,
- obtain background information or explanations,
- clarify ambiguities or contradictions in the story,
- check the accuracy of the information, and
- determine the relevance of aspects of the story.

You should also ask questions to confirm the witness's qualifications to give evidence and to understand his or her motivations. Do this by asking different types of questions to test the witness's

- *competence to testify*—as a lay witness, that he or she actually saw or heard the events in some way; as an expert witness, that he or she possesses special knowledge, skill, experience, training, or education;
- *credibility*—about any matters that would tend to show whether the witness is honest; and
- *bias*—by determining whether the witness has an interest in the matter in question that would tend to prejudice his or her testimony.

Use different types of questions at various points during the interview. Consider the following types of questions and their uses:

- *Open-ended questions* allow the witness to choose the information he or she thinks is relevant to a particular subject—for example, "What do you know about the facts of this case?" or "Is there anything else about this matter I should know?" Asking open-ended questions may also reveal gaps in the story which you can attempt to fill later on in the interview by asking other types of questions listed below. However, using open-ended questions can also cause some problems. They may allow a witness to ramble on about irrelevant things. This requires you to exercise some control by helping the witness refocus on the story. Use this type of question at Step 3a and Step 4f in Table 7.1.
- *Narrow/closed questions* allow you to focus on both the subject matter and the specific aspect that the witness should address in the answer—for example, "What can you tell me about the condition of the apartment?" and "How fast were you driving?" Use this type of question at Step 3a and Step 4a.
- *Yes/no questions* are very specific about subject matter and allow the interview subject to answer only "yes" or "no." For example, "Did you pay a last month's rent deposit?" or "Were you talking on your cellphone at the time of the accident?" Use this type of question at Step 4a.
- *Leading questions* make a statement that asserts what is relevant, and by their form suggest that the witness agrees with the statement—for example, "You didn't give notice to terminate in writing, did you?" or "You were talking on your cellphone at the time of the accident, weren't you?" Use this type of question throughout Step 4 when confirming information with the interview subject or when dealing with a difficult interview subject. These types of questions can help get information from a witness that he or she may not otherwise provide. They are also helpful when confirming information with the witness or when dealing with a witness who is hard to understand. However, use leading questions sparingly throughout your interview, as they can make witnesses feel they are under attack. Leading questions can also distort the facts, because the witness may agree with your statement out of politeness even if the statement is incorrect.

Some further examples of these different types of questions are presented in Table 7.2.

TABLE 7.2 Types of Questions and Examples

Type of Question	Example
Open-ended	Tell me what happened.
	How can I help you?
	What happened after that?
	Describe what you saw.
Narrow/closed	Where were you going?
	Did the landlord give you anything?
	When did the accident happen?
	What did you ask him to install in your kitchen?
Yes/no	Were you wearing your seat belt?
	Did you pay last month's rent?
	Did you call the police?
	Did you sign a contract?
Leading	You weren't wearing your seat belt, were you?
	You didn't pay last month's rent, did you?
	You didn't call the police, isn't that so?
	You didn't sign anything, right?

Throughout the interview, ask the witness if he or she has any documents related to the matter and whether he or she can provide the originals. This may include an offence notice or summons (in a provincial offences case), an appearance notice or summons (in a criminal case), pleadings, photographs, drawings, letters, emails, text messages, medical records, financial records, and so on. If the witness has any documents with him or her during the interview, review the documents with the witness. It may help the witness remember certain facts.

Keep in mind that, depending on the type of case and the rules of the court or tribunal, your client may have to disclose all documents relating to the case to the other party. Rule 4.01(6) of the *Paralegal Rules of Conduct* states that

> (6) If the rules of a tribunal require the parties to produce documents, a paralegal, when acting as an advocate,
>
> (a) shall explain to his or her client the necessity of making full disclosure of all documents relating to any matter in issue and the duty to answer to the best of his or her knowledge, information and belief, any proper question relating to any issue in the action;

(b) shall assist the client in fulfilling his or her obligation to make full disclosure; and

(c) shall not make frivolous requests for the production of documents or make frivolous demands for information.

You have an obligation under Rule 4.01(6) of the *Paralegal Rules of Conduct* to explain to your client the necessity of making full disclosure of all documents relating to any issue in the case and to assist your client in doing so. Make sure you explain this to your client during the interview.

Box 7.1 lists examples of the documents that the advocate for each party in the Kitchen Renovation Case, the Liquor Licence Case, and the Landlord and Tenant Dispute may ask for during the witness interviews.

BOX 7.1

Examples of Documents Requested in the Kitchen Renovation Case, the Liquor Licence Case, and the Landlord and Tenant Dispute

Kitchen Renovation Case

The advocate for the Baldwin Brothers will ask them to provide all documents relating to the case, including

• the invoice for services rendered

The advocate for the Feys will ask them to produce all documents relating to the case, including

• the invoice rendered to them

Liquor Licence Case

The prosecutor will ask Police Constable Lee to provide all documents relating to the case, including

• copies of his police notes
• the Catering Notification Form

The advocate for Victoria Levens and Treetop Catering Inc. will ask Victoria to provide all documents relating to the case, including

• summonses
• the Catering Notification Form
• any photographs of the student lounge and/or patio
• any drawings or sketches of the student lounge and/or patio

Landlord and Tenant Dispute

The advocate for the tenants will ask them to provide all documents relating to the case, including

- the lease agreement with Jim Croce
- form N12 "Notice to End Your Tenancy Because the Landlord, a Purchaser or a Family Member Requires the Rental Unit"
- form N9 "Tenant's Notice to End the Tenancy"
- the lease agreement for the new apartment
- the invoice from Two Guys Moving

The advocate for the landlord will ask him to provide all documents relating to the case, including

- the lease agreement with Arlo and Alice Guthrie
- form N12 "Notice to End Your Tenancy Because the Landlord, a Purchaser or a Family Member Requires the Rental Unit"
- form N9 "Tenant's Notice to End the Tenancy"

Once you are fairly satisfied that you have the witness's entire story, tell the witness your understanding of the facts and ask whether he or she agrees with it. If the witness disagrees with your understanding of the facts, ask for and make any necessary corrections. Before you conclude the interview, ask the witness whether there is anything else he or she has not told you that the witness thinks you should know.

5. Conclude

Conclude the interview by getting the witness's complete address, telephone number, and other contact information (if you do not already have it) and by thanking the witness for participating in the interview. If the witness is your client, tell him or her what the next steps are in the case and when you will next be contacting him or her.

6. Create a Witness Statement / Take Notes

You must make notes of what the witness says as you conduct the interview. When the interview is finished, do not just put your notes into a file. You need to organize the information collected. Take the time to prepare a summary of the information you have collected or a chronological overview of the facts immediately after the interview while the information is fresh in your memory. This will help to identify any missing facts or information. You should also take the time to set out the information in a witness statement. Examples of the witness statements for the Kitchen Renovation Case, the Liquor Licence Case, and the Landlord and Tenant Dispute are provided in Chapter 6.

Tips for an Effective Witness Interview

- Don't record the interview. Even if the witness gives permission for you to record the interview, it will likely make him or her feel uncomfortable.

- Don't be distracted during the interview. Turn off your computer and put away your cellphone. If your telephone rings, do not answer it. Your full attention should be on the witness.

- Avoid distracting behaviours such as clicking your pen or tapping your pen against your notepad while you or your witness are speaking.

- Don't use legal jargon.

- Don't interrupt the witness while he or she is speaking.

- Be conscious of your body language. Don't sit with your arms crossed. This sends a negative message to the witness, such as "I don't believe you," and may discourage the witness from being open and honest with you.

- Don't rush through the interview.

- Never tell the witness that he or she is lying.

- Take a break if necessary. Sometimes all the questions and information can be overwhelming for a witness. Taking a break can help the client to refocus.

- Compliment the witness when he or she gives important information—for example, "Thank you for telling me that. It is very helpful to know." It helps put the witness at ease and encourage him or her to share information with you.

- Observe the witness's demeanour, tone, and body language when discussing certain topics. This might help you identify when the witness might be lying or hiding information.

- Personalize the interview by continuing to refer to the witness by name. Avoid following a standardized list of pre-formulated questions.

A sample witness interview with a witness from Fact Situation 2, the Liquor Licence Case, is presented in Box 7.2.

Sample Witness Interview with Victoria Levens (Liquor Licence Case)

Paralegal:	Hello, Ms. Levens; my name is Linda Thomas, and I am the licensed paralegal who will be meeting with you today. How are you?
Victoria Levens:	Okay, thanks.
Paralegal:	Did you find the office all right today?
Victoria Levens:	Yes, thank you.
Paralegal:	If you would just follow me back to my office, we will get started.
Victoria Levens:	All right.
Paralegal:	Can I get you something to drink? We have tea, coffee, and water.
Victoria Levens:	No, thank you.
Paralegal:	After talking briefly with you over the phone, I understand you were charged under the *Liquor Licence Act*. Before we start talking about that and what happened, I would just like to explain to you that the purpose of our meeting today is to understand what happened so I can determine what, if anything, should happen next and whether I can assist you. I will start by asking you to tell me what happened from beginning to end. Once you have told me everything you know and can remember, I will start asking you questions. Some questions may be very specific. This is because I am trying to piece together all the details of what happened. After that, I will talk to you about next steps and answer any questions you might have. I expect this meeting to take about 30 to 45 minutes, and I will be taking notes throughout the meeting to assist me. Is this okay with you?
Victoria Levens:	Yes. Sounds good to me.
Paralegal:	Also, it is really important that you be open and honest with me about what happened. Everything that you tell me here today will remain confidential between you and my firm in accordance with my duties under the *Paralegal Rules of Conduct*. In order to represent you to the best of my abilities, I need to know all the facts, good or bad.
Victoria Levens:	Okay. Thank you for that. It makes sense.
Paralegal:	All right. Let's get started. What happened?

Victoria Levens:	Well, I was recently served with two summonses which say I have been charged with permitting alcohol to leave the premises. I have a catering business and I was hired by the Simpson Academy Advocacy Club to cater an event for its members. Yes, we served alcohol. But I worked really hard to make sure everything was controlled.
Paralegal:	Tell me more.
Victoria Levens:	I hired a bartender and a security guard for the event. But apparently there was a noise complaint from a neighbour, and so the police showed up to check things out. I guess there were beer bottles and plastic wine glasses on the grass beyond the outside patio, so the police officer told me he would be charging me under the *Liquor Licence Act*. A few days later I received summonses.
Paralegal:	I'm sure you were not expecting something like that to happen. You must have been surprised.
Victoria Levens:	Yes, I was very surprised and shocked. This has never happened to me before. I have never been charged with anything. I am always very organized, and I always make sure I take all the required steps when catering an event where alcohol is going to be served. For the Simpson Academy event, I notified the Registrar of the Alcohol and Gaming Commission, police, fire, health, and building departments about the event and everything as required by the law.
Paralegal:	How did you do that?
Victoria Levens:	I sent them a copy of the Catering Notification Form.
Paralegal:	Do you have that notice form you sent?
Victoria Levens:	Yes, I do. I have the original at my office.
Paralegal:	You said you were served with two summonses. You were served with more than one?
Victoria Levens:	Yes. I was charged individually, and my business was charged as well. I am the sole director, officer, and shareholder of Treetop Catering Inc.
Paralegal:	Did you bring those summonses with you today?
Victoria Levens:	Yes. Here they are.
	[*paralegal briefly reviews the summonses*]
Paralegal:	Did you have a licence to serve alcohol at this particular event?
Victoria Levens:	Yes. My company, Treetop Catering, holds a Liquor Sales Licence, and I applied for and was granted a caterer's endorsement authorizing me to sell and serve liquor at the Simpson Academy event in the indoor lounge and the outdoor patio.

Paralegal:	It appears from your summonses that your first court appearance is scheduled for September 12, 2016. What do you want to see happen here?
Victoria Levens:	Basically, I think the charge is ridiculous, and I want it dismissed. I want to fight it.
Paralegal:	When did this event and the incident take place?
Victoria Levens:	The event took place on May 16, 2016, in the evening.
Paralegal:	Where did the event take place? I know you mentioned at the student lounge at the Simpson Academy, but do you have the address?
Victoria Levens:	The student lounge is located at the Simpson Academy at 1292 Olde Street, Toronto, Ontario M5S 5P5.
Paralegal:	When did guests start arriving to the event on May 16, 2016?
Victoria Levens:	I would say around 7:00 p.m. The event was scheduled from 7:00 p.m. to midnight.
Paralegal:	Can you describe the student lounge? What did the setup for the event look like?
Victoria Levens:	There was an indoor bar and a fenced outdoor patio area. There was also a buffet inside the lounge area near the bar.
Paralegal:	Was the entire student lounge licensed for the service of alcohol?
Victoria Levens:	Yes. Both inside the student lounge and the outside patio. Guests were permitted to have alcohol on the patio in accordance with the caterer's endorsement.
Paralegal:	Did you draw any sketches or diagrams of the layout of the patio, or do you know anyone who did?
Victoria Levens:	Yes I did. I made a diagram shortly after I visited the lounge on May 1, 2016 to inspect the layout of the premises.
Paralegal:	Do you still have that diagram you made?
Victoria Levens:	Yes. I think it's at home on my computer.
Paralegal:	Okay, great. Because we will likely need that diagram. Please arrange to deliver it to my office.
Victoria Levens:	Will do.
Paralegal:	Okay, thank you. You mentioned that a police officer showed up at the event as a result of a noise complaint. Is that correct?
Victoria Levens:	Yes.
Paralegal:	When did the police officer arrive at the event?
Victoria Levens:	I think it was just after 11:30 p.m. It was definitely before midnight.

Paralegal:	And what happened when the police officer arrived?
Victoria Levens:	He just told me that there had been a noise complaint. He walked around to take a look at what was going on. I ended up telling him that I would just ask the guests to leave at that point since it was almost midnight and the event ended at midnight.
Paralegal:	You mentioned that there were beer bottles and plastic wine glasses on the grass beyond the outside patio. How do you know this?
Victoria Levens:	The police officer told me that he saw them there.
Paralegal:	But you never saw them yourself, correct?
Victoria Levens:	That is correct. I never went outside onto the patio during the evening until the police officer arrived because I was busy all night helping with the buffet and other things inside.
Paralegal:	But alcohol was being served at the event?
Victoria Levens:	Yes, it was.
Paralegal:	What type of alcohol?
Victoria Levens:	We had beer and wine.
Paralegal:	How were these drinks served to guests?
Victoria Levens:	The bartender was taking care of this. The beer was served in bottles and the wine in plastic wine cups.
Paralegal:	Were there any other types of drinks being served?
Victoria Levens:	Yes. We had soft drinks and water, which were served in small cans.
Paralegal:	Tell me about this outdoor patio. Is there a fence or anything separating the patio from the grassy area beyond the patio?
Victoria Levens:	Oh, yes. I forgot to mention that the outdoor patio is fully fenced, with a gate leading from the patio to the grassy area beyond.
Paralegal:	You mentioned that you hired a security guard for this event. What is his name, and what were his responsibilities?
Victoria Levens:	His name is Calvin Hobbs, and he has been working as a security guard for about three years now. That night, he was responsible for making sure no guests left the outside patio with any drinks. He was on the patio for the entire evening, I believe.
Paralegal:	Did any guests actually leave the patio?
Victoria Levens:	Well, I don't know for sure, because like I said, I stayed inside the lounge the entire evening, helping with the buffet. But the security guard told me that he saw some people leave to have a smoke outside the patio but that he never saw anyone leaving with an alcoholic drink.

Paralegal:	So the patio was fenced, and there was a security guard stationed on the patio to make sure no guests left the patio with drinks. Was there anything else that would have prevented or discouraged guests from leaving the patio?
Victoria Levens:	Well, there were signs around the lounge telling guests that alcohol was prohibited outside the patio area.
Paralegal:	Where were those signs, exactly? Do you remember?
Victoria Levens:	Yes. There was one posted at the door leading out to the patio and another one on the patio gate leading out of the patio to the grassy area.
Paralegal:	Other than the summonses, Catering Notification Form, and diagram, do you have any other documents that relate to this event or the charge? Letters, emails, text messages, records of any kind?
Victoria Levens:	No.
Paralegal:	All right. To summarize, Ms. Levens: Your company, Treetop Catering Inc., and you were catering an event at the Simpson Academy student lounge on May 16, 2016. Guests started to arrive at around 7:00 p.m. You arranged for a buffet, bartender, and security guard. Alcoholic drinks of beer and wine were served at the event. Only the student lounge and outside patio were licensed for alcohol. The outside patio was fenced but had a gate opening to a grassy area. There were signs on the doors leading out to the patio and on the patio gate, advising guests that alcohol beyond the patio was prohibited. You hired a security guard for the event to make sure no guests took alcohol outside the patio. He was stationed on the patio for the entire evening. Sometime around 11:30 p.m. or so a police officer arrived advising there had been a noise complaint. He walked around the premises and then told you he had seen beer bottles and plastic wine glasses on the grass beyond the patio area. However, you never saw anyone leaving the patio with alcoholic drinks because you remained inside in the lounge all evening. Do you agree with those facts as described?
Victoria Levens:	Yes. That's what happened.
Paralegal:	Is there anything else that you haven't told me that you think I should know?
Victoria Levens:	No. That's all there is.
Paralegal:	All right. In terms of going forward, we will have to start preparing for a trial. This involves obtaining any disclosure from the prosecutor and interviewing any potential witnesses. I would like to interview your security guard, Calvin Hobbs, and I will need his

contact information. Also, please arrange to drop off the Catering Notification Form and the diagram you made.

I will be in touch over the next few weeks once I have interviewed Mr. Hobbs. I see I already have your contact information in the file, so I will be in touch soon.

Do you have any questions for me?

Victoria Levens: No. You have been very helpful. I will get those items together for you. I look forward to hearing from you soon.

Paralegal: Thank you, Ms. Levens. Have a great weekend, and I will speak to you soon.

NOTES

1 Law Society of Upper Canada, *Paralegal Rules of Conduct* (Toronto: LSUC, 2007), online: <http://www.lsuc.on.ca/paralegal-conduct-rules>.

2 Law Society of Upper Canada, *Paralegal Professional Conduct Guidelines* (Toronto: LSUC, 2014), online: <http://www.lsuc.on.ca/paralegal-conduct-guidelines>.

REVIEW QUESTIONS

1. What are the six stages of an effective witness interview? Briefly summarize each stage.

2. What are open-ended questions, and at what steps of a witness interview should you use them? Provide an example.

3. What are narrow or closed questions, and at what steps of a witness interview should you use them? Provide an example.

4. What are yes/no questions, and at what steps of a witness interview should you use them? Provide an example.

5. What are leading questions, and at what steps of a witness interview should you use them? Provide an example.

EXERCISES

1. Find a partner. Take turns sharing with each other a difficult experience you faced in your life. While one partner is speaking, the other partner will practise active listening skills. While listening to your partner, use verbal and non-verbal techniques to encourage your partner to share more information with you. Show that you are paying attention and that you understand what your partner is telling you. Once both partners complete the exercise, take turns discussing the following:

    a. What techniques did each person use in order to encourage the other person to share more information?

    b. What techniques did each person use to demonstrate understanding?

    c. What techniques did each person use to demonstrate sympathy?

    d. Did the listener summarize any information? If so, was it summarized accurately?

    e. What did the listener do, if anything, that made the speaker feel uncomfortable?

2. Find a partner. Each partner will take turns acting as a witness and as an interviewing paralegal using the witness statements of Alice Guthrie and Jim Croce in the Landlord and Tenant Dispute. The witness statements can be found in Chapter 6.

To start, Partner 1 will play the role of Alice Guthrie, using the witness statement in Box 6.5. Partner 2 will play the role of Alice's paralegal and will interview Alice using the six steps discussed in this chapter. Only Partner 1 can refer to the witness statement.

Once finished, Partner 2 will play the role of Jim Croce, using the witness statement in Box 6.6. Partner 1 will play the role of Jim's paralegal and will interview Jim using the six steps discussed in this chapter. Only Partner 2 can refer to the witness statement.

After the interviews are completed, discuss with your partner the following:

a. Did the paralegal make the witness feel comfortable? If so, how did he or she do so?

b. Did the paralegal demonstrate active listening? If so, what did he or she do?

c. What types of questions did the paralegal use to elicit information from the witness?

d. Were there any material facts that the paralegal was unable to draw from the witness? If so, what could the paralegal have done to get the witness to share these facts?

CHAPTER 8

Presentation Skills

As an advocate, you must not only plan and prepare for *what* you will say; you must also pay attention to *how* you will say it. While some people are naturally gifted public speakers, most are not, and will need to develop presentation skills to improve their performance at a trial or hearing. It is likely that, as a new advocate, you will be nervous about appearing in court or before a tribunal. This is perfectly normal. The best way to combat your nerves is to be as well prepared as possible. This preparation includes practising your presentation skills.

You will not become an award-winning advocate overnight. Good advocacy skills are developed over a long period of time through practice both inside and outside the courtroom. With time and practice, you will develop your own presentation style along with the confidence needed to excel as an advocate. This chapter discusses the key presentation skills that every advocate should keep in mind when preparing to appear in court or before a tribunal.

Appearance

Good advocacy starts with a good appearance. Dress appropriately for your trial or hearing. Pay attention to your hair, clothing, and accessories. First impressions can be very important and may influence the attitude of the judge, justice of the peace, or adjudicator toward you.

Body Language and Mannerisms

Stand straight and hold your head up during your presentation, and avoid slouching, pacing, shuffling about, or fidgeting. Try to be aware of any mannerisms you might have while speaking that might be irritating or distracting and that will detract from your presentation. For example, some people fidget with their keys, hair, jewellery, coins, or pen when nervous. Pens are particularly problematic. The best advice is to avoid holding a pen during your presentation. That way, you won't be tempted to wave or point it at the judge, justice of the peace, or adjudicator, or to play with the clicker, if the pen has one, a common distraction for judges and other decision-makers. To avoid fidgeting, place your hands on the podium or clasp them together in front of you.

Consider whether your hand gestures are distracting. Many people use excessive hand gestures when speaking. Natural hand gestures can be effective. However, long, sweeping hand movements from side to side throughout a presentation will distract the decision-maker from the content of what you are saying.

Make sure you do not walk around the courtroom or hearing room too much while you are speaking. Pacing back and forth is a common habit when people are nervous and can be very distracting. When speaking, stand at the counsel table or the podium in the middle of the room, if there is one. While you may need to approach the bench or a witness in the witness box to hand over something such as an exhibit, you must always ask permission from the decision-maker to do so, and you must then immediately return to the podium or counsel table.

Use of Language

Consider whether the language you are using is appropriate for an oral presentation. Often, words look fine on the page but sound awkward or unduly complicated when spoken. Sentences should be shorter and sentence structure simpler in an oral presentation. At the same time, in order to show respect for the court or tribunal, avoid using informal language or slang. For example, when answering a question, say "yes" rather than "yeah" or "yep." Say "no" rather than "nope." When asking the decision-maker or witness to repeat themselves, say "pardon me?" rather than "what?" Also, use words that you know how to pronounce. Make sure you check the pronunciation of unusual or foreign words that you will be using.

When speaking during the hearing, you will likely be nervous. You may be tempted to use filler words. Filler words are meaningless words or sounds that a speaker uses to gain a moment to think about what to say next. They are often used as a form of pause between sentences. Some examples include "um," "oh," "like," and "you know." Fillers can also take the form of saying "Your Honour" or "Your Worship" at the beginning or end of every sentence. Many people use filler words without noticing that they are doing so. In order to cut out these words from your presentation, start by paying attention to how often you use them. Once you are aware of the problem, you can practise speaking without those words. Speaking slowly, and pausing when you want to use a filler word, is helpful.

Many advocates also have a habit of starting every sentence with the words "and," "okay," "well," and "now." This is particularly the case when an advocate is examining a witness during a direct or cross-examination. It is distracting and can weaken your effectiveness as an advocate. Again, you can avoid this habit by speaking slowly and taking pauses.

Use introductory sentences to take the place of headings so that the judge or other decision-maker can follow what you are saying. This is especially important during the closing argument, when you transition from one issue or argument to the next. For example, you might say, "I will next address the second issue, which is whether the notice given to the tenant was valid."

Finally, make sure the language you use is appropriate for a courtroom. Never use language that expresses your personal opinion or belief such as "I believe," "I think," or "in my opinion." Rather, when expressing a position or argument, start the sentence with "I submit" or "It is the [party's] position that …" Also, use language that is courteous and respectful to the judge, justice of the peace, or adjudicator. When disagreeing with a judge or other decision-maker, don't say "That's not true," or "You're wrong, Your Honour." Rather, show respect for the decision-maker's authority by using the phrase, "With respect, Your Honour," or "Respectfully, Your Honour." Further, make sure you practise using the appropriate honorific for your particular case—Your Honour, Your Worship, Madam Adjudicator, as the case may be. It is easy to fall into the habit of calling every decision-maker "Your Honour" when it is not appropriate to do so.

Volume and Clarity

Ensure that your voice is loud enough, but not too loud. Adjust your volume to the size of the courtroom or tribunal room. Some courtrooms or tribunal rooms are large and the judge or other decision-maker may be seated quite a distance away from you, in which case you need to be able to project your voice and speak clearly in order to be heard.

Speed

Speaking too quickly is one of the most common mistakes new advocates make. Most people naturally speak too quickly, especially when they are nervous, and also do not realize they are speaking too fast. A common practice among new advocates is to write "SLOW DOWN" in red pen at the top of their speaking notes. Speak slowly to avoid other common mistakes, such as using filler words. Always speak more slowly than you think you need to. If you sound to yourself like you are speaking too slowly, it is probably the right speed. Keep in mind that the judge or other decision-maker will be taking notes and needs time to process what you are saying.

Pacing

Think of pacing as punctuation in a written presentation: in an oral presentation, pacing takes the place of commas, periods, and paragraphs. Pause briefly between sentences, and pause longer between ideas. There is a common misconception among many people that silence is bad. This is not true for oral advocacy. Pauses, at appropriate times, can help put emphasis on certain words and points you are making and allow the adjudicator time to digest what you have just said. Remind yourself to pause by leaving large blocks of white space in your speaking notes.

Expression

Use your voice expressively. Do not speak in a monotone. Raise or lower your volume as appropriate in order to give expression to what you are saying. Speak with strength in your voice rather than with hesitation. Avoid "up-talk"—raising the pitch at the end of your sentences, a tendency that makes statements sound like questions. "Up-talk" makes the speaker sound tentative and uncertain, and is extremely irritating to the listener. Pay attention to your intonation so that you appear confident and certain about whatever you are saying. When you appear confident, you are likely to be more persuasive.

Awareness

Always be attentive to the decision-maker. Watch the judge, justice of the peace, or adjudicator to help you monitor the speed of your presentation. If the judge or decision-maker is writing notes, pause until you see that he or she has stopped writing or has otherwise indicated that he or she is ready for you to proceed. If the judge or decision-maker appears lost in a documents brief, case brief, or other written materials, take a moment to ask if you can provide some assistance.

You must also be attentive to other people in the courtroom or hearing room, including a witness who is being examined. If you are conducting a direct examination of a witness, pay attention to what the witness says in response to your questions. If you are too focused on your notes you may miss something significant that the witness says. Do not adhere to a script of questions—this may cause you to move too quickly from question to question without noticing that your witness has not yet answered your previous question.

Eye Contact

Good eye contact is an important part of effective oral communication. Maintain direct eye contact with the judge, justice of the peace, or adjudicator while you are speaking to him or her. If you are examining a witness, maintain eye contact with the witness while at the same time being attentive to the decision-maker.

Have Notes but Do Not Read

Do not read from your prepared notes. Look at the judge or decision-maker and talk to him or her—talking sounds very different from reading. You should be so well prepared and familiar with your case that you will not have to read. You can, and should, use notes to help you with your delivery. But do not rely on them too heavily. Look at them to refresh your memory, pause, and then resume eye contact with the judge or decision-maker. Prepare your notes so that they will help you in your delivery. Use large print and large blocks of white space to remind you to look at the judge or decision-maker. This also encourages you to read only small bits of text at a time and helps you to find your place easily when you need to check your notes.

You might want to avoid writing out a prepared speech to reduce the risk of reading the text word for word, especially if you are nervous. Instead, prepare a short outline with key topic sentences and words that remind you of the most important points you want to make.

Never memorize a prepared script. Memorizing a script decreases the effectiveness of the delivery by making it sound stilted and robotic. It also decreases an advocate's ability to remain flexible during the hearing. Good advocacy means being able to think on your feet. A judge, justice of the peace, or adjudicator may ask you questions during the hearing. If you have memorized a script, you will likely have trouble answering those questions. On the other hand, if you prepare well and practise your presentation, you will be able to use your notes to engage in a dialogue with the judge, justice of the peace, or adjudicator.

Never attempt to speak at a hearing or trial without any notes. Even if you think you have memorized everything you want to say, there is always a chance that you will forget a key fact or point. Also, there is nothing worse than being asked a question that you cannot answer because it was not part of the script you memorized! Again, notes are good as long as you do not read from them. Even the most experienced advocates use notes. The key is learning how to use your notes effectively.

Practise

Finally, practise your presentation before your court or tribunal appearance! Stand in front of a mirror or, better yet, ask someone to observe your presentation and critique your delivery and demeanour. Try videotaping yourself and watching it. You will likely surprise yourself the first time you watch your presentation on video. Many people are not aware of all the distracting things they do while speaking. Videotaping yourself is one of the best ways to improve your oral advocacy skills because it helps you identify any weaknesses you have such as speaking too fast, using slang or filler words, or making distracting hand gestures. Once you are aware of your weaknesses, you can work at improving them.

Practising your public speaking skills starts before you arrive at the court or tribunal for a trial or hearing. Seize every opportunity to practise your public speaking skills. This is the best way to combat nerves and become comfortable speaking in front of people. There are many opportunities, both in school and in the community, to practise these skills in order to develop the confidence you need to present in the court or hearing room. For example, Toastmasters International is a non-profit educational organization that helps people develop their public speaking and leadership skills. The organization has thousands of branches around the world. Consider joining one of its local clubs near you.[1]

---

1   More information about Toastmasters International can be found at <https://www.toastmasters.org>.

EXERCISES

1. You are attending the Law Society of Upper Canada's annual awards ceremony. You are asked to present the Distinguished Paralegal Award[2] to the recipient, Ms. Olga Lehmann. The Distinguished Paralegal Award is awarded to a paralegal who has demonstrated one or more of the following:

- outstanding professional development

- contribution to the development of the profession

- devotion to professional duties, adherence to best practices

- a history of community service

- personal character that brings credit to the paralegal profession

Olga Lehmann has worked as a paralegal for eight years. She represents clients in Small Claims Court and Landlord and Tenant Board matters. She appears regularly as a panel member for various continuing professional development programs on the topic of practice management and provides training and mentorship to newly licensed paralegals. Ms. Lehmann also volunteers for a number of non-profit organizations that work to increase access to justice for low-income individuals.

In front of an audience, introduce Olga Lehmann and present her with the Distinguished Paralegal Award using the presentation skills discussed throughout the chapter. You may make up any facts you require to introduce her as the recipient of the award. The introduction must be 40 to 60 seconds in length.

2. Find a partner. Take turns interviewing each other to learn about each other's backgrounds, interests, career goals, and so on. Find six things that you and your partner have in common. In front of an audience, take turns introducing each other, including the six things you each have in common. The introduction must be 40 to 60 seconds in length.

---

2 The Distinguished Paralegal Award is an annual award created by the Law Society of Upper Canada (<http://www.lsuc.on.ca/distinguished-paralegal-award>).

PART IV

The Trial or Hearing

CHAPTER 9

The Opening Statement

LEARNING OUTCOMES

After reading this chapter, you will understand

▨ what an opening statement is

▨ why an opening statement is important

▨ how to prepare an opening statement

▨ how to present an opening statement

There is a basic rule in public speaking: start by telling your audience what you are going to tell them; tell them; then tell them what you have told them. If a trial or hearing were a speech, the opening statement is the advocate's way of telling the audience (the judge or other decision-maker) what the advocate is going to say.

The purpose of the opening statement is to inform the judge or other decision-maker about the case he or she is about to hear. The judge or other decision-maker may already have read the pleadings and may therefore have some idea about the matter. However, it is still helpful for the judge or other decision-maker to hear an overview of the case from the perspective of each side, including the result each desires. An opening statement puts the legal and factual issues in context for the judge. It is like a map, telling the judge where you intend to go in the case.

This chapter discusses the opening statement—why it is important, how to prepare one, and how to present it.

Why Prepare an Opening Statement?

At the Superior Court level, the Crown, plaintiff, or applicant is always entitled to make an opening statement, in both jury and non-jury trials, before presenting evidence. Counsel for the accused, defendant, or respondent will usually then make an opening statement after the completion of the Crown's, plaintiff's, or applicant's case and just before calling their own evidence. In a non-jury trial, the accused, defendant, or respondent may be permitted to give the opening statement directly after that of the Crown, plaintiff, or applicant.

In practice, counsel appearing at the Superior Court level rarely make an opening statement in non-jury trials, and there are generally no opening statements in Small Claims Court or Provincial Offences Court trials, or in administrative tribunal hearings.

However, it is still a good idea to prepare an opening statement. Preparing an opening statement helps you focus your thinking about your case, and is an excellent way to prepare for a trial or hearing. Although the judge, justice of the peace, or adjudicator may not ask you to deliver a formal opening statement, he or she may, at the outset of the trial or hearing, ask you to summarize what your case is about or ask you other questions about your case. If you have prepared an opening statement, you will be able to respond in a clear and concise manner. This is the first opportunity you have to gain credibility with the judge or other decision-maker and set the tone for your case. Preparing and presenting a good opening statement will create a positive first impression.

Preparing Your Opening Statement

When preparing your opening statement, ask yourself, "If I were the judge or adjudicator, what would I want to know to help me understand the case and the evidence?" Your opening statement should set out the facts that you intend to prove at trial, and why those facts are significant. Your opening statement is the "blueprint" for your case; it essentially outlines your theory of the case for the judge or other decision-maker. It provides the framework of your case without going into a lot of detail.

When you are preparing an opening statement, your goal is to include all the necessary information that the judge or other decision-maker needs in order to understand what the case is about (from your perspective), both factually and legally. Having said that, an opening statement does not give a detailed legal argument, but simply sets out the legal issues to be decided in the case. The actual law, and how it should be interpreted and applied, are saved for the closing argument (see Chapter 14).

Start the preparation of your opening statement by reviewing your theory of the case, because your theory of the case provides the foundation for your opening statement.

Format of Opening Statement

Although there is no prescribed format or structure for an opening statement, the following suggested format will help you accomplish your goals.

1. State the theme of your case.
2. Identify the parties.
3. State the cause of action (plaintiff or applicant) or defence (defendant).
4. State the facts of the case consistent with your theory.
5. State the legal issues.
6. State the outcome you desire.

1. State the Theme of Your Case

Start your opening statement by telling the judge or other decision-maker the theme of your case. The theme of your case is derived from your theory of the case: it is your theory reduced to one or two sentences—just enough so that the judge or decision-maker gets a sense of the general area of law involved and your take on the matter. It should be the answer you would give to a friend who asks you, "What is your case about?" For example, "This is a case about a homeowner who did not pay for the supply of materials by the contractor," or "This is a case about a tenant who did not terminate a tenancy properly."

A good theme helps put the facts and issues of the case into context for the judge or other decision-maker. As an advocate, your role is to persuade the judge or other decision-maker to accept your version of the facts and to find in favour of your client. You do this through effective storytelling, which begins in the opening statement with a good theme.

2. Identify the Parties

Briefly explain who the parties are and how they fit into the overall picture. For example, "The plaintiff is a contractor who agreed to provide materials and services to the defendant homeowner." Such a statement helps the judge better understand each party's role in the case. Because the plaintiff presents its opening statement first, only the plaintiff needs to identify the parties. There is no need for the defendant to restate this information during the defendant's opening statement.

3. State the Cause of Action or Defence

The plaintiff states the cause of action of the case—for example, "This case involves the tort of battery." The cause of action provides the structure for the facts and the law. The defendant states his or her defence—for example, "The defendant's defence is that the plaintiff consented to the contact."

4. State the Facts of the Case Consistent with Your Theory

This is the main part of your opening statement: it sets out your version of the facts of the case and will help the judge to follow the testimony of your witnesses and to understand the importance of what they say.

Highlight the main facts and draw the decision-maker's attention to anticipated evidence that will be important in your case. To do so, use such phrases as, "The evidence will show that …" or "Mr. Smith will testify that … ." You may also state whom you will be calling as a witness and what the witness will testify about. However, in doing so, there are two things to remember.

First, do not make promises that you cannot keep. If you are not confident a witness will testify or what he or she will testify about, do not refer to it in your opening statement. Similarly, do not refer to evidence that is inadmissible or which may be declared inadmissible. If you fail to deliver on a promise made in your opening statement, you will likely lose credibility with the decision-maker.

Second, in highlighting the facts and anticipated evidence, be careful you do not start making legal arguments. Legal arguments have no place in opening statements because there is no actual evidence before the court yet. For example, do not tell the decision-maker what conclusions he or she should draw from the evidence that will be presented. The time for these statements is during your closing argument once the decision-maker has heard all the evidence.

Remember to state your version of the facts in a way that is understandable and believable, and makes sense. This involves presenting the facts in a logical way that reinforces your theme and leads the judge or other decision-maker to the only logical conclusion: your conclusion.

5. State the Legal Issues

Identify the legal issues raised by the facts of the case. Issues are usually introduced by the word "whether"—for example, "The legal issue in this case is whether the tenancy was properly terminated," or "The legal issue in this case is whether the homeowner breached the contract." In some cases there may be only one issue; in other cases there may be several. Set out all of the legal issues and identify the issues only. While you must not make legal arguments, refer to the law in detail, or state how the law should be interpreted, it may be helpful to briefly refer to the relevant law or statute. If you are the plaintiff or applicant, you can mention what the law requires in order to prove the case. If you act for the defendant in a criminal or provincial offences case, you may want to state that the prosecutor will not meet its burden of proof.

6. State the Outcome You Desire

Conclude your opening statement with a brief statement of the outcome you desire in the case. If you are claiming an amount of money in damages, however, this is not the time to go into detail about the dollar amounts you are seeking. For example, you should simply say, "The plaintiff is claiming one month's rent" and omit the dollar amount at this time. Defendants will usually request that the plaintiff's case be dismissed. In a criminal or provincial offences case, the prosecutor will ask that the judge or justice of the peace find the defendant guilty and that a conviction be entered against the defendant. The defendant will ask to be acquitted of the charge(s).

Adjust Your Language for Oral Presentation

Keep in mind that you will be delivering your opening statement orally; the judge or other decision-maker will not be reading what you have written. Accordingly, after you prepare your opening statement using the above format, read through it and adjust your language so that it is appropriate for an oral presentation. The following pointers may be helpful:

- *Keep your sentence structure simple and your sentences short.* Complex sentences that seem clear when read may be difficult for a listener to understand.

- *Use introductory sentences to take the place of headings.* State what you will be talking about at the start of each part of your opening statement—for example, "There are three issues in this case. The first issue is … The second issue is … The third issue is …"

- *Use words you know how to pronounce.* Make sure you will be able to deliver your opening statement without tripping over any unfamiliar words.

Box 9.1 contains a sample opening statement for the plaintiff in Fact Situation 1, the Kitchen Renovation Case.

BOX 9.1

Plaintiff's Opening Statement in the Kitchen Renovation Case

Good morning, Your Honour. My name is Smith, initial A, and I am the licensed paralegal for the plaintiff in this case.

This is a case about homeowners who did not pay the full contract amount for a kitchen renovation completed by the contractor.

The plaintiff is a small contracting company. The defendants hired the plaintiff to make some minor renovations to the kitchen in their home.

The plaintiff's claim is for damages for breach of contract.

The facts are as follows:

About six months ago, the plaintiff entered into a contract with the defendants. The parties agreed that the plaintiff would perform the following work in the defendants' kitchen: install a new countertop, paint the cabinets, install new hardware on the cabinet doors, paint the walls and ceiling, and install five pot lights. It was also agreed that additional pot lights could be installed at a cost of $250 each. The contract price was $7,500, and the defendants gave the plaintiff a deposit in the amount of $2,500. At the request of the defendants, the plaintiff installed three additional pot lights. The plaintiff completed the job and gave the defendants an invoice for $8,250 (the original contract price of $7,500 plus $750 for the supply and installation of the three additional pot lights). The defendant paid $5,000 but refused to pay the balance owing in the amount of $750.

The legal issue in this case is whether the defendants breached the contract in failing to pay the cost of the additional three pot lights.

The plaintiff claims damages for the unpaid balance of the contract price.

Box 9.2 contains a sample opening statement for the prosecution in Fact Situation 2, the Liquor Licence Case.

BOX 9.2

Prosecution's Opening Statement in the Liquor Licence Case

Good morning, Your Worship. My name is Smith, initial A, and I am the licensed paralegal appearing on behalf of her Majesty the Queen.

This is a case about a holder of a liquor licence who allowed the removal of alcohol from the licensed premises.

The corporate defendant, Treetop Catering Inc., held a liquor licence and a caterer's endorsement. The individual defendant, Victoria Levens, is the sole director, officer, and shareholder of Treetop Catering Inc.

It is the Crown's position that the defendants permitted the removal of alcohol from the licensed premises contrary to the *Liquor Licence Act*.

The facts are as follows:

On May 16, 2016 a party took place at the Simpson Academy student lounge. The defendant, Victoria Levens, was the owner of Treetop Catering Inc. and the organizer of the event. Treetop Catering Inc. held a Liquor Sales Licence and had a caterer's endorsement for the event. The boundaries of the event premises were the student lounge and outdoor fenced patio at the Simpson Academy. Witness testimony will show that party guests were observed on the lawn beyond the patio, and empty beer bottles and plastic wine glasses were found on the grass just beyond the patio fence.

The legal issue in this case is whether the defendants, Treetop Catering and Victoria Levens, committed an offence under the *Liquor Licence Act* by permitting the removal of alcohol from the premises.

The prosecution is seeking a finding of guilt and is asking that a conviction be entered against the defendants for committing the offence.

Box 9.3 contains a sample opening statement for the tenants in Fact Situation 3, the Landlord and Tenant Dispute.

Tenants' Opening Statement in the Landlord and Tenant Dispute

Good morning, Madam Adjudicator. My name is Smith, initial A, and I am the licensed paralegal for the tenants in this case.

This is a case about a landlord who served a notice of termination for personal use in bad faith.

The tenants were tenants in a two-unit building owned by the landlord.

The tenants' claim is for compensation for their increased rent and moving costs.

The facts are as follows:

The tenants had a one-year written lease with the landlord. At the end of their one-year lease, the landlord served a notice of termination of their tenancy so that his daughter could move into the apartment. As a result of the notice, the tenants moved out. They could not find a similar apartment for the same rent, but did find a suitable apartment in the same neighbourhood at a higher rent. The tenants also incurred moving expenses. The landlord's daughter did not move into the apartment. Instead, the landlord put the apartment up for lease at a higher rent than the tenants had been paying.

The legal issue in this case is whether the landlord gave the notice of termination in bad faith, and is therefore responsible to reimburse the tenants for their expenses caused by the move.

The tenants claim reimbursement of their increased rent for one year and their moving expenses.

Practise Your Opening Statement

Practise delivering your opening statement so that your delivery will add to, and not detract from, your statement's effectiveness.

You should be familiar enough with your opening statement so that you do not have to read it. Instead, try to talk to the judge or other decision-maker and tell him or her about your case. Do not memorize your opening statement. If you do, the delivery will be stilted and boring. Prepare and practise so that the delivery of your opening statement is more of a conversation with the judge, justice of the peace, or adjudicator rather than a speech. You may look at your notes, read a passage, pause, and look at the judge. Use your notes to help with your pacing. Good pacing reinforces the organization and meaning of your opening statement.

Use large print or bulleted points so that you will be forced to read only small bits at a time and will not lose your place. You might want to use an outline rather than writing out your opening statement word for word. Leave lots of white space between ideas to remind yourself to pause. Pause between sentences; pause longer between paragraphs. Pauses are good. They help the decision-maker digest what you just said.

Skills such as speaking slowly and loudly will make the delivery of your opening statement more persuasive. Speaking slowly, for example, ensures the decision-maker will be able to follow and absorb what you have to say. Speak with expression in order to maintain the attention of the decision-maker. Avoid speaking in a monotone, which will bore the decision-maker and lose his or her attention. See Chapter 8 for a more complete discussion of presentation skills.

Tips for an Effective Opening Statement

- Don't express your personal opinions or beliefs. Never say, "I believe," "I think," or "In my opinion." Instead say, "I submit" or "It is the plaintiff's (applicant's/Crown's/defendant's/respondent's) position that …"

- Never refer to settlement negotiations or offers to settle. Unless otherwise agreed by the parties, offers to settle are always **without prejudice**.

- Don't make statements about the credibility of your client or witnesses. This is a matter for the judge to decide.

- Don't hide unfavourable facts or weaknesses in your case. If you are the plaintiff or applicant, address them and explain them in a way that makes sense in the context of your client's story. If you don't, the defendant or respondent's advocate will certainly point them out to the decision-maker in a worse light.

- Don't make inflammatory statements about the other party or advocate. Remember your professional obligations, including the duty of civility under the *Paralegal Rules of Conduct* (as discussed in Chapter 2).

- Be flexible. If you are the defendant or the respondent, the plaintiff or applicant will present their opening statement first. Listen carefully to that opening statement. You may wish to add a few sentences to your opening statement in order to respond to something the other advocate said, such as unfavourable facts that undermine your client's story.

- Be prepared to go off-script if you have a script. The judge or decision-maker may interrupt you while you are presenting your opening statement, or ask you questions. You must always take direction from the decision-maker and not remain attached to a script. This ability comes with good preparation and knowing the details of your case.

---

without prejudice: cannot be referred to in court or used as evidence against a party in a legal proceeding

KEY TERM

without prejudice, 123

REVIEW QUESTIONS

1. What is the purpose of the opening statement?

2. What is the recommended format for an opening statement? Briefly describe what should be included in each step.

3. How and why should you adjust the language of your opening statement so that it is appropriate for an oral presentation?

4. Why is it important to practise delivering your opening statement?

5. How should you practise your opening statement?

EXERCISES

1. Read Box 9.1: Plaintiff's Opening Statement in the Kitchen Renovation Case. Prepare an opening statement for the defendants.

2. Read Box 9.2: Prosecution's Opening Statement in the Liquor Licence Case. Prepare an opening statement for the defendants.

3. Read Box 9.3: Tenants' Opening Statement in the Landlord and Tenant Dispute. Prepare an opening statement for the landlord.

4. Practise delivering the plaintiff's opening statement in the Kitchen Renovation Case, the prosecution's opening statement in the Liquor Licence Case, and the tenants' opening statement in the Landlord and Tenant Dispute.

CHAPTER 10

Exhibits

Judges, justices of the peace, and adjudicators make decisions in cases by applying the law to the facts of the particular case. Before making a decision, a judge or other decision-maker must first determine what happened in the case. Usually, the two sides in a case have different versions of what happened—sometimes slightly different, other times vastly different. The judge or other decision-maker has to choose between the two versions. You tell your version of what happened (your theory of the case) through the direct examination (also known as **examination-in-chief**) of your witnesses.

In addition to oral testimony, many cases also involve some sort of physical evidence—a signed contract, a letter, a photograph, a diagram, the sunglasses that were allegedly stolen—something that you can show to the decision-maker to help prove your case. These objects cannot walk into the witness box and testify, but instead must be introduced as exhibits through the oral testimony of witnesses.

This chapter discusses the purpose of exhibits and sets out the steps for introducing exhibits as evidence.

Definition and Purpose of Exhibits

An **exhibit** is an object that is introduced as evidence at a trial or hearing. An exhibit is any non-oral evidence that is made part of the record of the trial or hearing. Exhibits include documents, such as letters or contracts; physical evidence, such as property; and demonstrative evidence, such as photographs or diagrams.

An exhibit can provide objective, physical evidence to support and strengthen a witness's oral testimony. For example, assume a landlord is alleging that a tenant caused damage to the rental unit. The landlord can give oral testimony describing the damage; however, a picture of the unit showing the damage is far more compelling and, as the saying goes, "A picture is worth a thousand words." As you prepare the direct examination of your witnesses, always consider whether exhibits are available to support your witnesses' testimony. To be useful, an exhibit should either, in and of itself, prove a fact, or it should help the judge or other decision-maker better understand the evidence.

---

examination-in-chief: also known as a direct examination of a witness, it is the questioning of your own witness(es) under oath

exhibit: an object that is introduced as evidence at a trial or hearing

Using Exhibits

Exhibits may be introduced during the direct examination of your witnesses or during the cross-examination of the other side's witnesses. In Chapter 11 we discuss the purpose of and preparation for the direct examination of your witnesses, and provide examples of direct examinations that include the introduction of exhibits. In Chapter 12 we discuss the purpose of and preparation for the cross-examination of the other party's witnesses, together with examples of cross-examinations that include the introduction of exhibits.

Using Exhibits in Direct Examination

Exhibits may be introduced during direct examination to confirm a fact to which a witness is testifying. For example, assume your witness testifies that he or she had a written contract setting out the terms of a renovation project. You should introduce the contract itself as an exhibit. Doing so helps to prove that the contract exists and that it was signed by both parties. The judge or other decision-maker can then actually read the terms of the contract. Or, assume your witness testifies about damage done to his or her sweater by a dry cleaner. Instead of merely describing the damage, you should introduce the sweater as an exhibit to allow the judge or other decision-maker to see the actual damage. Exhibits may also be used to help the decision-maker better understand the witness's testimony. For example, a diagram or photograph of an accident location may clarify the witness's testimony regarding the accident.

Using Exhibits During Cross-Examination

Exhibits may be introduced during cross-examination to help you discredit the witness's testimony. For example, suppose the opposing witness, your client's landlord, has testified that he never received notice from your client that your client's apartment was in need of repairs. You should introduce as an exhibit a copy of the letter your client sent to the landlord complaining about the damage.

Introducing Exhibits into Evidence

You cannot simply give an object to the judge or other decision-maker to consider; you must introduce it as an exhibit through the testimony of a witness who has direct knowledge of the object and is able to verify its authenticity. You must also be able to establish that the exhibit is relevant to the facts of the case—the primary test of admissibility of all evidence—and that you have followed any other procedural steps required for admissibility. For example, under Rule 18 of the *Rules of the Small Claims Court*, a written statement or document that has been served on all parties at least 30 days before the trial date must be received in evidence, unless the trial judge orders otherwise.

An exhibit may be introduced by asking a limited number of questions, and the process usually does not take long. However, those questions must cover a number of steps to properly introduce and use the exhibit.

1. Establish a context for the exhibit.
2. Set up the exhibit.
3. Show the exhibit to the witness and to the other side.
4. Have the witness authenticate the exhibit.
5. Enter the exhibit into evidence.
6. Use the exhibit.

1.   Establish a Context for the Exhibit

Inexperienced advocates often introduce an exhibit first and then try to explain how it fits into the evidence. Instead, you should establish a context for the exhibit before you introduce it by steering the direct examination toward the matters or facts to which the exhibit relates.

2.   Set Up the Exhibit

Once you have established a context for the exhibit, focus your questions on the exhibit itself, making sure to include enough information so that it is clear exactly what the exhibit is. For example, "I'm going to show you a lease agreement dated February 1, 2016." Your set-up should establish that the exhibit has **probative value** or will assist the witness with his or her oral testimony. Often, this is obvious by the very nature of the exhibit.

The following examples illustrate the right way and the wrong way to establish a context for an exhibit and set it up (that is, steps 1 and 2).

Your client is a landlord and has testified that the original rent for an apartment was $1,000 per month. You are now trying to establish that the rent has been increased to $1,014 by way of a notice of rent increase (as required by legislation).

The wrong way:

Paralegal: I'm showing you a notice of rent increase dated December 1, 2016. Can you explain what this is?

The right way:

Paralegal: Is the monthly rent still $1,000 per month?
Landlord: No. I increased the rent effective March 1, 2017.

---

probative value: is sufficiently useful to prove something in a trial

Paralegal: What did you do to increase the rent?

Landlord: I served the tenant with a notice of rent increase.

Paralegal: I'm showing you a notice of rent increase dated December 1, 2016. Is this the notice of rent increase you served?

Landlord: Yes.

3. Show the Exhibit to the Witness and to the Other Side

Show the exhibit to the witness and then hand it to him or her. You must also show the exhibit to the other side, unless you have already provided a copy, in which case, tell the judge or other decision-maker that you have done so.

4. Have the Witness Authenticate the Exhibit

Once the witness has the exhibit, you must connect it to the witness to establish that the witness is qualified to testify about it. In other words, the witness must have some direct involvement with or knowledge of the exhibit. For example, a party would be qualified to give evidence in court about an exhibit if he or she

- prepared the exhibit,
- received the exhibit from another party, or
- discovered the exhibit.

Make sure that the witness confirms the identity of the document. For example:

Paralegal: I'm showing you a notice of rent increase dated December 1, 2016. Is this the notice of rent increase you served?

Landlord: Yes, it is.

You must also prove that the exhibit is authentic—in other words, it is what you say it is. If the exhibit is property, such as a sweater damaged by a dry cleaner, you must establish that it has not been tampered with in any way before trial. If the exhibit is a photograph or diagram, you must establish that it is accurate and does not in any way distort the evidence it illustrates. If the exhibit is a document, you must show that it has not been amended or modified in any way.

5. Enter the Exhibit into Evidence

After the witness identifies the exhibit, take it back and hand it to the judge or other decision-maker (or to the clerk, if there is one, who will hand it to the decision-maker). Ask the decision-maker to enter it into evidence as an exhibit by stating, "I would ask that this (document) be introduced as Exhibit (X)." The decision-maker will briefly state the nature of the exhibit and then assign it a number. For example, if you introduce a lease as the second exhibit of a trial, the judge might state: "Lease agreement dated February 1, 2015, marked as Exhibit 2."

Keep a list of all the exhibits entered during the trial or hearing. Record the number of each exhibit and a brief description. The list will help you both to keep track of the number that will be assigned to the next exhibit and to retrieve an exhibit if you need to use it again. If you are about to enter an exhibit and cannot remember what its number should be, simply ask that it be marked as the next exhibit.

6. Use the Exhibit

Having gone to all this trouble to enter the exhibit, make sure that you actually use it! Ask your witness questions about the exhibit. You may use the exhibit to help your witness with details of his or her evidence. For example, your witness may have testified that he or she signed a written contract for the renovation of a bathroom, and you entered the contract as an exhibit. Have your witness look at the exhibit while asking questions about the terms of the contract instead of having the witness recall the details of the contract from memory. At the very least, draw the attention of the decision-maker to the key aspects of the exhibit.

The decision-maker may ask you whether you want the exhibit back after it is marked and entered into evidence. If you are not asked, then ask the decision-maker or clerk for the exhibit and give it to the witness. Then, ask questions about it. When you are finished with the exhibit, be sure to return it to the decision-maker or clerk.

Working with Exhibits That Have Already Been Entered

You may want to refer a witness to an exhibit that has been entered into evidence earlier in the trial through another witness. In that case, ask for the exhibit using the number and description assigned to it by the judge or other decision-maker, for example, "Your Honour, may I please have Exhibit 5, the lease agreement." Present it to the witness by saying, "I am showing you Exhibit 5." Remember to return the exhibit to the decision-maker or clerk when you are finished using it.

Some Examples

Here are examples of how to work with several different types of exhibits.

A Contract

Your client is a home renovator who entered into a written contract for the renovation of a bathroom, and is now suing for money owing under the contract.

Paralegal: You said that you had an agreement with Harry Homeowner for the renovation of his bathroom. Was that agreement oral or in writing?

Witness: It was in writing.

Paralegal: I'm going to show you a written agreement dated February 1, 2016.

The paralegal shows the exhibit to the advocate acting for the other side and then to the witness.

Paralegal: Is this the agreement you are referring to?

Witness: Yes, it is.

Paralegal: And is that your signature on page 2?

Witness: Yes, it is.

Paralegal: And is that the defendant's signature below yours?

Witness: Yes, it is.

Paralegal: Your Honour, I would request that the agreement be introduced as Exhibit 1.

The paralegal hands the exhibit to the judge or court clerk. After the exhibit is entered into evidence, the paralegal asks for the exhibit back. The paralegal hands the exhibit to the witness.

Paralegal: Can you show me the paragraph that sets out the cost of the renovation?

Witness: *(Points to paragraph)*

Paralegal: Please tell me what that paragraph says.

The paralegal can then refer the witness to that paragraph and ask questions about additional paragraphs in the agreement.

A Photograph

Your client's dog was attacked by a neighbour's dog, and your client is suing for the cost of the veterinary bills.

Paralegal:	You said that your dog was attacked by the defendant's dog. Did your dog suffer any injuries as a result of the attack?
Witness:	Yes, to his neck and to one of his ears.
Paralegal:	Did you do anything to document those injuries?
Witness:	Yes. I took a photograph.
Paralegal:	*(After showing the photograph to the advocate for the defendant)* I'm showing you a photograph of a dog. Is that the photograph you took of your dog?
Witness:	Yes, it is.
Paralegal:	When and where was this photograph taken?
Witness:	It was taken about half an hour after the attack, while we were waiting in the veterinarian's office for my dog to be seen.
Paralegal:	Does this photograph accurately show the injuries that your dog suffered?
Witness:	Yes, it does.
Paralegal:	Your Honour, I would request that the photograph be introduced as Exhibit 1.

The paralegal hands the exhibit to the judge or court clerk. After it is entered into evidence, the paralegal asks for the exhibit back. The paralegal hands the exhibit to the witness.

Paralegal:	Can you please point out your dog's injuries in the photo.
Witness:	You can see where his left ear is bloody, and where the skin on his back has been pulled back.

A Diagram

Your client was involved in a traffic accident and is suing for the cost of repairing the damage to her car.

Paralegal:	You said that the accident occurred at the corner of Pine Street and Elm Street?
Witness:	Yes, that is correct.
Paralegal:	I am showing you a diagram entitled "Scene of Accident." Do you recognize this diagram?
Witness:	Yes. I drew the diagram.
Paralegal:	*(After showing the diagram to the advocate for the defendant)* What does the diagram show?
Witness:	It shows the intersection of Pine Street and Elm Street.
Paralegal:	Is the diagram an accurate depiction of the intersection?

Witness: Yes. It accurately depicts the intersection as it looked on the date of the accident.

Paralegal: Your Honour, I would request that the diagram be introduced as Exhibit 1.

The paralegal hands the exhibit to the judge or court clerk. After it is entered into evidence, the paralegal asks for the exhibit back. The paralegal hands the exhibit to the witness.

The paralegal can then ask the witness to explain various aspects of the accident with reference to the diagram.

KEY TERMS

examination-in-chief, 126
exhibit, 126
probative value, 128

REVIEW QUESTIONS

1. What is an exhibit? Give an example.

2. Why are exhibits useful at trial?

3. Give an example of how exhibits may be used during direct examination.

4. Give an example of how exhibits may be used during cross-examination.

5. What are the six steps you should follow to properly introduce and use an exhibit? Briefly summarize each step.

6. How do you use an exhibit that has already been entered into evidence earlier in the trial through another witness?

EXERCISE

Your witness is a residential landlord who entered into a written tenancy agreement with Tom Tenant on January 15, 2016 for a one-year term starting February 1, 2016 at a monthly rent of $1,000. Prepare the part of the landlord's direct examination in which you introduce the tenancy agreement as an exhibit, and question the landlord about the exhibit.

CHAPTER 11

Direct Examination of Witnesses

LEARNING OUTCOMES

After reading this chapter, you will understand

▓ what a direct examination of a witness is

▓ how to prepare a direct examination

▓ how to prepare your witness for direct examination

▓ how to conduct a direct examination

▓ the process for having a police officer refer to his or her notes during a direct examination

▓ the *Paralegal Rules of Conduct* relating to communicating with witnesses giving testimony in the context of a direct examination of a witness

As part of the decision-making process, the judge, justice of the peace, or adjudicator in your case must first determine the facts of the case. You tell the judge or other decision-maker your version of the facts—what happened between the parties—through the oral testimony of your witnesses and the physical evidence, in the form of exhibits, introduced through their oral testimony. You get your witnesses to tell their story to the judge by conducting a direct examination (also known as examination-in-chief). This chapter discusses the purpose of and the preparation for the direct examination of your witnesses.

Meaning and Purpose of Direct Examination

Direct examination is the questioning of your own witness(es) under oath. The purpose is to elicit from your witnesses the evidence you need to satisfy all of the elements of your claim or defence. Your goal in direct examination is to have your witness(es) introduce the undisputed facts and to present the more persuasive version of the disputed facts. To achieve this goal, you must design your questions in such a way that, when answered, a logical, complete, believable, and understandable story unfolds. There should be no factual gaps in the story. You must also anticipate where your version of the story will differ from that of the other side and then focus your direct examination on these points—and convince the court that your story is more believable. Through direct examination, you have the opportunity to put forward your client's version of the disputed facts in a controlled and persuasive manner. The purpose of direct examination is to establish the facts only. It is not the time to argue the law or draw conclusions from the evidence.

Preparing Yourself for Direct Examination

You cannot achieve the objectives of direct examination without extensive preparation. To prepare for direct examination, start by asking yourself the following questions.

What Facts Do You Need to Prove?

You address this question when you develop your theory of the case. As discussed in Chapter 6, you review the law to determine the facts you must prove to establish your cause of action or defence.

How Will You Prove Each Fact?

You also address this question when you develop your theory of the case. Again, as discussed in Chapter 6, make a list of each fact you must prove and, for each one, ask yourself what evidence is required to prove that fact and how that evidence will be produced at trial: What witness will you call? Do you have documentary evidence to support the fact?

Who Are Your Witnesses?

Who has direct knowledge of the facts of your case? Make a list of all of your potential witnesses and the aspect of your case on which each can testify. Each witness must have personal knowledge of the facts to which he or she will testify. For example, Witness A can testify to the fact that the contract was signed because she signed it, and Witness B can testify to the fact that the contract price was paid because he paid the moneys.

In What Order Will You Call Your Witnesses?

Consider how best to tell the story so that it makes sense and will be understood and remembered by someone with no familiarity with the facts. Ideally, the witness who knows most of the story and can provide an overall context should give evidence first. Usually, this will be a party to the case (plaintiff, applicant, defendant, or respondent).

What Do You Want the Witness to Say and in What Sequence? Are There Any Documents to Be Introduced?

Go back through your list of facts and your witness statements. Take all of the facts about which the witness can testify and put them in a logical order. Make a note of any supporting documents that the witness can identify. These documents will be introduced into evidence as exhibits. The process for introducing and using exhibits is discussed in Chapter 10.

Eliminate Any Unnecessary Repetition of Evidence

You may have two or more witnesses who can give evidence on the same fact. In that case, you must consider whether you need more than one witness to testify about that fact—in other words, to **corroborate** evidence of that fact already given by another witness. You do not need to corroborate evidence about a fact that is not in dispute. Corroboration is also generally not required to prove an objective fact— for example, the fact that a contract was signed. In such cases, the corroborating evidence will be unnecessarily repetitive and may bore the judge or other decision-maker. However, corroboration is recommended if you are trying to prove a fact that is in dispute or a subjective fact—for example, that a tenant's behaviour was disturbing other tenants. If two witnesses testify about the tenant's behaviour, this fact becomes more believable and convincing than if only one witness testifies.

Develop the Witness's Story

Now that you have finalized the facts to be covered in the witness's testimony and the sequencing of those facts, write out the facts as a narrative that flows naturally. Ask yourself, "If the witness told a perfect story, what would it sound like?" Write out that story. You should end up with a detailed, logical, understandable, and persuasive story.

Pay particular attention to those areas in which your version of the facts differs from that of the other side. Do not omit unfavourable facts: include them and try to explain them away in a plausible manner. Your witness will be more convincing if he or she does not appear to be hiding anything. Focus on the areas that are in dispute. Anticipate the other side's theory, and develop the aspects on which your witness is likely to be cross-examined.

Avoid **hearsay**—for example, "The landlord told me that other tenants complained." Also avoid irrelevant detail.

---

corroborate: confirm or support with additional evidence

hearsay: a statement, originally made out of court, that is repeated in court for the truth of its contents

Prepare Your Questions

Only now, after having developed the story, are you ready to write out your questions. The most common mistake of novice advocates is to start with their questions instead of starting with the story. The result is a stilted direct examination in which there are too many questions, and the focus is on the advocate and the questions rather than on the witness and the witness's story. When preparing your questions, focus on the story you want told, and not on your questions. In other words, the questions are driven by the story. Write out the story first, and then insert questions designed to elicit each part of that story. It is your job to design your questions so that when they are answered, a complete story unfolds. This will keep the focus on the witness, not you, and will result in a story that flows naturally.

Start your direct examination with questions about the witness's background. Questions such as "What do you do for a living?" and "Where do you live?" help to personalize or humanize the witness, and will help to put the witness at ease.

Your final notes should then set out each question you intend to ask, followed by the answer you want to that question. (See the section "Formulating Your Questions," below, for more guidance.)

Preparing Your Witnesses for Direct Examination

It is not enough to prepare yourself for direct examination. You will not accomplish very much if you are prepared but your witnesses are not, because it is the witnesses, not you, who will be presenting the evidence at the hearing. You will need to prepare each witness in the following areas:

- What the witness will say
- How the witness will say it
- Where the witness will say it
- What the other side will ask the witness in cross-examination

What the Witness Will Say

Start by explaining to the witness why his or her evidence is important and how it fits into the entire case. Review your questions with the witness in advance of the trial so that the witness is familiar with you and your questions. The witness should know what information you are looking for when you ask a particular question. If you will be introducing any exhibits through the witness, make sure the witness has seen them and knows how to identify them.

You may also want to explain some basic rules of evidence so that the witness understands the nature of your questions. Your witness should know that generally you cannot ask leading questions during direct examination, and what a leading question is. That way, he or she may be able to help you out when it is difficult for you to ask a non-leading question. You should also explain to the witness that the decision-maker is not interested in the witness's opinion, unless, of course, the witness is being called as an expert witness. Finally, witnesses should be reminded that they may testify only about the facts of which they have direct knowledge. Hearsay is not admissible, and the witness should therefore know not to repeat what someone else has told him or her.

How the Witness Will Say It

You want your witnesses to tell the truth, and you want them to be believed, so it is a good idea to "coach" them on how to present their testimony so that they do not appear to be lying. Tell your witnesses to be polite, to speak clearly and in a loud enough voice, and to maintain eye contact with you when answering questions. Remind them to dress in a conservative and respectable manner.

Where the Witness Will Say It

Witnesses are usually very nervous about having to be in court—they are scared of courtrooms and judges, and they are especially nervous about being cross-examined! You can help your witnesses feel more comfortable by preparing them for the courtroom experience.

Go over the trial or hearing process with your witness and the order in which things will happen. It may also be helpful to show your witness the courtroom before the trial and to explain who the various people are and what they do. Show the witness where he or she will testify, and explain the process of being sworn in or affirmed.

What the Other Side Will Ask the Witness in Cross-Examination

For most witnesses, cross-examination is the scariest part of the trial or hearing, and for good reason. Cross-examination is the part of the trial or hearing that cannot be rehearsed or scripted. Unlike direct examination, where the witness knows you and is familiar with your questions, the witness does not know the other side's advocate, nor does the witness know what questions the advocate will ask.

Cross-examination involves the unknown, which makes witnesses very nervous. You must counter the unknown by preparing your witness extremely well for the cross-examination. The best way to do this is to conduct a mock cross-examination of the witness. Pretend that you are the opposing side's advocate, and ask the questions that you anticipate will be asked of this witness. This preparation will give the witness a good sense of what to expect during cross-examination at the trial or hearing. Tell your witness to listen to the questions very carefully and to answer only the question asked—the witness should never volunteer any additional information. Your witness should know that he or she is entitled to say "I don't know," or "I don't remember," or "I don't understand the question" if any of these is the case. If your witness cannot respond to a question with only a "yes" or "no," he or she is entitled to explain. Advise your witness to remain calm and polite throughout, and always to tell the truth. Finally, remind your witness to stop speaking if you make an **objection**. (See Chapter 12 for more about cross-examination; see Chapter 16 for more about objections.)

Formulating Your Questions

There are some basic rules to follow in formulating the questions for your witnesses during direct examination.

Ask One Question at a Time

Ask one question at a time rather than multiple-part questions. For example, don't ask, "Was a deposit paid, or was the entire amount owing due on completion?" If the witness says "yes," it is not clear which question he or she is answering. Break the question down into two separate questions.

Use Simple Language

Use simple language so that the witness and the decision-maker will understand what you are asking. For example, instead of asking, "What was the completed value of the projected construction renovation you were undertaking?" Ask instead, "How much did the renovation cost?"

Ask Open-Ended Questions

In direct examination, the focus should be on the witness only. The advocate's role is simply to elicit the facts from the witnesses needed to establish the theory of the case. The storytelling must come from the witness, not the advocate. Keep the focus on the witness by asking open-ended questions. Open-ended questions usually start with the following introductory language: *Who, what, where, when, why, how; Tell me about …* ; *Describe …* These types of questions invite explanations and descriptions

---

objection: statement directed to the decision-maker that a question asked, an answer given, or an object introduced by the opposing party is improper

from the witness—for example, "Where were you on the evening of June 1, 2016?" or "Describe what you saw when you were driving along Sullivan Street."

Do Not Ask Leading Questions

In direct examination, you are not allowed to ask leading questions. A **leading question** is one that suggests a desired answer or one that assumes a fact in dispute that has not yet been proved. Disallowing such questions prevents you from "feeding" answers to your witness. For example, consider the following question: "You were angry, weren't you?" This question clearly suggests the answer "yes." You should instead ask, "How did you feel?" A question such as "When did you deliver the appliances?" is leading if there has been no evidence before the court that the appliances had, in fact, been delivered, because it assumes this fact.

When preparing your direct examination questions, think about whether the question either assumes a fact or suggests a desired answer. If either of these is the case, rephrase the question so that it is non-leading, using the language discussed above regarding open-ended questions.

Table 11.1 contains examples of leading versus non-leading questions.

TABLE 11.1 Leading Versus Non-Leading Questions

Leading Questions	Non-Leading Questions
You met with the landlord on March 1, didn't you?	Whom did you meet with on March 1?
Were you going to talk to the landlord about terminating your lease?	Why were you at the landlord's office?
Was the landlord angry when she heard the news?	How did the landlord react when she heard the news?
Did the landlord yell at you after you told her the news?	What did the landlord do after you told her the news?
Did the landlord demand that you leave?	What did the landlord do next?
You sold alcohol at the event, correct?	Did you sell beverages at the event? What type of beverages did you sell at the event?
You hired a security guard to ensure guests didn't take alcohol beyond the licensed area, didn't you?	What steps did you take to avoid guests taking alcoholic beverages outside the licensed area?

leading question: question that suggests a desired answer or that assumes a fact in dispute that has not yet been proven

As you can see, leading questions can usually be answered only with "yes" or "no," while non-leading questions are open-ended.

The general rule is that you should not ask leading questions during direct examination, but there are some exceptions to this rule. For example, you can lead your witness when asking about a matter that

- is introductory—for example, "Do you work at Alice's Appliances?" or "Are you a student at Simpson Academy?"
- is undisputed—for example, "Did you purchase a fridge?"
- is directing the witness to a specific subject, by way of introduction—for example, "At some point you had a meeting with the landlord; is that correct?" After the witness says "yes," you can go on to ask, "Can you tell me when that was?"

Tips for Direct Examination

When preparing and conducting the direct examination of your witness, you should follow these basic tips.

Always Introduce the Witness

Never start a direct examination of a witness without eliciting some basic background facts about the witness, and in particular, the witness's relationship to the facts of the case. For example, you might ask the witness what his or her relationship is to your client. It's also a good idea to ask for some personal information about the witness. For example, you might ask the witness's age, what he or she does for a living, or whether he or she has a family. You can then transition into questions relating to the case so as to start the storytelling of what happened.

There are also certain background facts you should establish if you are conducting a direct examination of a police officer in a criminal or provincial offences trial. For example, you should establish that the witness is employed as a police officer, the municipality and division where the officer works, and how long he or she has been employed as a police officer. You should also ask whether the officer was on duty on the date in question and what the officer's responsibilities were. There are other special considerations involving the examination of a police officer, which are discussed below.

Keep the Focus on the Witness

As Thomas Mauet wrote, "[A] witness will be believed and remembered because of the manner and content of his or her testimony, not because the questions asked were so brilliant."[1] The focus should be on the witness, not on you. Avoid behaviour that may distract the judge or other decision-maker from listening to what the witness is saying. For example, if you start pacing while your witness is speaking, you will draw attention to yourself and away from the witness. Also, many advocates have a habit of repeating the witness's answer. This is distracting and annoying, so do not do it. To have the testimony unfold as if the witness is telling a story, it should sound "natural" even though you have rehearsed it with your witness.

Listen to What Your Witness Says

Although you want to remain passive while the witness speaks, you should still show interest in what your witness is saying. Pay attention to and maintain interest in your witness's testimony. Make sure that the witness has answered your question fully. It is important to make sure you get the answer you need for each question before moving on to the next question. If the witness has not answered your question fully, ask additional questions. Failing to listen carefully can result in your failing to establish important facts that are integral to your theory of the case. Also, if the witness anticipates and answers several of your prepared questions at once, make sure you don't ask the questions that have already been answered.

Direct the Witness's Testimony

You are the "director" of the examination, and your goal is to keep the testimony moving in a clear and logical manner. You accomplish this by directing the witness to the topics you will cover and then by asking questions that elicit a story that is understandable, logical, and convincing. The judge or other decision-maker (and the witness) should know where you are headed with your questions. For example, assume your case involves a meeting that took place between a landlord and tenant on March 1. Do not simply ask the witness, "What did you do on March 1?" The witness probably did many things that day that have absolutely nothing to do with your case. Instead, you should say, "Ms. Lahari, you told us earlier about a problem you were having with your apartment. Did you ever meet with the landlord to discuss that problem?"

Admit Your Weak Facts

You can be sure that the other side has anticipated your theory and identified the weaknesses of your case. You can also be sure that if you do not mention your weak facts during direct examination, the opposing advocate will raise them in cross-examination! It is far better to admit your weak facts as part of your direct examination because you can control how and when the information comes out. More importantly, the witness can explain away the weakness in a logical and reasonable manner, something that may not be possible during cross-examination. Admitting weaknesses up front also enhances the credibility of your case—it shows that you have nothing to hide.

Remember That Facts Outweigh Opinion

You call witnesses to testify at a trial or hearing because they have personal knowledge of events that are relevant to your case. In other words, they have directly seen, heard, or done something that is relevant to the issues in the case. When testifying, witnesses should relate facts, not their opinions. Factual evidence has more value than opinion evidence unless the witness is an expert (see below). For example, if a witness says, "I could see that the defendant was very upset," that is merely an opinion. You should then ask, "Why do you say that?" In this way, you can draw out the facts that caused the witness to form that opinion. The witness can then say, for example, "He became very quiet; he sat down; he had tears in his eyes."

Control the Speed of the Testimony

Many advocates rush through the witness's testimony. While both the advocate and the witness are familiar with the story, the judge or other decision-maker is not—this is the first time that he or she is hearing the story. You must pay attention to make sure that the decision-maker has enough time to absorb what is being said and to write it down. Take your time. Pause after your witness answers a question—make sure the evidence is being heard and understood. If your witness is speaking too fast, slow him or her down. If your witness answers a question with a lot of information at once, be certain the decision-maker has taken it all in. If you are in doubt, break down the witness's answer into small parts and review each part.

Finally, try to hold the decision-maker's attention. If your questions are disorganized, irrelevant, or repetitive, the decision-maker may become bored, inattentive, and annoyed. Thorough preparation will help you maximize the impact of your direct examination.

Special Witnesses

There are additional considerations for certain types of witnesses.

Expert Witnesses

An **expert witness** is a witness who, because of education, skill, or experience, has more knowledge than the average person about a particular subject matter in dispute. By virtue of his or her expertise, training, and specialized knowledge in a particular subject, the witness is considered to be an expert in that subject. Expert witnesses

---

expert witness: a witness who is permitted to testify at a trial or hearing because of special knowledge or proficiency in a particular field that is relevant to the case

are allowed to give their opinions on matters that involve their area of expertise, even though they do not have personal knowledge of events relating to the case. For example, a plumber can testify about the probable cause of toilet damage, even without having been present when the toilet was damaged. If you call an expert witness, you must first demonstrate that the witness has the necessary background and expertise to give an opinion. The other side's advocate may challenge the witness's credentials and qualification as an expert, in which case it is up to the judge or other decision-maker to determine whether the witness qualifies.

Police Officer as a Witness

In a criminal or provincial offences matter, the prosecutor will usually call the police officer who responded to the scene or who laid the charge, to testify about the facts needed to establish the elements of the offence. Police officers are trained to write notes during or immediately after an investigation. A police officer may need to refer to his or her notes during direct examination to refresh his or her memory as to dates, times, and specific details regarding his or her conversation with the defendant or other witnesses. A judge or justice of the peace may allow a police officer to refer to his or her notes during a direct examination in order to refresh his or her memory; however, the prosecutor must establish the following facts:

1. That the police officer made notes
2. That those notes were made around the time of the incident
3. That there have been no alterations, deletions, or additions to the notes since they were made
4. That the police officer has an independent recollection of the event or incident in question and needs to refer to the notes only to refresh his or her memory

Once the prosecutor has established these facts through the questioning of the police officer, the prosecutor must ask the judge or justice of the peace permission for the officer to refer to his or her notes for the purpose of refreshing memory. For an example of how this is done, see the direct examination of Police Constable Matthew Lee in the Liquor Licence Case (Box 11.3, below).

Paralegal Rules of Conduct Respecting Witnesses in the Context of a Direct Examination

Rule 4.03 of the *Paralegal Rules of Conduct* imposes restrictions on a paralegal's ability to speak with a witness giving testimony. These restrictions depend on whether the witness is sympathetic or unsympathetic to the paralegal's cause and at what point during the testimony the paralegal wishes to communicate with the witness. A **sympathetic witness** is a witness who gives evidence that is favourable to your client's case. An **unsympathetic witness** is one who gives evidence that is unfavourable to your client's case.

Rules 4.03(1)(a) through (c) deal with a paralegal's communication with witnesses giving testimony during and immediately after a direct examination:

> 4.03(1) Subject to the direction of the tribunal, a paralegal shall observe the following rules respecting communication with witnesses giving evidence:
>
> (a) During examination-in-chief, the examining paralegal may discuss with the witness any matter that has not been covered in the examination up to that point.
>
> (b) During examination-in-chief by another licensee of a witness who is unsympathetic to the paralegal's cause, the paralegal not conducting the examination-in-chief may discuss the evidence with the witness.
>
> (c) Between completion of examination-in-chief and commencement of cross-examination of the paralegal's own witness, the paralegal ought not to discuss the evidence given in chief or relating to any matter introduced or touched on during the examination-in-chief.

Rule 4.03(2) allows a paralegal to discuss a matter with a witness that may otherwise breach Rule 4.03(1) as long as the paralegal obtains the consent of the opposing licensee or the tribunal:

> 4.03(2) With the consent of the opposing licensee or with leave of the tribunal, a paralegal may enter into discussions with a witness that might otherwise raise a question under this rule as to the propriety of the discussions.

Sample Direct Examinations in the Kitchen Renovation Small Claims Court Case

In Chapter 1, Fact Situation 1 set out the basic facts of a Small Claims Court dispute involving a kitchen renovation contract. In Chapter 6, we developed the theory of both the plaintiff's and the defendants' cases, and we provided witness statements for the plaintiff's two witnesses and the defendants' two witnesses.

Box 11.1 contains the sample direct examinations of the plaintiff's witnesses, Alec Baldwin and Stephen Baldwin, along with the exhibit referred to in Stephen's direct examination. Compare the direct examination of each witness to the witness statements in Chapter 6, and see how the questions are designed to elicit the story of each witness. Note how the exhibit is introduced in the direct examination of

---

sympathetic witness: a witness who gives evidence that is favourable to your client's case

unsympathetic witness: a witness who gives evidence that is unfavourable to your client's case

Stephen Baldwin. Note also how each witness gives evidence only on the matters of which he has direct knowledge. Finally, note how the direct examinations are designed to eliminate unnecessary overlap between the testimony of the two witnesses.

BOX 11.1

Kitchen Renovation Case: Direct Examinations of the Plaintiff's Witnesses

Direct Examination of Alec Baldwin

Q: What is your relationship to Baldwin Brothers Construction?

A: I'm an owner of the business together with my brother Stephen.

Q: Can you tell me a little bit about the business?

A: We're licensed contractors and have been in business for ten years. We do general contracting work, specializing in small renovation projects.

Q: What is your relationship with the defendants?

A: Six months ago, Tina Fey hired us to renovate her kitchen.

Q: What renovations were you hired to do?

A: Tina told us she wanted the kitchen cabinets painted, new hardware installed on the doors, a new countertop, and the existing lighting replaced with pot lights. She also wanted the kitchen walls and ceiling painted.

Q: How many pot lights were you supposed to install?

A: We talked about how many pot lights she would need to make her kitchen bright. I told her that pot lights normally cost $250 each installed, and that five would be the right number for her kitchen.

Q: Did you talk about the possibility of additional lights?

A: Yes. She asked what would happen if she wanted more light, and I said, "Then we can install more," even though I was sure five would be enough.

Q: Did you and Ms. Fey agree on a contract price?

A: Yes. Based on our discussions I gave her a price of $7,500 for all the work, and she agreed.

Q: Did you ask for a deposit before starting the work?

A: Yes, Ms. Fey gave me a deposit of $2,500.

Q: And did you in fact do the work?

A: Yes. We went to the house the following week to start the work. We installed the new countertop. After that I went to another job, and my brother completed the work at the Feys.

Q: How long did it take to complete the work?

A: Less than a week.

Q: Did you give the Feys an invoice for your work?

A: My brother dealt with the invoice and payment.

Direct Examination of Stephen Baldwin

Q: What is your relationship to Baldwin Brothers Construction?

A: I'm an owner of the business together with my brother Alec.

Q: What is your relationship with the defendants?

A: Six months ago, we were hired by Tommy and Tina Fey to renovate their kitchen.

Q: What renovations were you hired to do?

A: We were hired to paint the kitchen and the cabinets, install a new countertop, and install pot lights. My brother Alec negotiated the contract with the Feys.

Q: Did you do the work?

A: My brother and I came a week later to start the work.

Q: Did you have any discussions with either defendant about the number of pot lights to be installed?

A: Yes. Tommy Fey was at home during the renovation. When it was time to install the pot lights, I checked with him about the location of the five lights I was planning to install.

Q: What did Mr. Fey say?

A: Tommy told me he didn't think that five lights would provide enough light. I told him to tell me how many he wanted and that I could install more. He told me he wanted three more, and I said fine.

Q: Did you discuss with him the cost of the additional lights?

A: He never asked me what it would cost, so we never discussed money.

Q: Did you complete the work?

A: Yes. The job was finished within a week.

Q: Were the defendants satisfied with your work?

A: We did a good job, and the Feys seemed happy with our work. Everything was fine until I gave Tommy the bill.

Q: I'm showing you an invoice from Baldwin Brothers Construction dated June 30, 2016. Is this a copy of the invoice that you gave to Mr. Fey?

A: Yes, it is.

(The paralegal shows the invoice to the advocate for the defendant and then gives it to the judge or court clerk and says: "Your Honour, I would ask that this invoice be introduced as Exhibit 1." After the judge states, "Invoice from Baldwin Brothers Construction

dated June 30, 2016, marked as Exhibit 1," the paralegal asks for the exhibit back and gives it to the witness.)

Q: How much was the invoice for?

A: The bill was for $8,250.

Q: How was that amount calculated?

A: The original contract price of $7,500 plus $750 for supplying and installing three additional pot lights.

(The paralegal asks for the exhibit from the witness and hands it back to the judge)

Q: What was Mr. Fey's reaction?

A: He asked what the extra $750 was for, and I said it was for three extra pot lights at $250 each, over and above the five lights that were included in the contract.

Q: What did Mr. Fey do then?

A: He said the contract included "all necessary lights" and he wouldn't pay any more than the $7,500 originally agreed to. And he gave me a cheque for $5,000.

FIGURE 11.1   **Exhibit 1 in the Kitchen Renovation Case: Invoice from Baldwin Brothers Construction**

INVOICE

BALDWIN BROTHERS CONSTRUCTION

56 LASMERE AVENUE — WESTON, ON M9L 2N3 — TEL 416 555-8902

TO: *Tommy and Tina Fey*   DATE: *June 30, 2016*

Kitchen Renovation as agreed:	*$7,500.00*
Painting kitchen cabinets, installing new hardware on doors, installing new countertop, installing five pot lights.	
Installing 3 additional pot lights @ $250	*750.00*
	8,250.00
Less deposit	*2,500.00*
Balance owing (including HST)	*$5,750.00*

Box 11.2 contains the sample direct examination of the defendant Tina Fey. Again, compare her direct examination to her witness statement in Chapter 6. You'll get a chance to prepare the direct examination of Tommy Fey as an exercise at the end of this chapter.

BOX 11.2

Kitchen Renovation Case: Direct Examination of the Defendant, Tina Fey

Q: What is your relationship to the plaintiff?

A: Six months ago, I hired the plaintiff to renovate my kitchen.

Q: What renovations did you hire the plaintiff to do?

A: I met with Alec Baldwin and told him that I wanted the kitchen cabinets painted, new hardware installed on the doors, a new countertop, and the existing lighting replaced with pot lights. I also wanted the kitchen walls and ceiling painted.

Q: Did the plaintiff agree to do that work?

A: Yes, for $7,500.

Q: Did you discuss with the plaintiff how many pot lights he was going to install?

A: I told Alec that I wanted enough pot lights to make my kitchen bright.

Q: What was Alec's response?

A: He assured me that he would install the necessary number of pot lights as part of the contract price.

Q: Did you and Alec agree on an exact number of pot lights?

A: Alec told me that five would be enough, but when I asked him what would happen if I needed more lights, he said that he could install more.

Q: Did you and Alec have any discussions about an additional cost if you were to need more than five pot lights?

A: No. He never said that there would be an extra charge.

Q: Did you give the plaintiff a deposit?

A: Yes, I gave Alec a deposit of $2,500 when he and his brother Stephen started the work a week later.

Q: And was the work completed?

A: Yes.

Q: How long did it take to complete the work?

A: Less than a week.

Q: Did the plaintiff give you an invoice for the work?

A: My husband dealt with the invoice and payment.

Sample Direct Examinations in the Liquor Licence Case

In Chapter 1, Fact Situation 2 set out the basic facts of a provincial offences case involving a charge under the *Liquor Licence Act*. In Chapter 6, we developed the theory of both the prosecution's and the defendants' cases, and we provided witness statements for the prosecution's two witnesses and the defendants' two witnesses.

Box 11.3 contains the sample direct examinations of prosecution witnesses Constable Matthew Lee and Patrick Elder, along with the exhibit referred to in the direct examination of Constable Lee. Again, compare the direct examination of each witness to the witness statements in Chapter 6, and see how the questions are designed to elicit the story of each witness. Note how the exhibit is introduced in the direct examination of Constable Lee. Note also how each witness gives evidence only on the matters of which he has direct knowledge. Finally, note how the direct examinations are designed to eliminate unnecessary overlap between the testimony of the two witnesses.

BOX 11.3

Liquor Licence Case: Direct Examinations of the Prosecution Witnesses

Direct Examination of Police Constable Matthew Lee

Prosecutor:	Good afternoon, Constable Lee. Are you currently employed as a police constable with the Toronto Police Service, 14 Division?
Witness:	That is correct.
Prosecutor:	How long have you been employed as a police constable?
Witness:	I've been working as a police constable for about ten years.
Prosecutor:	Were you employed and working as a police constable with the Toronto Police Service on May 16, 2016?
Witness:	Yes, I was. I started my shift at 6:00 p.m. on that date.
Prosecutor:	What were your responsibilities that shift?
Witness:	I was responsible for patrolling the neighbourhood and responding to various scenes as required and directed by dispatch.
Prosecutor:	Were you dispatched to the Simpson Academy on May 16, 2016?
Witness:	Yes. A few hours after I started my shift that day, I was dispatched to the Simpson Academy to investigate a noise complaint involving an event.

Prosecutor:	Where is the Simpson Academy campus located?
Witness:	The campus is located at 1292 Olde Street in Toronto.
Prosecutor:	I see that you are looking at something that is in front of you.
Witness:	Yes, I am.
Prosecutor:	What is it that you are looking at?
Witness:	I have with me the notes I made on May 16, 2016.
Prosecutor:	When did you make those notes?
Witness:	I made these notes both during and immediately after attending the Simpson Academy student lounge to investigate the noise complaint on May 16, 2016.
Prosecutor:	Have there been any alterations, deletions, or additions to those notes since you made them?
Witness:	No.
Prosecutor:	Do you require the use of these notes to refresh your memory regarding certain details relating to the event in question?
Prosecutor:	Yes, I do.
Prosecutor:	Do you have an independent recollection of what took place on May 16, 2016?
Witness:	Yes, I do.
Prosecutor:	Your Worship, may the officer be permitted to refer to his notes for the purposes of refreshing his memory?
Justice of the Peace:	Any objections from the defence?
Paralegal for the defendant:	No objections.
JP:	The officer is permitted to refer to his notes for the purposes of refreshing his memory.
Prosecutor:	I would like to take you back to May 16, 2016 and your attendance at the Simpson Academy student lounge. What time did you arrive at the campus on that date?
Witness:	I arrived at the campus at about 11:30 p.m.
Prosecutor:	Did you arrive with any other officers?
Witness:	No. I was working on my own.
Prosecutor:	Please describe what happened when you arrived at the Simpson Academy on May 16, 2016.
Witness:	Upon my arrival at the campus, I made my way to the student lounge, where I observed a party taking place.
Prosecutor:	What did you see when you arrived at the student lounge?

Witness:	I immediately noticed an indoor bar and doors leading out to an outdoor patio area. I walked over to the bar, where there was a bartender behind it. I observed beer and wine bottles behind the bar, and the bartender was in the process of pouring wine into plastic wine glasses.
Prosecutor:	Were the premises licensed to serve alcohol?
Witness:	Yes.
Prosecutor:	How do you know that?
Witness:	When I walked over to the bar, I saw a Liquor Sales Licence and Catering Notification Form posted over the bar in the name of Treetop Catering Inc. I had also received a copy of the Catering Notification Form at my headquarters on May 2, 2016.

(The prosecutor provides a copy of a document to the defence and to the witness)

Prosecutor:	I am showing you a Catering Notification Form dated May 2, 2016. Is this the Catering Notification Form that you saw posted above the bar that evening?
Witness:	Yes, it is.
Prosecutor:	Has the document been amended or modified in any way since you saw it on May 16, 2016?
Witness:	No, it hasn't.
Prosecutor:	Your Worship, I would ask that this document be introduced as Exhibit 1.
JP:	Any objections from the defence?
Paralegal for the defendant:	No objections.
JP:	The Catering Notification Form dated May 2, 2016 is marked as Exhibit 1.
Prosecutor:	What is the purpose of a Catering Notification Form?
Witness:	A Catering Notification Form is provided by a holder of a valid Liquor Sales Licence with a catering endorsement to the Alcohol and Gaming Commission of Ontario, local police, fire, building, and health departments in order to notify them of the licensee's intention to cater an event in a specific area that will include service of alcoholic beverages at premises that are unlicensed. It identifies the nature and details of the event as well as the name and information of the sponsor of the event and licensee information.
Prosecutor:	Does this Catering Notification Form that you saw posted on May 16, 2016 identify the details of the event, sponsor, and licensed area?

FIGURE 11.2 **Exhibit 1 in the Liquor Licence Case: Catering Notification Form for Treetop Catering Inc.**

Alcohol and Gaming
Commission of Ontario
Inspection and Investigation Branch
90 Sheppard Ave. E. Suite 200
Toronto, ON M2N 0A4
416.326.8700 or 1 800.522.2876 toll free in Ontario

Catering Notification Form

This form must be received by the AGCO **at least ten (10) days prior to an event or thirty (30) days prior to an event using a Temporary Tiered Seating Approval.** Please complete all sections and **drop off, mail or fax the completed form to 416.326.0300.** Incomplete forms will be returned.

1. Event Information

Nature of Event (wedding, reception, birthday, etc.)

RECEPTION FOR STUDENTS

Date of Event	Room Capacity	No. in Attendance	Approximate Hours of Liquor Sale & Service
MAY 16, 2016	60	40	7:00 P.M. to 12:00 A.M.

Name of Event Premises	Tel. No of Event Premises
SIMPSON ACADEMY, STUDENT LOUNGE	(416) 222 – 5151

Address of Event Premises (street number and name, city, postal code)	Boundaries & Room Name/Number
1292 OLDE STREET, TORONTO, ONTARIO M5S 5P5	Student Lounge & Patio

Will the sale, service or consumption of liquor take place in tiered seating at the event? ☐ Yes ☐ No (If **Yes**, see Requirement 2 below)

2. Sponsor Information

Name of Sponsor (person/organization holding the event)

SIMPSON ACADEMY ADVOCACY CLUB (SIMPSON ACADEMY)

Address of Sponsor	Tel. Nº of Sponsor
1292 OLDE STREET, TORONTO, ONTARIO M5S 5P5	(416) 222 – 5151

3. Contact Information

Name of Contact (person whom the AGCO can contact regarding the event)	Tel. Nº of Contact
VICTORIA LEVENS	(905) 900 – 3131

4. Licensee Information

Licensee (person/organization to whom the liquor sales licence with catering endorsement is issued)	Liquor Sales Licence Number
TREETOP CATERING INC.	729191

Name of Licensed Establishment	Tel. Nº of Licensed Establishment
TREETOP CATERING INC.	(905) 922 – 3131

5. Licensee Signature

Print Name	Signature	Date
VICTORIA LEVENS	*Victoria Levens*	MAY 2, 2016

Requirements:

1. Catering Event: In addition to advising the AGCO at least ten (10) days prior to the event, the licence holder must also notify the local police, fire, building and health departments at least ten (10) days prior to the event.
2. Temporary Tiered Seating: This form must be submitted at least thirty (30) days prior to the event and include the following: (a) copies of the notification letters to the police, fire, building, health and municipal clerks departments; and (b) a sketch showing the area where the temporary tiered seating will be located. **You must have a Temporary Tiered Seating Approval on your licence.**
3. The event must be sponsored by a person other than the licence holder.
4. The licence holder or employee should carry a copy of the liquor sales licence when transporting liquor to and from the event, and post a copy of the liquor sales licence and this catering notification form at the event; The licence holder or employee should only transport and sell and serve liquor that is purchased under the liquor sales licence.

5. Post a Sandy's Law warning sign at the event (download the sign at http://www.agco.on.ca/en/whatwedo/signs_sandyslaw.aspx).
6. Ensure light meals are available at the event.
7. Allow only the licensee or its employees to sell and serve liquor at the event and ensure that all employees are trained in accordance with the regulations on server training.
8. Do not cater an event exceeding ten (10) consecutive days in length, operate an ongoing business with a sponsor or promote an event.
9. Do not sell and serve liquor at an event held in a residence.
10. As long as it is not a residence, the specified location for the catered event shall be deemed to be a licensed establishment during the time of the event and the licensee shall ensure compliance with the applicable sections of the *Liquor Licence Act* and Regulations.
11. Failure to comply with the *Liquor Licence Act* and Regulations can result in disciplinary action, including a suspension or revocation of the licensee's endorsement and/or liquor sales licence.

For more information, contact AGCO Customer Service at **416.326.8700** or **1 800.522.2876** (toll-free in Ontario) or online at **www.agco.on.ca/en/services/ licence_endorsement_cater_LSL.aspx**

1240 (11/08)   Catering Notification Form

Witness:	It describes the event as a "reception for students" at the Simpson Academy student lounge and, in particular, the student lounge and patio. The form states that the approximate hours of liquor sale and service would be 7:00 p.m. to midnight on May 16, 2016 and that the licensee was Treetop Catering Inc.
Prosecutor:	Who was sponsoring the event?
Witness:	The Simpson Academy Advocacy Club.
Prosecutor:	Was there anyone in charge of the service at the event that evening?
Witness:	Yes, Victoria Levens. At that time, she was the owner of Treetop Catering Inc. The bartender introduced me to her shortly after I arrived.
Prosecutor:	How did you know the person you were introduced to was Victoria Levens?
Witness:	She identified herself to me as Victoria Levens and as the owner of Treetop Catering Inc., the organizer of the event.
Prosecutor:	Do you see the defendant, Victoria Levens, in the courtroom now?
Witness:	Yes. She is sitting over there to the left. *(Points to identify the defendant)*
Prosecutor:	Your Worship, let the record show that the witness has identified the defendant in court today. Constable Lee, what did you say to Ms. Levens after you were introduced to her?
Witness:	I told her that there had been a noise complaint.
Prosecutor:	And then what happened?
Witness:	At this point, it was already close to midnight and the event was almost over. The defendant said she would tell the guests that the party was over. We then walked outside to the patio.
Prosecutor:	What did you see when you walked out to the patio?
Witness:	I saw a few things. I noticed many people standing around on the patio. I also noticed that the patio was enclosed with a fence which had a gate opening to a grassy area beyond the patio.
Prosecutor:	Did you see anything else?
Witness:	I saw a number of empty beer bottles and plastic wine glasses on the grassy area just beyond the fence surrounding the patio.
Prosecutor:	How do you know they were empty beer bottles and plastic wine glasses?
Witness:	I walked over to them to get a closer look. I also picked them up to inspect them. They were the same type of clear plastic wine glasses that I saw the bartender using a few minutes before. The beer bottles were the standard glass beer bottles. They had a green label on them. They also smelled like alcohol.

Prosecutor:	How did you know they smelled like alcohol?
Witness:	I have smelled alcohol many times before in my professional capacity during bar inspections and in my personal capacity. In this case, I could smell a strong odour of beer coming from the empty beer bottles.
Prosecutor:	Was the grassy area included in the boundaries of the licensed area for this event?
Witness:	No. The Catering Notification Form indicated that the boundaries for this event included only the student lounge and outside patio. The patio is enclosed by a fence which separates the patio from the lawn and grounds of the campus.
Prosecutor:	What did this fence look like?
Witness:	It was a wooden fence. It was quite low. As previously mentioned, there was a gate that was part of the fence which opened onto the grassy area.
Prosecutor:	Was the gate open when you arrived on the patio?
Witness:	It wasn't wide open. But it wasn't completely closed, either. It was open about 3 inches or so.
Prosecutor:	Did you see anything else while you were there?
Witness:	I noticed a security guard standing on the patio.
Prosecutor:	How many security guards did you see that evening at the event?
Witness:	Just one security guard.
Prosecutor:	How did you know this person you saw was a security guard?
Witness:	He was wearing a black t-shirt with the word "Security" across the front of the t-shirt.

Direct Examination of Patrick Elder

Prosecutor:	Good afternoon, Mr. Elder. What do you do for a living?
Witness:	I'm retired. I used to work as an accountant, but I retired about five years ago.
Prosecutor:	Where do you live?
Witness:	I live at 1310 Olde Street, Unit 501, in Toronto.
Prosecutor:	What type of building is this?
Witness:	It's a ten-storey apartment building.
Prosecutor:	Describe the location of the apartment building.
Witness:	It's located on the northwest corner of Olde Street and New Avenue. My building is right next door to the Simpson Academy campus. There are also a few restaurants and a pub across the street.
Prosecutor:	What floor is your unit on?

Witness:	Fifth floor.
Prosecutor:	Does your unit have a balcony?
Witness:	Yes, it does.
Prosecutor:	What direction does your balcony face?
Witness:	It faces east. It overlooks the outside patio of the Simpson Academy student lounge and adjoining lawn.
Prosecutor:	How far is your balcony from this outside patio?
Witness:	I would say about 20 feet or so.
Prosecutor:	Do you enjoy living in your apartment building, Mr. Elder?
Witness:	Most of the time. However, the noise from all the students on campus can be hard to deal with sometimes.
Prosecutor:	And did you have a problem with the Simpson Academy students on May 16, 2016?
Witness:	Yes. Starting at around 7:00 or 7:30 p.m., I could hear that there was some kind of event taking place at the Simpson Academy. At first it was just the usual sound of people outside talking and laughing, but as the evening wore on, the voices got louder and louder.
Prosecutor:	What did you do about it?
Witness:	At the beginning, nothing much other than closing my window. However, as the evening wore on, the voices got louder and louder. By about 11:00 p.m. the party was so loud that I couldn't get to sleep.
Prosecutor:	What did you do next?
Witness:	I got out of bed and walked out onto my balcony.
Prosecutor:	Describe what you saw when you were out on your balcony.
Witness:	I saw a large crowd of people on the patio and the grassy area around the patio.
Prosecutor:	How many people did you see out there?
Witness:	At least 20.
Prosecutor:	What did you do?
Witness:	I went inside my apartment to call the police to make a complaint regarding the noise.

Box 11.4 contains the sample direct examination of the defendant, Victoria Levens. Again, compare her direct examination to her witness statement in Chapter 6. You will get a chance to prepare the direct examination of Calvin Hobbs as an exercise at the end of this chapter.

Liquor Licence Case: Direct Examination of the Defendant, Victoria Levens

Paralegal: Good afternoon, Ms. Levens. What do you do for a living?

Witness: I run a catering business called Treetop Catering Inc.

Paralegal: Are you the owner of Treetop Catering Inc.?

Witness: Yes. I am the sole director, officer, and shareholder of the company. I run the company on my own, including organizing and managing all the events we cater.

Paralegal: Did you organize an event on May 16, 2016?

Witness: Yes, I did.

Paralegal: Please tell us about that particular event.

Witness: Well, in April 2016 I was contacted by the Simpson Academy Advocacy Club to organize and manage a party for its members at the Simpson Academy student lounge at 1292 Olde Street in Toronto on May 16, 2016.

Paralegal: What were you hired to provide?

Witness: By the terms of our agreement, I was to provide a light buffet, beer, wine, and soft drinks for 40 guests.

Paralegal: How were the beverages served?

Witness: Beer came in dark brown glass bottles and the wine was served in small white plastic wine cups. Soft drinks were served in small cans.

Paralegal: Who was responsible for serving and selling alcohol to the guests?

Witness: The bartender I hired for the event. He served all the beverages from behind the bar.

Paralegal: Did you have a licence to serve and sell alcohol?

Witness: Yes, I did. I also applied for and was granted a caterer's endorsement, which authorized me to sell and serve liquor at the Simpson Academy student lounge for this particular event.

Paralegal: Were you required to notify anyone of your intention to serve and sell alcohol at the event on March 16, 2016?

Witness: Yes. On May 2, 2016, shortly after making a site visit at the lounge, I completed the Alcohol and Gaming Commission's Catering Notification Form and sent it to the Registrar of the Alcohol and Gaming Commission. I also sent it to the local police, fire, health, and building departments, as required.

Paralegal: Your Worship, I would like to recall Exhibit 1, being the Catering Notification Form.

(The court clerk provides the exhibit to the paralegal)

Paralegal:	Ms. Levens, I am showing you Exhibit 1. Is this the Catering Notification Form that you completed and provided to the Alcohol and Gaming Commission, local police, fire, health, and building departments?
Witness:	Yes, it is.
Paralegal:	Is that your signature at the bottom of the page?
Witness:	Yes.
Paralegal:	What does the form say about the boundaries and room number where the event would be taking place?
Witness:	It notes the boundaries for the event to be the student lounge and outside fenced patio.
Paralegal:	Describe for His Worship the student lounge and outside fenced patio.
Witness:	Well, the student lounge room included an indoor bar, and then there were doors in that room leading outside to a fenced patio. The fence had a gate that opened onto a grassy lawn which was part of the campus grounds. At the event, I had set up a small buffet inside the student lounge room.
Paralegal:	How big was the outside patio?
Witness:	I would say approximately 30 feet by 30 feet. It could fit about 20 to 25 people comfortably.
Paralegal:	Was there anything else?
Witness:	Yes. There were signs posted around the premises that stated "No alcoholic beverages permitted outside the patio."
Paralegal:	You mentioned that you made a site visit to the lounge before the event. When did you make this site visit?
Witness:	On May 1, 2016.
Paralegal:	What did you do at the site when you arrived?
Witness:	I walked around the lounge and the patio to see what the facilities were like in order to plan for the event. I needed to know where I could set up the buffet and what the bar looked like, and determine the licensed areas for service of alcohol.
Paralegal:	Did you do anything to document what you saw when you were inspecting the venue?
Witness:	Yes. I made a diagram of the lounge and outside patio once I got back to my office after the site visit.

(The paralegal hands a copy of a diagram to the prosecutor and an original diagram to the witness)

FIGURE 11.3   **Exhibit 2 in the Liquor Licence Case: Victoria Levens's Diagram of the Simpson Academy Student Lounge and Patio**

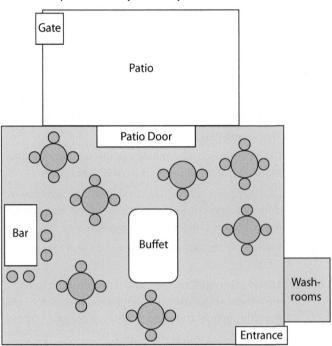

Simpson Academy Student Lounge and Patio—
Simpson Academy Advocacy Club Event

Paralegal:	I'm showing you a diagram entitled "Simpson Academy Student Lounge and Patio—Simpson Academy Advocacy Club Event." Do you recognize this diagram?
Witness:	Yes. I made the diagram on my computer. I then printed the diagram using my printer to produce this document.
Paralegal:	When did you make this diagram?
Witness:	I made it on May 1, 2016 shortly after my site visit.
Paralegal:	What does the diagram show?
Witness:	It shows the layout of the Simpson Academy student lounge and patio.
Paralegal:	Does this diagram accurately show the set-up and premises of the Simpson Academy student lounge on May 16, 2016, the date of the event?
Witness:	Yes, it does.

Paralegal:	Your Worship, I would ask that this document be introduced as Exhibit 2.
JP:	Any objections from the prosecution?
Prosecutor:	No objections.

(The paralegal hands the exhibit to the court clerk)

JP:	The diagram is entered as Exhibit 2.

(Once the exhibit is entered into evidence, the paralegal takes the exhibit back from the court clerk and hands it to the witness)

Paralegal:	How many signs stating "No alcoholic beverages permitted outside the patio" were posted on May 16, 2016 during the event?
Witness:	There were two.
Paralegal:	Can you please point out where the signs stating "No alcoholic beverages permitted outside the patio" were posted?
Witness:	*(Witness points to the diagram)* One sign was posted there on the doors leading out to the patio. There was also one on the gate leading out to the patio to the grassy lawn area.
Paralegal:	Starting with your arrival, how did the event proceed on May 16, 2016?
Witness:	I hired some staff to assist with the event, including a bartender, so we arrived at the student lounge around 5:00 p.m. that day to set up everything. Guests started to arrive at about 7:00 p.m.
Paralegal:	What was your role at the event?
Witness:	I was responsible for setting everything up, including the buffet, and for helping with the buffet. I also kept an eye on things to make sure that everything went smoothly.
Paralegal:	When did the event end?
Witness:	The event was scheduled for 7:00 p.m. to midnight, but a police officer arrived shortly after 11:30 p.m. to check things out. He advised me that there had been a noise complaint. The event ended shortly after that.
Paralegal:	What did you do when the police officer arrived?
Witness:	Because it was close to midnight, I told the officer that I would tell the guests that the party was over and to go home. I then walked outside onto the patio and told the security guard, Calvin Hobbs, to ask the guests to leave.
Paralegal:	What happened next?
Witness:	Shortly after that, Police Constable Lee told me that he would be charging me with the offence of permitting the removal of alcohol

from the premises due to the empty beer bottles and plastic wine glasses on the grassy lawn area outside the enclosed patio and licensed area.

Paralegal: At any point in time that evening did you see any guests with alcohol standing on the grass beyond the enclosed patio?

Witness: No, I didn't. I didn't even see any guests at all on the grassy area when I walked outside to tell my security guard to ask the guests to leave.

Paralegal: You mentioned that you hired a security guard for this event. Why did you hire him?

Witness: Well, it is my standard practice to hire at least one security guard for every event that I cater. I wanted to make sure that nothing got out of control and that guests did not leave the patio with any alcohol, because the lounge and patio were the only areas licensed for alcohol.

Paralegal: What other things prevented guests from leaving the patio with alcohol?

Witness: As I mentioned earlier, the outside patio was enclosed by a fence around the entire perimeter. There were also signs posted on the doors leading out to the patio and on the fence's gate advising guests that alcohol was not permitted beyond the patio.

Sample Direct Examinations in the Landlord and Tenant Tribunal Dispute

In Chapter 1, Fact Situation 3 set out the basic facts of a landlord and tenant dispute involving the termination of a tenancy. In Chapter 6, we developed the theory of the tenants' and the landlord's cases and provided the witness statements for both of the tenants' witnesses and both of the landlord's witnesses.

Box 11.5 contains the sample direct examinations of the tenants, Alice Guthrie and Arlo Guthrie. Again, compare the direct examination of each witness to the witness statements in Chapter 6, and see how the questions are designed to elicit the story of each witness. Note how the exhibits (Figures 11.4 through 11.8) are introduced in the direct examination of both witnesses. Note also how each witness gives evidence of only the matters of which he or she has direct knowledge. Finally, note how the direct examinations are designed to eliminate unnecessary overlap between the testimony of the two witnesses.

Landlord and Tenant Dispute: Direct Examinations of the Tenants

Direct Examination of Alice Guthrie

Q: What is your relationship to Jim Croce?

A: My husband Arlo and I rented a one-bedroom apartment from him at 234 Sycamore Street in Toronto.

Q: Did you have a written tenancy agreement?

A: Yes.

Q: I'm showing you a tenancy agreement dated May 1, 2015. Is that the agreement you signed?

(The paralegal shows the agreement to the advocate for the landlord, then gives it to the adjudicator and says, "Madam Adjudicator, I would ask that this agreement be introduced as Exhibit 1." After the adjudicator states, "Tenancy agreement dated May 1, 2015 marked as Exhibit 1," the paralegal asks for the exhibit back and hands it to the witness.)

Q: What were the terms of your tenancy?

A: The lease was for one year starting on May 1, 2015 and ending on April 30, 2016 at a monthly rent of $1,250.

(The paralegal returns the exhibit to the adjudicator)

Q: What sort of building was the apartment located in?

A: The building had two units. The apartment was a great place to live. Jim and his wife Julia lived in the other unit.

Q: What was your relationship with the landlord like?

A: We got along well with Jim and Julia. We paid our rent on time and never had any problems with the landlord.

Q: Do you still live in the apartment?

A: No.

Q: Why?

A: On March 1, 2016 Jim knocked on our door and handed me a notice terminating our tenancy.

Q: I'm showing you a form N12 "Notice to End Your Tenancy Because the Landlord, a Purchaser or a Family Member Requires the Rental Unit" dated March 1, 2016. Is that the form you are referring to?

FIGURE 11.4   Exhibit 1 in the Landlord and Tenant Dispute: Alice and Arlo Guthrie's Tenancy Agreement

TENANCY AGREEMENT

ADDRESS: *234 Sycamore Street, Apt. 2, Toronto*

Name of Tenant(s):   *Alice Guthrie and Arlo Guthrie*

Name of Landlord: *Jim Croce*

Term: *One Year*   from   *May 1, 2015*   to   *April 30, 2016*

Monthly rent: $ *1,250.00*   payable on the first day of each month.

Rent includes all utilities.

Dated: *May 1, 2015*

Tenant's signature(s)   *Alice Guthrie*

Arlo Guthrie

Landlord's signature   *Jim Croce*

A: Yes.

(The paralegal shows the form N12 to the advocate for the landlord, then gives it to the adjudicator and says, "Madam Adjudicator, I would ask that this notice be introduced as Exhibit 2." After the adjudicator states, "Form N12 dated March 1, 2016 marked as Exhibit 2," the paralegal asks for the exhibit back and hands it to the witness.)

Q: What did the form say?

A: It said that we had to move out by April 30, 2016 because Jim's daughter intended to move into the rental unit.

(The paralegal returns the exhibit to the adjudicator)

Q: Did the landlord say anything to you when he gave you the form?

A: Yes, Jim told me that his daughter Cynthia was finishing her studies at the University of Ottawa and was moving back to Toronto.

FIGURE 11.5   **Exhibit 2 in the Landlord and Tenant Dispute: Landlord's Notice to End Tenancy**

Notice to End your Tenancy
Because the Landlord, a Purchaser or a Family Member Requires the Rental Unit
N12

To: (Tenant's name) include all tenant names	From: (Landlord's name)
ALICE GUTHRIE AND ARLO GUTHRIE	JIM CROCE

Address of the Rental Unit:

234 SYCAMORE STREET, APT. 2, TORONTO, ON M2J 1X5

> **This is a legal notice that could lead to you being evicted from your home.**

The following information is from your landlord

I am giving you this notice because I want to end your tenancy. I want you to move out of your rental unit by the following termination date: 3 0 / 0 4 / 2 0 1 6 .
dd/mm/yyyy

My Reason for Ending your Tenancy

I have shaded the circle next to my reason for ending your tenancy.

⊙   **Reason 1**: The following person intends to move into the rental unit:

☐ Me   ☐ My spouse   ☒ My child

☐ My parent   ☐ My spouse's child   ☐ My spouse's parent

Or ☐ A person who provides or will provide care services to:

☐ Me   ☐ My spouse   ☐ My child

☐ My parent   ☐ My spouse's child   ☐ My spouse's parent

○   **Reason 2:** I have signed an Agreement of Purchase and Sale of the rental unit and the following
      person intends to move into the rental unit:

☐ The purchaser   ☐ The purchaser's spouse   ☐ The purchaser's child

☐ The purchaser's   ☐ The purchaser's spouse's   ☐ The purchaser's spouse's
   parent   child   parent

Or ☐ A person who provides or will provide care services to:

☐ The purchaser   ☐ The purchaser's spouse   ☐ The purchaser's child

☐ The purchaser's   ☐ The purchaser's spouse's   ☐ The purchaser's spouse's
   parent   child   parent

OFFICE USE ONLY: File Number ☐☐☐☐☐☐☐☐☐☐☐

Delivery Method: ○ In Person ○ Mail ○ Courier ○ Email ○ Efile ○ Fax   FL ☐

v. 30/11/2015   Page 1 of 2

FIGURE 11.5   **Concluded**

Important Information from the Landlord and Tenant Board

The termination date	The termination date the landlord sets out in this notice must be at least **60 days** after the landlord gives you this notice.
	Also, the termination date must be the last day of the rental period. For example, if you pay rent on the first of each month, the termination date must be the last day of a month.
	Finally, if the tenancy is for a fixed term the termination date cannot be earlier than the last day of the fixed term. For example, if you signed a one-year lease, the termination date cannot be earlier than the last day of the one-year period set out in the lease.
A tenant can give 10 days' notice to end the tenancy	You can terminate the tenancy sooner than the date set out in this notice as long as you give the landlord at least **10 days'** notice that you intend to move out of the rental unit. You must use the Landlord and Tenant Board's Form N9 *Tenant's Notice to End the Tenancy* to give your written notice to the landlord.
What if you disagree with the notice?	You do not have to move out if you disagree with what the landlord has put in this notice. However, the landlord can apply to the Board to evict you. The Board will schedule a hearing where you can explain why you disagree.
What if you move out?	If you move out of the rental unit by the termination date, your tenancy ends on that date.
What if the landlord applies to the Board?	The landlord can apply to the Board to evict you immediately after giving you this notice. If the landlord applies to the Board to evict you, the Board will schedule a hearing and send you a copy of the application and the *Notice of Hearing*. The *Notice of Hearing* sets out the date, time and location of the hearing. At the hearing, the landlord will have to prove the claims they made in this *Notice to End your Tenancy* and in the application and you can respond to the claims your landlord makes. If the Board issues an order ending your tenancy and evicting you, the order will not require you to move out any earlier than the termination date included in this notice.
How to get more information	For more information about this notice or your rights, you can contact the Landlord and Tenant Board. You can reach the Board by phone at 416-645-8080 or 1-888-332-3234. You can visit the Board's website at sjto.ca/LTB.

Signature   ◉ Landlord   ◯ Representative

First Name

J	I	M																													

Last Name

C	R	O	C	E																									

Phone Number

(	4	1	6	)	5	5	5	-	1	2	1	2

Signature *Jim Croce*	Date (dd/mm/yyyy) 01/03/2016

Representative Information (if applicable)

Name	LSUC #	Company Name (if applicable)
Mailing Address		Phone Number
Municipality (City, Town, etc.)	Province	Postal Code	Fax Number

Page 2 of 2

Q: What did you do after getting the notice?

A: Arlo and I began to hunt for another apartment the next day. We wanted another one-bedroom apartment in the same neighbourhood.

Q: And how did the hunt go?

A: We searched online, checked newspaper ads, walked the neighbourhood looking for "For Rent" signs, and asked our friends. We weren't able to find a similar apartment for the same rent, but, after almost two weeks, we managed to find a suitable apartment in the same neighbourhood for $1,350 per month, available on April 1, 2016.

Q: And did you rent that apartment?

A: Yes. We signed a one-year lease on the new apartment.

Q: I'm showing you a tenancy agreement dated March 13, 2016. Is that the lease you signed?

A: Yes, it is.

(The paralegal shows the tenancy agreement to the advocate for the landlord, then gives it to the adjudicator and says, "Madam Adjudicator, I would ask that this tenancy agreement be introduced as Exhibit 3." After the adjudicator states, "Tenancy agreement dated March 13, 2016 marked as Exhibit 3," the paralegal asks for the exhibit back and hands it to the witness.)

FIGURE 11.6   **Exhibit 3 in the Landlord and Tenant Dispute: Alice and Arlo Guthrie's New Tenancy Agreement**

TENANCY AGREEMENT

ADDRESS: *35 WAVERLY STREET, APT. 3, TORONTO*

Name of Tenant(s): *ALICE GUTHRIE & ARLO GUTHRIE*

Name of Landlord: *CARLO ROSSO*

Term: *1 YEAR* from *APRIL 1, 2016* to *MARCH 31, 2017*

Monthly rent: $ *1,350.00* payable on the first day of each month.

Rent includes all utilities.

Dated: *MARCH 13, 2016*

Tenant's signature(s)   *Alice Guthrie*

Arlo Guthrie

Landlord's signature   *Carlo Rosso*

Q: What were the terms of this new lease?

A: The lease was for one year starting on April 1, 2016 at a rent of $1,350 per month.

(The paralegal returns the exhibit to the adjudicator)

Q: And did you move out of the apartment on March 31st?

A: Yes.

Q: This was earlier than the termination date set by the landlord in his notice. How did you arrange that?

A: On March 15th, Arlo prepared a form N9 to terminate our tenancy as of March 31, 2016 and gave it to Jim.

Direct Examination of Arlo Guthrie

Q: What is your relationship to Alice Guthrie?

A: She is my wife.

Q: And what is your relationship to the landlord?

A: Alice and I rented a one-bedroom apartment from Jim Croce at 234 Sycamore Street in Toronto.

Q: And do you still live in that apartment?

A: No. We moved out on March 31, 2016.

Q: How did that come about?

A: Jim served us with a notice terminating our tenancy as of April 30, 2016 on the basis that he needed the apartment for his daughter. Alice and I found another apartment to move to available on April 1st. So I served him with a notice terminating our tenancy earlier.

Q: I'm showing you a form N9 "Tenant's Notice to End the Tenancy" dated March 15, 2016. Is this the notice that you served?

A: Yes, it is.

(The paralegal shows the form N9 to the advocate for the landlord, then gives it to the adjudicator and says, "Madam Adjudicator, I would ask that this notice be introduced as Exhibit 4." After the adjudicator states, "Form N9 dated March 15, 2016 marked as Exhibit 4," the paralegal asks for the exhibit back and hands it to the witness.)

Q: And what is the termination date in this notice?

A: March 31, 2016.

Q: And when did you serve this notice on the landlord?

A: I handed the notice to Jim at his apartment on March 16, 2016.

(The paralegal returns the exhibit to the adjudicator)

FIGURE 11.7 **Exhibit 4 in the Landlord and Tenant Dispute: Tenants' Notice to End Tenancy**

Tenant's Notice to End the Tenancy
N9

To: (Landlord's name)	From: (Tenant's name) include all tenant names
JIM CROCE	ALICE GUTHRIE AND ARLO GUTHRIE

Address of the Rental Unit:

234 SYCAMORE STREET, APT. 2,
TORONTO, ON M2J 1X5

I am giving this notice because I want to move out of the rental unit.

The last day of my tenancy will be | 3 | 1 | / | 0 | 3 | / | 2 | 0 | 1 | 6 | **. This is the termination date.**
dd/mm/yyyy

I will move out of the rental unit on or before the termination date.

Important Information from the Landlord and Tenant Board

The termination date

For most types of tenancies (including monthly tenancies) the termination date must be at least **60 days** after the tenant gives the landlord this notice. Also, the termination date must be the last day of the rental period. For example, if the tenant pays on the first day of each month, the termination date must be the last day of the month. If the tenancy is for a fixed term (for example, a lease for one year), the termination date cannot be earlier than the last date of the fixed term.

Exceptions:
- The termination date must at least **28 days** after the tenant gives the landlord this notice if the tenancy is daily or weekly (the tenant pays rent daily or weekly). Also, the termination date must be the last day of the rental period. For example, if the tenant pays rent weekly each Monday, the termination date must be a Sunday. If the tenancy is for a fixed term, the termination date cannot be earlier than the last date of the fixed term.
- A special rule allows **less than 60 days' notice** in situations where the tenant would normally be required to give 60 days notice (for example, monthly tenancies). The tenant can give notice for the end of February no later than January 1st and can give notice for the end of March no later than February 1st.

The landlord can apply to end the tenancy

The landlord can apply to the Board for an order to end the tenancy and evict the tenant as soon as the tenant gives the landlord this notice. However, if the Board issues an order ending the tenancy, the order will not require the tenant to move out any earlier than the termination date the tenant included in this notice.

When a tenant can give 10 days' notice

The termination date set out in this notice can be **10 days** (or more) after the tenant gives this notice to the landlord if the landlord has given the tenant either an **N12 Notice to End your Tenancy** or an **N13 Notice to End your Tenancy**. The termination date does not have to be the last day of a rental period.

Ending the tenancy when the landlord refused to allow the tenant to assign the rental unit

The tenant can use this notice to end the tenancy if the tenant asked the landlord for permission to assign the rental unit to someone else, and the landlord refused. The termination date must be:
- at least **28 days** after the tenant gives the notice to the landlord if the tenancy is daily or weekly, or
- at least **30 days** after the tenant gives the notice to landlord if the tenancy is anything other than daily or weekly.

The termination date does not have to be the last day of a rental period or the last day of a fixed term.

v. 30/11/2015   Page 1 of 2

FIGURE 11.7   Concluded

Ending the tenancy in a care home	If the tenant lives in a care home, the termination date in this notice can be **30 days** (or more) after the tenant gives the notice to the landlord. The termination date does not have to be the end of a rental period or the last day of a fixed term.
	If a tenant who lives in a care home gives this notice to the landlord, they can also give the landlord a 10-day notice for the landlord to stop providing care services and meals. If the tenant gives the landlord the 10-day notice, the tenant is not required to pay for care services and meals after the end of the 10-day period.
Tenants can't be required to sign this notice	A landlord cannot require the tenant to sign an N9 *Tenant's Notice to End the Tenancy* as a condition of agreeing to rent a unit. A tenant does not have to move out based on this notice if the landlord required the tenant to sign it when the tenant agreed to rent the unit.
	Exceptions: A landlord can require a tenant to sign an N9 *Tenant's Notice to End the Tenancy* as a condition of agreeing to rent a rental unit in the following two situations:
	• The tenant is a student living in accommodation provided by a post-secondary institution or by a landlord who has an agreement with the post-secondary school to provide the accommodation.
	• The tenant is occupying a rental unit in a care home for the purposes of receiving rehabilitative or therapeutic services, and
	• the tenant agreed to occupy the rental unit for not more than 4 years,
	• the tenancy agreement set out that the tenant can be evicted when the objectives of providing the care services have been met or will not be met, and
	• the rental unit is provided to the tenant under an agreement between the landlord and a service manager under the *Housing Services Act, 2011*.
The tenant must move out by the termination date	The tenant must move out and remove all their personal possessions from the rental unit by the termination date set out on page 1. If the tenant moves out by the termination date set out above, but leaves behind personal possessions, the tenant will no longer have any rights to those possessions and the landlord will be allowed to dispose of them.
How to get more information	For more information about this notice or your rights, you can contact the Landlord and Tenant Board. You can reach the Board by phone at **416-645-8080** or **1-888-332-3234**. You can visit the Board's website at sjto.ca/LTB.

Signature   ⦿ Tenant   ◯ Representative

First Name

A	R	L	O																											

Last Name

G	U	T	H	R	I	E																							

Phone Number

(	4	1	6	)	5	5	5	-	2	3	4	5

Signature *Arlo Guthrie*	Date (dd/mm/yyyy) 15/03/2016

OFFICE USE ONLY:	File Number										

Delivery Method: ◯ In Person   ◯ Mail   ◯ Courier   ◯ Email   ◯ Efile   ◯ Fax   FL

Page 2 of 2

Q: Did you use a moving company to move to your new apartment?

A: Yes. We hired Two Guys Moving to move our belongings to the new apartment.

Q: And how much did the move cost?

A: Two Guys gave us a bill for $750.

Q: I'm showing you an invoice from Two Guys Moving dated March 31, 2016 for $750. Is this the bill?

A: Yes, it is.

(The paralegal shows the invoice to the advocate for the landlord, then gives it to the adjudicator and says, "Madam Adjudicator, I would ask that this invoice be introduced as Exhibit 5." After the adjudicator states, "Invoice dated March 31, 2016 marked as Exhibit 5," the paralegal asks for the exhibit back and hands it to the witness.)

Q: Did you pay this bill?

A: Yes, I did.

(The paralegal returns the exhibit to the adjudicator)

Q: Did you have any further dealings with the landlord after moving out?

A: Yes. On April 15, 2016, I took a walk past the Sycamore Street apartment and saw a sign on the front lawn advertising a one-bedroom apartment for rent for $1,375 per month available May 1, 2016. I saw Jim working in the front garden, so I asked him about the sign.

FIGURE 11.8   **Exhibit 5 in the Landlord and Tenant Dispute: Invoice from Two Guys Moving**

INVOICE

TWO GUYS MOVING

25 LAFITE AVENUE — TORONTO, ON M9L 2N3 — TEL 416 555-9000

TO: *ALICE & ARLO GUTHRIE*   DATE: *31/03/16*

Moving apartment contents from 234 Sycamore St. Toronto, to 35 Waverly Street Toronto	*$750.00* *(HST included)*

Q: And what did Jim say?

A: He told me that his daughter decided not to move back to Toronto after all because she got a job in Ottawa.

Q: And what do you want from the landlord now?

A: We're asking for an order that Jim pay our increased rent for one year and our moving costs of $750.

Box 11.6 contains the sample direct examination of the landlord, Jim Croce. Again, compare his direct examination to his witness statement in Chapter 6. Note how the previously admitted exhibits are used in the questioning of the witness. You'll get a chance to prepare the direct examination of Cynthia Croce as an exercise at the end of this chapter.

BOX 11.6

Landlord and Tenant Dispute: Direct Examination of the Landlord, Jim Croce

Q: What is your relationship to 234 Sycamore Street in Toronto?

A: I've owned the building since 2002. It's a two-unit building. My family and I have always lived in the downstairs two-bedroom unit and rented out the upstairs one-bedroom unit.

Q: Who exactly lived with you in your unit?

A: My wife Julia and our daughter Cynthia, until she graduated high school in 2012 and moved to Ottawa to attend university.

Q: And what was to happen when Cynthia graduated from university?

A: It was always our intention that Cynthia would move back to Toronto and into the one-bedroom apartment after she graduated.

Q: What is your relationship with Alice and Arlo Guthrie?

A: In 2015, we rented the upstairs unit to Alice and Arlo Guthrie. They signed a one-year lease.

(The paralegal asks the adjudicator for Exhibit 1 and shows it to the witness)

Q: Is this the lease that you're referring to?

A: Yes.

Q: What were the terms of the lease?

A: It was for one year, starting on May 1, 2015 and ending on April 30, 2016 at a monthly rent of $1,250.

Q: Were the Guthries good tenants?

A: Yes. They paid their rent on time and never caused any problems.

Q: Are the Guthries still living in the apartment?

A: No.

Q: How did that come about?

A: In February 2016, Cynthia told my wife and me that she was on track to graduate that spring and would probably be moving back to Toronto. So, I prepared a form to terminate the tenancy so that Cynthia could move into the unit.

(The paralegal asks the adjudicator for Exhibit 2)

Q: I'm showing you a form N12 "Notice to End Your Tenancy Because the Landlord, a Purchaser or a Family Member Requires the Rental Unit" dated March 1, 2016. Is that the form you are referring to?

A: Yes.

Q: What did the form say?

A: It said that the tenants had to move out by April 30, 2016.

(The paralegal returns the exhibit to the adjudicator)

Q: Did you give the form to the tenants?

A: Yes. I gave the form to Alice at the apartment on March 1, 2016.

Q: And did you say anything to the tenant?

A: Yes, I told Alice that my daughter Cynthia was finishing her studies at the University of Ottawa and was moving back to Toronto.

Q: And did the tenants move out on April 30th as you requested?

A: They moved out on March 31, 2016.

Q: And how did that come about?

A: On March 15th, Arlo knocked on my door and handed me a notice terminating the tenancy as of March 31, 2016.

(The paralegal asks the adjudicator for Exhibit 4)

Q: I'm showing you a form N9 "Tenant's Notice to End the Tenancy" dated March 15, 2016. Is this the notice that you received?

A: Yes, it is.

(The paralegal returns the exhibit to the adjudicator)

Q: Did your daughter Cynthia move into the apartment vacated by the Guthries?

A: No. On April 8, 2016 Cynthia called home and told me that she had just gotten a job in Ottawa and would not be returning to Toronto after all.

Q: Did you tell the tenants that they didn't have to move?

A: No. They had already moved out.

Q: So what did you do?

A: I had to find a new tenant for the apartment, and figured that I could try to get a higher rent than Arlo and Alice had been paying. I made up a sign advertising the apartment for rent for $1,375 per month starting May 1, 2016.

Q: How did the Guthries find out about what happened?

A: I was working in the garden about a week later when Arlo happened to walk by the house and see the "For Rent" sign. He asked me about it, and I told him that Cynthia had decided not to move back to Toronto after all because she got a job in Ottawa.

NOTE

1　Thomas A Mauet, "Direct Examination" in *Fundamentals of Trial Techniques* (New York: Little, Brown, 1980) at 85-86.

KEY TERMS

REVIEW QUESTIONS

1. What is direct examination, and what is its purpose?

2. How should you design your direct examination questions?

3. How should you prepare yourself for direct examination?

4. In what areas must you prepare each witness?

5. What are the basic rules to follow when formulating the questions for your witnesses during direct examination?

6. What are the basic guidelines to follow when preparing and conducting the direct examination of your witnesses?

7. What is an expert witness, and how may an expert's evidence differ from that of other witnesses?

DISCUSSION QUESTION

Marcus is a licensed paralegal who represents Luna in a Small Claims Court action. Luna alleges that her dog was attacked three times by the dog of Francis He, the defendant. She is suing Francis for $5,000 plus interest and costs. At trial, Marcus calls a third-party witness to the attack to testify in support of Luna's claim. Marcus completes the direct examination of the witness. Before Francis's lawyer starts the cross-examination of the witness, the judge calls a lunch break. Marcus wants to speak to the third-party witness during the break about what he said during the direct examination and to prepare him for the cross-examination by Francis's lawyer. Can Marcus speak to the third-party witness during the break? Explain your answer.

EXERCISES

1. You are a licensed paralegal working as a prosecutor. You are prosecuting Ms. Larissa Bodin, who was charged with the offence of racing a motor vehicle contrary to section 172(1) of the *Highway Traffic Act*, RSO 1990, c H.8. It is the day of the trial, and you are conducting a direct examination of Police Constable Linda Wong, who attended at the scene of the incident and charged Ms. Bodin with the offence. You know the police officer wrote notes relating to the incident. Prepare the part of the officer's direct examination in which she refers to her notes to refresh her memory regarding the incident.

2. Prepare a direct examination of Tommy Fey in the Kitchen Renovation Case.

3. Prepare a direct examination of Calvin Hobbs in the Liquor Licence Case.

4. Prepare a direct examination of Cynthia Croce in the Landlord and Tenant Dispute.

Cross-Examination of Witnesses

You present your version of the facts of your case through the direct examination of your witnesses, but your version of the facts does not go unchallenged. The advocate for the other side has the right to challenge your version of the facts by way of cross-examination of your witnesses. In addition, the other side will present another version of the facts through the direct examination of its own witnesses. However, you too have the right to challenge those witnesses by cross-examination.

The importance of cross-examination to the success or failure of a case is generally overrated. In a criminal trial, cross-examination takes on more importance if the defence chooses not to call any witnesses, but in a civil case, the theory of your case is presented through the direct examination of your own witnesses, and it is that evidence that will win your case. Cross-examination of the other party's witnesses generally serves only to confirm that evidence. However, cross-examination is probably the most dreaded part of a trial—for both the questioner and the witness. That is because it involves the unknown. Unlike direct examination, you do not have an opportunity to practise with the witness you are questioning; in fact, you do not know the witness at all, and you do not know for sure what the witness will say. Yet, it is possible to limit the risk inherent in cross-examination, and therefore the anxiety, through proper preparation.

This chapter discusses the purpose of, and preparation for, the cross-examination of the other party's witnesses.

Definition and Purpose of Cross-Examination

Cross-examination is the questioning of a witness who was produced by the other side. It takes place immediately after the direct examination of that witness.

The two main goals of cross-examination are

- to get the witness to give evidence that is favourable to your case and

- to get the witness to give evidence that will discredit testimony given by that witness on direct examination that is unfavourable to your case.

---

cross-examination: questioning of a witness who was produced by the other side that takes place immediately after the direct examination of that witness

In almost every case, the destruction of the witness is *not* your goal. Keep in mind that most witnesses are not lying when they testify in court. They may be mistaken or relying on bad information, but generally they are not lying. Even if your goal is to discredit the witness, your approach should be to attack the evidence, not the witness.

Preparing for Cross-Examination

Just because you cannot practise your cross-examination with the witness (as you were able to do with your direct examination) does not mean that you do not have to prepare. In fact, the opposite is true. Because there is the element of the unknown, planning and preparing are all the more important.

Prepare for cross-examination by doing the following:

- Before the trial or hearing,
    - know your case well and
    - select target areas for cross-examination.
- During the trial or hearing,
    - listen to what the witness says in direct examination,
    - listen to what the witness says during cross-examination, and
    - know when not to cross-examine.

Preparation Before the Trial or Hearing

The bulk of your preparation for cross-examination takes place before you go to court or appear before a tribunal.

Know Your Case Well

Learn everything you can about the evidence involved in your case. Review again the pleadings and documents. Think about who will be testifying for the other side. For each witness, ask:

- Why is this witness being called?
- What can this witness say to help the other side's case?
- What can this witness say to hurt your case?

Find out what the witness has already said about the case—for example, by way of a written statement or previous sworn testimony.

Select Target Areas for Cross-Examination

Your goals are to get the witness to give evidence that is favourable to your case, or to get the witness to give evidence that will call into question unfavourable testimony given by the witness on direct examination. Consider how each witness fits within your theory of the case, and focus on the matters that are in dispute. Think about what you might say about this witness's evidence in closing, and then structure your cross-examination around these matters. For example, if you intend to prove that the witness's recollection of an event is unreliable, focus on facts that will support this: the witness was distracted by other events, the witness was talking to someone else at the time, and so on. You should have a purpose for every question you ask. If a question has no purpose, don't ask it.

Preparation During the Trial or Hearing

Given the nature of cross-examination, you cannot be fully prepared before the trial or hearing starts. You must continue to prepare even as the trial or hearing is going on.

Listen to What the Witness Says in Direct Examination

Take notes as the witness testifies. Pay particular attention to what the witness says in your target areas. Leave room at the margin of your notes to insert, where appropriate, the questions you have already drafted. That way, when you ask the questions, you can refer to the witness's own testimony on the point. As you listen to the witness's testimony, you may need to change your questions, add questions, or abandon questions.

Listen to What the Witness Says During Cross-Examination

Your preparation for cross-examination continues until the minute you end it. Every time the witness answers one of your questions, you must decide what to do next: Continue the line of questioning as previously planned? Pursue a new line of questioning? Abandon the line of questioning? You must be able to think on your feet!

Know When Not to Cross-Examine

As you listen to a witness's testimony, ask yourself whether the witness has said anything that hurts your case. If not, don't cross-examine unless you think you can get the witness to say something that will help your case.

Formulating Your Questions

The key to a successful cross-examination is control. You control the witness by asking leading questions. As discussed in Chapters 7 and 11, a leading question is one that suggests a desired answer or assumes a fact not yet proved. Unlike in direct examination, where generally you are not allowed to ask leading questions, in cross-examination you not only can, but should, lead the witness. By asking leading questions you tell the witness what to say; you suggest desired answers. The best way to maintain control of the witness is to ask short, single-fact questions that can be answered only by "yes" or "no."

While it is permissible and wise to use leading questions in cross-examination, do not make the mistake of trying to turn every question into a leading question. The use of open-ended questions can be effective if you are reasonably sure of the answer that you will get and if you can phrase your question in a way that limits the breadth of the response. Sometimes, you will have to ask an open-ended question to get the information you need. However, you should avoid questions that invite explanation. For example, you should never ask a question during cross-examination that starts with "why." Any question that gives the witness an opportunity to simply repeat his or her direct examination, or to explain or clarify, is a mistake.

The following pointers will help you plan and execute an effective cross-examination.

Keep It Short

Keep your cross-examination as short and succinct as possible. There are many opportunities for disaster in a cross-examination. The less time you spend cross-examining, the less likely you are to get into trouble. You should have only a few target areas for your cross-examination—once you hit them, stop. If you question in too many irrelevant areas, you risk boring the judge or other decision-maker, who may then not pay attention when you ask a question about something important.

Be Organized

Deal with one target area at a time; do not jump around from one unrelated question to another. While moving around from subject to subject may keep the witness off-balance, it is also likely to confuse the judge or other decision-maker, who may then miss it when you make an important point.

Be Subtle

Within each target area, frame your questions so that you extract small pieces of information at a time. This approach has several advantages. First, the witness does not see where you are going until it is too late. Second, if the witness gives you answers that you do not like, you can readjust your questioning before too much damage is done.

Do Not Ask the Witness to Agree with Your Conclusion

Within each target area, ask only the questions that will get you the facts you need to support your conclusion about the evidence. Do not ask the witness to agree with your conclusion. First, you don't need the witness to agree with your conclusion; you need the judge or other decision-maker to agree with it. Think of the picture puzzle "connect the dots." Each dot is part of a picture that is not visible until all the dots are connected. In cross-examination, you know the picture you want to draw, and you are getting the witness to establish the dots for you. Do not ask the witness to connect the dots; you will do that when you present and discuss the evidence in your closing argument.

Second, if you do ask the witness to agree with your conclusion, the odds are that the witness will not only disagree, but will explain away the facts you have already elicited that support your conclusion. For example, assume that you want to establish that a witness was not really paying attention when he claims he saw an event take place. That is your "picture"; your "dots" are the facts that support this conclusion—that he was distracted by a noise; that he turned away; that he bent down to tie his shoe; and so on. Ask questions only about these facts. In your closing, remind the judge of this evidence and submit that, as a result, the witness was not really paying attention. Do not ask the witness, "Since you were tying your shoes, you really weren't paying attention, were you?" First, this approach is unnecessary, and second, you will give the witness an opportunity to explain how he could do both at the same time. Leave the conclusions to the judge.

Do Not Invite an Explanation

Focus your questions on getting only the facts you need to support your conclusions. Always avoid questions that invite an explanation. If the witness's answer does not make sense, or is false, avoid asking, "What do you mean?" or "How can you say that?" The answer will likely explain away the confusion and restore the witness's credibility. Avoid questions that are vague or contain a conclusion or judgment— these types of questions tend to provoke an explanation. Use questions that contain objective facts instead. For example, instead of asking, "You were distracted, weren't you?" you should ask, "You were talking to Ms. Bertelli at that moment, right?" or "You answered a phone call, isn't that right?"

Keep Your Questions Clear and Simple

Use short, simple questions that focus on your target, and always use plain, basic words. As noted above, each question should be intended to elicit one fact only. For example, do not ask: "You were travelling in an easterly direction when you were operating your motor vehicle and it was dark out, isn't that right?" Instead ask, "You were driving your car east, is that right?" After the response, then ask, "And it was dark out, wasn't it?" Complex questions open the door to explanations. If your question invites an explanation, the witness must be given the opportunity to explain; you cannot cut the witness off. Shorter, more carefully phrased questions are more likely to result in single-word responses.

Keep It Civil

A witness will be more cooperative, and therefore more likely to give you the answers you are after, if you are polite and gentle than if you are rude and a bully.

Pay Attention

Listen carefully to the answers given in cross-examination. If the witness does not answer your question, ask it again. If the witness offers more or different information than you expected, think about cross-examining on this new information. Pay attention to the answers and not to your next question!

Know the Answer Before You Ask the Question, or at Least Know the Risk

The conventional wisdom regarding cross-examination is to ask only questions to which you already know the answer. However, it is difficult to achieve this level of certainty at tribunal and lower-level courts, because you do not have an opportunity to examine the other party under oath before the actual trial or hearing. If you are not sure what the answer to a question will be, weigh the potential benefit from the answer you want against the potential risk from the answer you do not want. If an unfavourable answer to a question can really hurt your case, it may be better not to ask that question. If an unfavourable answer will not really hurt, while a favourable answer will really help, you may want to risk asking the question.

Do Not Repeat the Other Side's Direct Examination

Do not give the witness an opportunity to repeat his or her testimony from the direct examination. That evidence helps the other side. You do not want the judge to hear it twice!

Paralegal Rules of Conduct

The *Paralegal Rules of Conduct* impose restrictions on a paralegal's ability to speak with a witness giving testimony. In Chapter 11, we discussed the rules that apply during and after a paralegal's direct examination of a witness. There are also rules that apply during and after a paralegal's cross-examination of a witness. The restrictions that apply to a paralegal depend on whether the witness is sympathetic or unsympathetic to the paralegal's cause.

Rules 4.03(1)(d) through (g) deal with a paralegal's communication with witnesses giving testimony during and immediately after a cross-examination:

> 4.03(1) Subject to the direction of the tribunal, a paralegal shall observe the following rules respecting communication with witnesses giving evidence: …
>
> (d) During cross-examination by an opposing licensee, the witness's own representative ought not to have any conversation with the witness about the witness's evidence or any issue in the proceeding.
>
> (e) Between completion of cross-examination and commencement of a re-examination, a paralegal who is going to re-examine the witness ought not to have a discussion about evidence that will be dealt with on re-examination.
>
> (f) During cross-examination by the representative of a witness unsympathetic to the cross-examiner's cause, the paralegal may discuss the witness's evidence with the witness.
>
> (g) During cross-examination by the representative of a witness who is sympathetic to that licensee's cause, any conversations ought to be restricted in the same way as communications during examination-in-chief of one's own witness.

While Rule 4.03(1)(f) permits a paralegal who is conducting a cross-examination of a witness who is unsympathetic to that paralegal's cause to discuss the evidence with that witness during the cross-examination, the witness is under no obligation to speak to the paralegal when not testifying on the witness stand. For example, assume Henry Lee represents the plaintiff in a Small Claims Court case and is half-way through a cross-examination of a witness who is unsympathetic to Henry's case when the judge calls a ten-minute recess. Henry can approach the witness in the hallway to discuss the evidence (as long as the witness does not have legal representation). However, the witness is not obliged to speak to Henry about anything, including the evidence, until the cross-examination resumes.

Once the examining paralegal completes the cross-examination of an unsympathetic witness, there may be a re-examination by the opposing licensee who first conducted the examination-in-chief. If there is, Rule 4.03(1)(e) makes it clear that the paralegal who is going to re-examine the witness should not discuss with that witness the evidence that will be dealt with on re-examination. This rule ensures that the paralegal does not influence the testimony of the witness during re-examination. Chapter 13 discusses the purpose and preparation of a re-examination of a witness.

Sample Cross-Examinations

In Chapter 1 we gave you three fact situations: Fact Situation 1 set out the basic facts of a Small Claims Court dispute, Fact Situation 2 the basic facts of a provincial offences case, and Fact Situation 3 the basic facts of a landlord and tenant dispute.

In Chapter 6 we developed the theory of the case of both sides in each of the fact situations, and provided you with witness statements for all of the witnesses for both sides of each case. In Chapter 11 we provided you with sample direct examinations of three witnesses in each of the cases and asked you to prepare the direct examinations of the other witnesses. Here we present three cross-examinations for each of the fact situations.

In preparing to cross-examine each witness, you must identify the target areas of your cross-examination. Those areas will come from those facts of the case that are in dispute. Read the commentary before each cross-examination to see how the target areas of each examination have been chosen. Note that the cross-examinations are short. Note also the use of both leading and open-ended questions.

The Kitchen Renovation Small Claims Court Case

Box 12.1 contains the sample cross-examinations of the plaintiff's witnesses, Alec Baldwin and Stephen Baldwin.

BOX 12.1

Cross-Examination of the Plaintiff's Witnesses
Alec Baldwin

In this case, Alec Baldwin's evidence is that there was an agreement to install five pot lights as part of the contract price and that installation of additional pot lights would cost $250 each. Tina Fey's evidence, on the other hand, is that there was an agreement to install all necessary pot lights, whatever number that would be. Alec suggested that five lights would be enough, but agreed to install more lights if necessary. He never said they would cost extra.

In cross-examining Alec Baldwin, the defendant's advocate will focus on the exact wording of the discussion between Alec and Tina, and try to establish that there was no clear agreement that she would have to pay extra if more than five lights were installed.

Q: You stated in your direct examination that you told Ms. Fey that five lights would be the right number for her kitchen. Is that correct?

A: Yes, that's correct.

Q: And you stated that you could install more lights if she wanted more?

A: Yes.

Q: Did you specifically tell her that any additional lights would cost extra?

A: I told her that pot lights cost $250 each.

Q: But did you specifically tell her that additional lights would cost extra?

A: No.

Stephen Baldwin

In this case, Stephen Baldwin's evidence is that, after asking Tommy about the location of the five pot lights he was planning to install, Tommy asked him to install three additional pot lights, and Stephen agreed. He never said that they would cost extra. In cross-examining Stephen Baldwin, the defendant's advocate will focus on the exact wording of the discussion between Stephen and Tommy, and try to establish that there was no clear statement that the additional pot lights would cost extra.

Q: You stated in your direct examination that you asked Mr. Fey about the location of the five pot lights that you would be installing. Is that correct?

A: Yes, that's correct.

Q: And Mr. Fey stated that he didn't think that five lights would provide enough light. Is that correct?

A: Yes.

Q: And you stated that you could install more lights if he wanted more?

A: Yes.

Q: And did he ask for more lights?

A: Yes, he asked for three more lights.

Q: Did you tell him that these lights would cost extra?

A: No. He never asked me what they would cost, so we never discussed money.

Q: So you did not specifically tell him that the three additional lights would cost extra. Is that correct?

A: Yes.

Box 12.2 contains the sample cross-examination of the defendant, Tina Fey. You'll get a chance to prepare the cross-examination of Tommy Fey as an exercise at the end of this chapter.

BOX 12.2

Cross-Examination of the Defendant, Tina Fey

In this case, Tina Fey's evidence is that there was an agreement to install all necessary pot lights, whatever number that would be. Alec suggested that five lights would be enough, but agreed to install more lights if necessary. He never said they would cost extra. Alec Baldwin's evidence, on the other hand, is that there was an agreement to install five pot lights as part of the contract price and that installation of additional pot lights would cost $250 each. In cross-examining Tina Fey, the plaintiff's advocate should focus on the exact wording of the discussion between

Alec and Tina, to try to establish that it was clear that she would have to pay extra if more than five lights were installed.

Q: You stated in your direct examination that you discussed the number of pot lights with Alec, is that right?

A: Yes.

Q: When you discussed the number of pot lights with Alec, did he mention the cost of each pot light?

A: Yes.

Q: How much did each pot light cost?

A: $250.

Q: You stated in your direct examination that Alec Baldwin suggested five lights would be the right number for your kitchen. Is that correct?

A: Yes, that's correct.

Q: You stated in your direct examination that when you asked Alec about installing more than five pot lights, he said he could install more.

A: Yes, that's correct.

Q: Did you ask Alec about any extra costs for installing more than five pot lights?

A: No.

The Liquor Licence Case

Box 12.3 contains the sample cross-examinations of prosecution witnesses Patrick Elder and Constable Matthew Lee.

BOX 12.3

Cross-Examination of Prosecution Witnesses

Patrick Elder

In this case, Patrick Elder's evidence is that he heard and saw people on the patio and the grass at the Simpson Academy student lounge. Victoria Levens's evidence is that she never saw any guests standing on the grass outside the patio. Calvin Hobbs's evidence is that he stood on the patio all evening long and did not see any guests carrying alcoholic drinks as they left the patio.

In cross-examining Patrick Elder, the defendant's advocate will try to focus on what Patrick Elder saw from his balcony and try to establish that he did not see any guests holding alcoholic beverages while on the grassy area.

Paralegal: Good afternoon, Mr. Elder. You stated in your direct examination that on May 16, 2016 you saw a large crowd of people on the

	patio and grassy area around the patio at the Simpson Academy student lounge. Is that correct?
Witness:	Yes, that's correct.
Paralegal:	About 20 people or so you said, right?
Witness:	That's what I said.
Paralegal:	Where were you standing when you saw these people?
Witness:	I was standing on my balcony overlooking the student lounge and patio.
Paralegal:	When you were standing on your balcony and saw the crowd of people, what time was it?
Witness:	It was around 11:00 p.m.
Paralegal:	Was it dark outside at that time?
Witness:	Yes.
Paralegal:	When you saw the crowd of people standing on the grassy area, could you see their hands?
Witness:	Yes.
Paralegal:	Did you actually see any of those people standing on the grassy area holding beverages in their hands?
Witness:	No.
Paralegal:	Did you see any of these people you saw on the grassy area holding beer bottles?
Witness:	No, I didn't.
Paralegal:	Did you see any of these people you saw on the grassy area holding wine glasses of any sort?
Witness:	No, I didn't.

Police Constable Matthew Lee

In this case, Police Constable Lee's evidence is that he observed empty beer bottles and plastic wine glasses on the grass just beyond the fence of the patio. Victoria Levens's evidence, on the other hand, is that she did not see any guests standing on the grassy area and that she hired a security guard to make sure the guests did not take alcohol outside the patio. Her evidence is also that the patio was enclosed by a fence separating the patio from the grassy area. Calvin Hobbs's evidence is that he stood on the patio all evening long and did not see any guests carrying alcoholic drinks as they left the patio.

In cross-examining Police Constable Matthew Lee, the defendant's advocate will try to focus on the set-up of the event including the signs, the fence, and the security guard on the patio. The advocate will also focus on the evidence that Police Constable Lee did not see any guests on the grass beyond the licensed area.

Paralegal:	Good afternoon, Mr. Lee. You stated in your direct examination that you saw empty beer bottles and plastic wine glasses on the grassy area outside the patio on May 16, 2016. Is that correct?
Witness:	Yes, that's correct.
Paralegal:	You stated that this grassy area was outside the licensed area for alcohol for this event. Is that right?
Witness:	Yes.
Paralegal:	Did you actually see any guests standing on the grassy area beyond the patio holding alcohol beverages?
Witness:	No, I didn't.
Paralegal:	Did you even see any guests standing on the grassy area beyond the patio?
Witness:	No, I didn't.
Paralegal:	Were all the guests you saw that evening within the fenced outside patio perimeters?
Witness:	Yes.
Paralegal:	You stated that you inspected the empty beer bottles and plastic wine glasses on the grassy area. Is this correct?
Witness:	Yes, it is.
Paralegal:	When you went to inspect them, how did you get from the patio area to the grassy area?
Witness:	I walked through the gate in the fence.
Paralegal:	You didn't step over the fence, right?
Witness:	No, I didn't.
Paralegal:	When you went out onto the patio that evening, what did you see?
Witness:	I saw a rather large gentleman wearing a black t-shirt with the word "Security" across the front.
Paralegal:	Where was this gentleman standing?
Witness:	I can't remember exactly where he was standing, but he was standing on the patio somewhere near the gate.
Paralegal:	Did you also see a sign on the gate door?
Witness:	Yes.
Paralegal:	What did this sign say?
Witness:	It said "No alcoholic beverages permitted outside the patio."
Paralegal:	You also noticed the same sign on the door leading out to the patio from the inside?
Witness:	Yes, I did.

Box 12.4 contains the sample cross-examination of the defendant, Victoria Levens. You'll get a chance to prepare the cross-examination of Calvin Hobbs as an exercise at the end of this chapter.

Cross-Examination of the Defendant, Victoria Levens

In this case, Victoria Levens's evidence is that there was a sign posted at the door leading out to the patio and one on the gate leading out of the patio to the grassy area stating "No alcoholic beverages permitted outside the patio." Her evidence is also that she hired a security guard to make sure that guests did not take alcohol outside the patio and that there was a fence surrounding the patio separating the licensed patio area from the non-licensed grassy area.

Police Constable Lee's evidence is that the fence was a low fence and that he did observe empty beer bottles and plastic wine glasses on the non-licensed grassy area beyond the fenced patio.

In cross-examining Victoria Levens, the prosecutor will try to focus on Victoria's duties during the event, including the fact that she was busy with the buffet all evening and did not go outside onto the patio until Police Constable Lee arrived. The prosecutor will also focus on the set-up of the event, including the height of the patio fence, the number of signs, and the number of security guards to show that Victoria could have done more to ensure that alcohol did not leave the licensed area.

Prosecutor:	Good afternoon, Ms. Levens. You stated in your direct examination that you never saw any guests with alcohol standing on the grass beyond the enclosed patio that evening. Is this correct?
Witness:	That's correct.
Prosecutor:	What were you doing all evening?
Witness:	I was helping with the buffet.
Prosecutor:	Was the buffet located inside the student lounge?
Witness:	Yes, it was.
Prosecutor:	Did you ever go outside the student lounge at all that evening?
Witness:	No, I didn't. I stayed inside until the police officer arrived.
Prosecutor:	So you wouldn't have been able to see anyone standing on the grassy area holding alcohol all evening, then?
Witness:	Not from inside.
Prosecutor:	But guests could purchase alcohol from the bar and then walk outside to the patio?
Witness:	Yes.

Prosecutor:	Did you see guests going from inside the student lounge to outside toward the patio?
Witness:	Yes.
Prosecutor:	During your direct examination, you described a fence enclosing the outside patio. Is this correct?
Witness:	Yes. There was a fence that surrounded the entire patio.
Prosecutor:	Was the fence very high?
Witness:	No.
Prosecutor:	Could guests successfully step over it if they tried?
Witness:	Yes.
Prosecutor:	Ms. Levens, how many signs were posted on the premises that evening stating "No alcoholic beverages permitted outside the patio"?
Witness:	There were two signs.
Prosecutor:	Have you catered events at other venues where there have been more than two signs advising guests where alcohol is prohibited?
Witness:	Yes. It all depends on the particular venue and the number of guests.
Prosecutor:	Ms. Levens, were there signs posted along the fence outside the patio advising guests that no alcoholic beverages were permitted beyond the fence?
Witness:	No.
Prosecutor:	Was there a sign at the front door of the venue advising guests who walked in that alcohol was prohibited beyond the fenced patio?
Witness:	No.
Prosecutor:	Was there a sign at the bar advising guests who were purchasing alcohol that alcohol was prohibited beyond the fenced patio?
Witness:	No.
Prosecutor:	Ms. Levens, you stated in your direct examination that you hired a security guard for this event, isn't that so?
Witness:	Yes.
Prosecutor:	How many security guards did you hire for this event?
Witness:	One.
Prosecutor:	Only one security guard for an event with 40 guests?
Witness:	Yes.
Prosecutor:	So you didn't hire another security guard to monitor the grassy lawn area on the campus beyond the patio?
Witness:	No.

The Landlord and Tenant Dispute

Box 12.5 contains the sample cross-examinations of the tenants in the Landlord and Tenant Dispute, Alice Guthrie and Arlo Guthrie.

BOX 12.5

Cross-Examination of the Tenants, Alice and Arlo Guthrie

In this case, the main issue is the good faith, or lack thereof, of the landlord in serving the notice of termination. Alice has no evidence to give on that point. However, if the landlord is found to have acted in bad faith, the landlord may be ordered to pay the increased rent that the tenants have incurred for one year after vacating the rental unit, and reasonable moving expenses incurred by the tenants.

Alice Guthrie

Alice has given evidence that she and Arlo were unable to find a similar apartment for the same rent, and so rented an apartment for $1,350 per month. In cross-examining Alice Guthrie, the landlord's advocate should focus on their efforts to find another apartment, to try to establish that they did not take reasonable steps to find an apartment for the same price.

Q: You stated in your direct examination that, after receiving the notice of termination from the landlord, you and your husband began to hunt for another apartment, but you did not find an apartment for the same rent, is that correct?

A: Yes.

Q: And so you rented a more expensive apartment, is that correct?

A: Yes.

Q: And you stated that you were looking for another one-bedroom apartment in the same neighbourhood, is that correct?

A: Yes.

Q: Did you look for apartments in other neighbourhoods?

A: No.

Q: You said that you searched online, checked newspaper ads, looked for "For Rent" signs, and asked your friends, is that correct?

A: Yes.

Q: Did you ever speak to a real estate agent?

A: No.

Q: How long did you look for an apartment before agreeing to rent the more expensive apartment?

A: Two weeks.

Q: When was that apartment available?

A: April 1, 2016.

Q: But you were not required to vacate your apartment until April 30, 2016—is that correct?

A: Yes.

Arlo Guthrie

Arlo, like Alice, has no evidence to give on the point of good faith. However, if the landlord is found to have acted in bad faith, he may be ordered to pay the increased rent that the tenants have incurred for one year after vacating the rental unit, and reasonable moving expenses incurred by the tenants.

Arlo has given evidence that he and Alice incurred moving expenses of $750. In cross-examining Arlo Guthrie, the advocate should focus on the couple's efforts to hire a moving company, to try to establish that they did not take reasonable steps to find a mover at a reasonable price. There is a risk that Arlo will say that he shopped around before hiring the moving company, but that answer will not really hurt the case.

Q: In your direct examination, you stated that you hired Two Guys Moving to move your belongings to your new apartment. Is that correct?

A: Yes.

Q: And the move cost $750, is that correct?

A: Yes.

Q: Did you get quotes from any other moving companies before hiring Two Guys?

A: No.

Box 12.6 contains the sample cross-examination of the landlord, Jim Croce. You'll get a chance to prepare the cross-examination of Cynthia Croce as an exercise at the end of this chapter.

BOX 12.6

Cross-Examination of the Landlord, Jim Croce

Again, the main issue in this case is the good faith, or lack thereof, of the landlord in serving the notice of termination. Jim has given evidence that he terminated the tenancy because he required the apartment for his daughter Cynthia. In cross-examining Jim Croce, the tenants' advocate should focus on the exact wording of the conversation(s) he had with Cynthia about her return to Toronto to try to establish that it was not certain that she was returning to Toronto at the time the notice was served.

Q: In your direct examination, you stated that it was your intention that your daughter Cynthia would move back to Toronto and into the one-bedroom apartment when she graduated from university. Is that correct?

A: Yes.

Q: And you stated that in February 2016, Cynthia told you that she was about to graduate that spring and would probably be moving back to Toronto. Is that correct?

A: Yes.

Q: And you were happy at the thought that she would be coming home, weren't you?

A: Yes.

Q: That was something that you and your wife both wanted?

A: Yes.

Q: Cynthia said that she would probably be moving back to Toronto?

A: Yes.

Q: Did she ever say that it was a certainty that she would be moving back?

A: No.

Q: And in fact, by April 8th, she told you that she wouldn't be returning to Toronto after all, is that correct?

A: Yes.

KEY TERMS

cross-examination, 180

REVIEW QUESTIONS

1. What is cross-examination, and when does it take place?

2. What are the two main goals of cross-examination?

3. What questions should you ask yourself when preparing for cross-examination before the trial or hearing?

4. What should you consider when selecting target areas for cross-examination?

5. How should you prepare for cross-examination during the trial or hearing?

6. When should you *not* cross-examine a witness?

7. Why should you use leading questions during cross-examination?

8. When should you use open-ended questions during cross-examination?

9. What types of questions should you always avoid during cross-examination?

DISCUSSION QUESTIONS

1. Tiana Larus represents the defendant in a provincial offences matter. She conducted a direct examination of the plaintiff earlier in the day, and the prosecutor just finished the cross-examination of the defendant. There is a 40-minute lunch recess before Tiana will conduct a re-examination of her client, the defendant. During the lunch recess, Tiana sees her client in the hallway and asks her how she's doing. Her client answers, "I'm okay. I just can't wait to start my vacation tomorrow!" Is Tiana in breach of the *Paralegal Rules of Conduct*? Explain your answer.

2. You represent Nathan, the defendant in a charge under the *Highway Traffic Act* for racing a motor vehicle. The prosecutor is halfway through her cross-examination of your client when the judge calls a 20-minute recess. You and Nathan walk out of the courtroom into the hallway. You tell Nathan he's doing really well but when he gets on the stand again to clarify that he never made a racing bet with his friend. Are you in breach of the *Paralegal Rules of Conduct*? Explain your answer.

EXERCISES

1. Prepare a cross-examination of Tommy Fey in Fact Situation 1, the Kitchen Renovation Case.

2. Prepare a cross-examination of Calvin Hobbs in Fact Situation 2, the Liquor Licence Case.

3. Prepare a cross-examination of Cynthia Croce in Fact Situation 3, the Landlord and Tenant Dispute.

Re-Examination

After the other side has finished cross-examining your witness, you have the chance to question your witness again by way of **re-examination**. Re-examination ends the questioning of the witness by the parties, and unless the judge has questions for the witness, the witness may return to his or her seat in the courtroom or hearing room.

Scope and Purpose of Re-Examination

The scope of re-examination is limited. You may question the witness only about matters arising out of the witness's answers in cross-examination. It is not an opportunity to have your witness repeat, correct, or add to evidence given in the direct examination. In other words, this is *not* a second chance at direct examination. This limitation arises as a matter of fairness: if you introduce new material after the cross-examination of your witness, that is evidence on which the other side has not had a chance to cross-examine.

The purpose of re-examination is to respond to, explain, or clarify matters raised during cross-examination, but only if explanation or clarification is needed. You can use re-examination to give your witness a chance to explain why a particular answer was given on cross-examination—especially helpful if the question limited your client to a "yes" or "no" answer. Of course, you should not ask for an explanation unless you are confident your client has one that is beneficial to your case.

In fact, it is often dangerous to re-examine. If your witness has given damaging evidence on cross-examination, and you cannot repair the damage, all you will do is reinforce or highlight the damaging information! If your client has given new information on cross-examination, but the information has not hurt your case, do not re-examine.

During re-examination, you may not use leading questions. Any explanation or clarification must come from the witness, not you. You cannot, for example, ask, "When you said Mr. Smith appeared confused, didn't you really mean he appeared drunk?" Instead, you would have to ask, "In your cross-examination, you stated that Mr. Smith appeared confused. Can you explain what you meant by that?"

---

re-examination: questioning of a witness after cross-examination to respond to, explain, or clarify matters raised during cross-examination

Preparing for and Conducting Re-Examination

Take notes while your witness is being cross-examined. Make a note of any new information given by your witness. Review this evidence to determine whether it is harmful. If so, consider whether your witness will improve the situation if you ask for an explanation.

If you decide to re-examine your witness, start each line of questioning with a reference to and a restatement of the particular evidence given on cross-examination, and then ask your questions—for example, "On your cross-examination you stated you didn't complain to the landlord about the other tenant; can you explain why you didn't complain?"

Paralegal Rules of Conduct

The *Paralegal Rules of Conduct* impose restrictions on the ability of a paralegal to communicate with a witness giving testimony during re-examination. The applicable rule follows from the other restrictions placed on paralegals at other stages of a witness's testimony as discussed in Chapter 11 (Direct Examination of Witnesses) and Chapter 12 (Cross-Examination of Witnesses).

You will recall from Chapter 12 that the *Paralegal Rules of Conduct* caution that a paralegal who is going to re-examine a witness ought not to discuss any evidence that will be dealt with on re-examination with that witness (Rule 4.03(1)(e)). In other words, once the examining advocate completes the cross-examination of the witness, a paralegal who is going to re-examine that witness should not discuss the evidence with that witness before the re-examination starts.

In addition, Rule 4.03(1)(h) states:

> (h) During re-examination of a witness called by an opposing licensee, if the witness is sympathetic to the paralegal's cause, the paralegal ought not to discuss the evidence to be given by that witness during re-examination. The paralegal may, however, properly discuss the evidence with a witness who is adverse in interest.

As you can see, the paralegal's ability to communicate with a witness giving testimony during re-examination depends on whether that witness is sympathetic or unsympathetic to the paralegal's cause.

It is important to remember that Rule 4.03(2) permits a paralegal to discuss with a witness matters that might cause the paralegal to breach the Rules on communicating with witnesses giving testimony in certain circumstances. Those circumstances include where the paralegal obtains consent from the opposing licensee or permission from the court or tribunal.

Rule 4.03(2) states:

4.03(2) With the consent of the opposing licensee or with leave of the tribunal, a paralegal may enter into discussions with a witness that might otherwise raise a question under this rule as to the propriety of the discussions.

KEY TERMS

re-examination, 200

REVIEW QUESTIONS

1. What is the scope of re-examination?

2. What is the purpose of re-examination?

3. Why can it often be dangerous to re-examine your witness?

4. What types of questions can you ask during re-examination?

5. Briefly discuss how to prepare for and organize your re-examination.

6. Explain the *Paralegal Rules of Conduct* that are applicable to the re-examination of a witness.

DISCUSSION QUESTION

Lester Harrison is a licensed paralegal representing the plaintiff in a Small Claims Court matter for breach of contract. The advocate for the defendant has just finished cross-examining the plaintiff. Lester is now preparing to re-examine the plaintiff on a new matter that arose during the cross-examination. Lester meets with the plaintiff during the lunch break to prepare and tells her the types of questions he will be asking her during the re-examination. Is Lester in breach of the *Paralegal Rules of Conduct*? Explain your answer.

CHAPTER 14

Closing Argument

LEARNING OUTCOMES

After reading this chapter, you will understand

■ the purpose of a closing argument

■ the order in which closing arguments are presented

■ how to prepare a closing argument

■ how to present a closing argument

After the last witness is excused, the advocate for each side is given an opportunity to summarize his or her case for the judge or other decision-maker in the form of a closing argument.

In Chapter 9, we told you the basic rule in public speaking: Start by telling your audience what you are going to tell them; tell them; then tell them what you have told them. Think of the trial or hearing as a speech: You tell the judge or other decision-maker what you are going to tell him or her in your opening statement; you do the telling with your evidence; and then you tell the judge or other decision-maker what you have told him or her in your closing argument. The closing argument is your last chance to persuade the judge or other decision-maker to decide the case in favour of your client.

This chapter discusses the closing argument—its purpose, how to prepare one, and how to present it.

Purpose of Closing Argument

The purpose of the closing argument is to persuade the judge or other decision-maker to choose your theory of the case over that of the other side.

At the conclusion of the trial or hearing, the judge, justice of the peace, or adjudicator will make a decision either for or against your client by first determining the facts of the case and then applying the relevant law to those facts. In order to win, you have to be successful on both the facts and the law, and a closing argument addresses both.

With respect to the facts, the purpose of the closing argument is to summarize your version of the facts and persuade the judge or other decision-maker to prefer your version of the facts to that of the other side. This is the time to "connect the dots" of your evidence—to advise the judge or other decision-maker of the reasonable inferences and logical conclusions to be drawn from the evidence presented during the trial, both through the direct examination of your witnesses and the cross-examination of the witnesses for the other side.

With respect to the law, the purpose of the closing argument is to advise the judge or other decision-maker of the relevant law and to demonstrate how the law should be applied to your facts so that you win.

The Order of Closing Arguments

After all the evidence has been given during the trial or hearing, the adjudicator will ask the advocates for both parties to make their closing arguments.

In a Small Claims Court trial, the plaintiff's advocate gives the first closing argument, followed by the defendant's advocate. In a criminal or provincial offences proceeding, the defendant's advocate presents the first closing argument, followed by the Crown. In a Landlord and Tenant Board hearing, the applicant presents the first closing argument, followed by the respondent.

Preparing Your Closing Argument

Most of your closing argument can be—and in fact should be—prepared before the trial or hearing starts. If you have properly prepared for your trial or hearing, you will have developed your theory of the case and will therefore know what the evidence will be and what the relevant law is. You should also be able to anticipate the evidence that will be presented by the other side and what your witnesses will be asked on cross-examination—although you cannot know for sure. As a result, you will have to finalize your closing argument during the trial or hearing, after all the evidence has been presented, to make sure that your conclusions and inferences are supported by the evidence as actually given. However, if you are well prepared going into the trial or hearing, there should not be too many, if any, surprises during the trial or hearing.

You should keep in mind the following guidelines as you prepare your closing argument.

Use Common Sense

Your closing argument should be logical, credible, and easy for the judge or other decision-maker to follow. It should be based on the facts and supported by the law, and not be based on wishful thinking.

Do Not Argue Facts Not in Evidence

You can refer only to evidence that has in fact been presented during the trial or hearing. Any conclusion that you draw must be supported by the facts established during direct examination of your witnesses or cross-examination of the witnesses of the other side. You cannot assume facts in your closing argument. You are, however, allowed to argue matters of general knowledge or common sense.

Do Not Misstate the Law or the Evidence

You must present the law and the evidence accurately. When summarizing or paraphrasing legal principles, be careful not to change their meaning. When referring to evidence, present it in an impartial and fair manner. Remain neutral—do not let your bias or prejudice in the case influence you to misrepresent the evidence.

Do Not State Your Personal Belief

Do not state your personal views about your client, your witnesses, or the case, and avoid using any language that may suggest a personal opinion or belief of the worthiness of your case or the credibility of your witnesses. For example, do not introduce arguments with the words "I believe" or "I think." Rather, use the words "I submit" or "It is the plaintiff's submission that ..." It doesn't matter what you think or believe; what matters is what the judge or other decision-maker is persuaded to think or believe. The facts and the law should speak for themselves.

Remember that your closing argument is your last opportunity to speak to the judge or other decision-maker—use it wisely! Weave all the evidence together into a compelling, logical, and persuasive argument that supports your theory of the case, and that is consistent with the facts and supported by the law.

Format of Closing Argument

Your closing argument should be a clear, concise, and persuasive synopsis of the issues, the evidence, and the law. It should walk the judge or other decision-maker through your theory of the case and lead him or her to the conclusion that your case should prevail. Proper organization is crucial.

There is no prescribed format for a closing argument, but the following structure is suggested:

1. Outline the issues you will deal with in your closing argument.
2. Deal with each issue in turn, addressing the facts and the law relating to the issue.
3. State the relief you are seeking.

1. Outline the Issues

Start by telling the judge or other decision-maker how many issues you will be dealing with—for example, "Your Honour, there are three issues in this case." Then, set out each issue: "The first issue is whether ..." These issues should be the same ones you set out in your opening statement. However, instead of simply stating the issues, you also state your position on each issue. For example, "Your Honour, there are three issues in this case. The first issue is whether there was a contract between the parties, and we submit that there was." Setting out the issues and your position on each issue provides a road map for the judge, justice of the peace, or adjudicator to follow during your closing argument. Keep in mind that the decision-maker will likely be taking notes during your closing argument, and setting out a road map will help the decision-maker to understand the structure of your submissions.

2. Deal with Each Issue

For each issue you identify, start by summarizing the evidence adduced at the trial or hearing in keeping with your theory of the case. Your goal is to convince the judge or other decision-maker to accept your version of the facts. Start with the evidence about which the parties agree. Then, discuss the evidence that is in dispute, and give the judge or other decision-maker some reason to prefer your version of the evidence. This is the time to draw logical inferences and conclusions that clearly favour your theory and support your view of the disputed evidence. Think of ways you can strengthen the evidence—for example, by convincing the judge or other decision-maker that your witnesses are more believable, and by identifying corroboration, consistency, and impartiality within the testimony. Raise inconsistencies, contradictions, or bias apparent in the evidence presented by the other side. Remind the judge, justice of the peace, or adjudicator of any promises your opponent made in his or her opening statement about the evidence to be presented and which he or she has failed to keep. Tie the evidence together to present a convincing case that supports your theory. Make sure you have explained away any unfavourable evidence—do not leave any loose ends.

After summarizing the facts, move on to a discussion of the relevant law—statute law, case law, or both—that applies to each issue. When referring to a statutory provision, state the name of the statute and the applicable section. If the section is not too long, read it; otherwise, summarize it, being careful not to change the meaning. When referring to case law, give the case name and then summarize the principle of law underlying the case. You may also quote directly from the case. When quoting directly from the case, make sure you identify the paragraph and/or page from which you are quoting so that the judge, justice of the peace, or adjudicator can follow along. For example, you might say: "I would like to refer Your Honour to the 2014 Ontario Small Claims Court decision of *Smith v Jones* at Tab 4 of the plaintiff's Book of Authorities. Specifically, I would like to refer Your Honour to paragraph 25 of that decision on page 10." As you refer to each statutory provision or case, state how the legal principle applies to the facts of the case. You should be sure to provide the judge or other decision-maker with a book of authorities, containing copies of the statutory provisions and/or cases to which you make reference. Also, refer the decision-maker to the appropriate pages in the book of authorities as you discuss each one. See Chapter 17 for a more complete discussion of the book of authorities.

After you have finished your discussion of the relevant statutes and cases, state your conclusion for the particular issue.

Repeat this process for each issue you identified in the introduction to your closing argument.

3. State the Relief You Are Seeking

When you are finished discussing each issue, state the relief or judgment you are seeking. For example, if you are representing a defendant, you will likely be asking that the plaintiff's case be dismissed.

Adjust Your Language for Oral Presentation

Keep in mind that you will be delivering your closing argument orally; the judge or other decision-maker will not be reading what you have written. Accordingly, after you prepare your closing argument using the above format, read through it and adjust your language so that it is appropriate for an oral presentation. The following pointers may be helpful:

- *Keep your sentence structure simple and your sentences short.* Complex sentences that may be simple to read are difficult for a listener to understand.

- *Use introductory sentences to take the place of headings.* State what you will be talking about at the start of each part of the closing argument. For example, when dealing with each issue, start by saying, "I would now like to deal with the second issue, which is … (restate the issue)" or "With respect to my third submission, which is … (restate that submission)." Doing so reminds the judge, justice of the peace, or adjudicator where you are in the structure of your submissions.

- *Use words you know how to pronounce.* Make sure you will be able to deliver your closing argument without tripping over any words.

- *Use language that is persuasive and respectful, not argumentative.* Although it is called a closing *argument*, you should never argue with the judge or other decision-maker! The term *argument* refers to the fact that you are trying to persuade the decision-maker. Use language and sentence structure that show respect for the authority of the decision-maker to make the final decision. Never tell the decision-maker what to do—for example, "You should prefer the evidence of the plaintiff." Instead, submit or suggest—for example, "I submit that the plaintiff's evidence should be preferred to that of the defendant." Also, do not use inflammatory language when speaking about the opposing party or opposing advocate. Remember your professional obligations under the *Paralegal Rules of Conduct* as discussed in Chapter 2. You must treat your opponent (and the court) with respect and maintain a professional tone.

Be Prepared for Questions from the Judge, Justice of the Peace, or Adjudicator

Your closing argument is a detailed submission on the law and the evidence. The judge, justice of the peace, or adjudicator may interrupt you during your closing argument to ask questions about the law including case law that you are relying on, so you should be prepared for questions.

In addition to knowing the facts of your own case and the relevant law, know the details of the cases you refer to in your submissions. You may wish to answer a judge's question by referring to a particular paragraph of a case you provided to the court.

Always think about what you intend to say before you answer the question. One of the biggest mistakes an advocate can make is rushing into answering a question without first having thought the answer through. Take a moment to think about your answer. Silence is okay. There is no need to rush. If you don't know the answer to a question, take a moment to think. Ask the judge for a moment to consult your notes by simply saying, "Your Honour, may I have a moment to consult my notes?" Taking a moment to think about the question and your answer is important, and the judge, justice of the peace, or adjudicator will respect that. If you have fully prepared for your trial or hearing, you will likely be able to answer any question the decision-maker poses.

Also, make sure you listen to the questions carefully. Always answer the decision-maker's question directly. If you don't understand the question asked, it is helpful to restate your understanding of the question to the adjudicator in order to clarify what he or she is asking.

Practise Your Closing Argument

Practise delivering your closing argument so that your delivery will enhance, and not diminish, your argument's effectiveness. Keep in mind the following tips for practising your closing argument. Refer to Chapter 8 for a more detailed discussion of key presentation skills for advocates.

You should be familiar enough with your closing argument so that you do not have to read it. Instead, try to talk to the judge or other decision-maker and tell him or her about your case. However, you do not have to memorize your closing argument. You may look at your notes, read a passage, pause, and then look at the decision-maker. Sometimes, working from memory may cause your delivery to be stilted. Instead, use your notes to help with your pacing. Block your argument out; use large print so that you will be forced to read only small bits at a time and will not lose your place. Leave lots of white space between ideas to remind yourself to pause. Refer to Chapter 8 for a more detailed discussion on how to use notes effectively throughout your presentation.

Practise speaking slowly so that the judge or other decision-maker will be able to follow and absorb what you have to say. Speak a lot more slowly than you think you need to.

Use pacing to reinforce the organization and meaning of your closing argument. Pause between sentences; pause longer between paragraphs. Your pacing takes the place of commas, periods, and paragraphs. Remember that pauses, at appropriate times, can help put emphasis on certain words and points you are making and allow the decision-maker time to digest what you have just said.

Practise using the appropriate honorific: Your Honour, Your Worship, Ms. Adjudicator, as the case may be.

Practise speaking loudly. The judge or other decision-maker must be able to hear you if he or she is to understand you.

Finally, practise speaking with expression. If you speak in a monotone, you will bore the decision-maker and lose his or her attention. Make a special effort to avoid "up-talk," the tendency, especially among young people, to express statements as if they were questions. "Up-talk" makes a speaker sound nervous and tentative rather than confident and persuasive.

Box 14.1 contains a sample closing argument for the plaintiff in the Kitchen Renovation Case. You'll get a chance to prepare a closing argument for the defendant as an exercise at the end of this chapter.

BOX 14.1

Plaintiff's Closing Argument in the Kitchen Renovation Case

Your Honour, the issue in this case is whether the defendants breached their contract with the plaintiff by failing to pay the cost of installation of three pot lights, and we submit that they have.

The facts of the case are as follows:

Both parties agree that they entered into a contract for minor renovations to the defendants' kitchen in the amount of $7,500. Both parties also agree that the contract required the plaintiff to install pot lights in the kitchen. The evidence of the parties differs, however, with respect to the exact number of pot lights that were included in the contract price. The defendants' evidence is that the contract price included the installation of all necessary pot lights to make the kitchen bright. The plaintiff's evidence is that the contract price included the installation of only five pot lights, and that any additional pot lights requested would cost extra.

We submit that the evidence of the plaintiff should be preferred on this point because it is not reasonable to assume that a contractor would agree to provide an undefined number of lights.

This case involves common law principles of contract law, in particular, contract interpretation. We submit that there is clearly a contract between the parties, and the only issue is one of interpretation. We submit that, in interpreting contracts, the court should try to give effect to the intention of the parties based on the clear meaning of the words they used, and that each party must persuade the court that his or her interpretation of the contract is the correct one.

In this case, the evidence of the parties about the exact words used differs. However, if Your Honour prefers the evidence of the plaintiffs, as we submit Your Honour should, then Your Honour should conclude that the contract provided for five pot lights only, and additional pot lights were to cost extra.

We therefore submit that the defendants are responsible for the cost of supplying and installing the three additional pot lights at a cost of $250 each.

The plaintiffs therefore ask for damages in the amount of $750 for the cost of supplying and installing the additional three pot lights.

Box 14.2 contains a sample closing argument for the defendants in the Liquor Licence Case. You'll get a chance to prepare a closing argument for the Crown as an exercise at the end of this chapter.

BOX 14.2

Defendants' Closing Argument in the Liquor Licence Case

Your Worship, the issue in this case is whether the defendants, Treetop Catering and Victoria Levens, committed the offence of permitting the removal of alcohol from the licensed premises contrary to the *Liquor Licence Act*, and we submit that the defendants did not.

We have two submissions to make. Our first submission is that the Crown has failed to prove beyond a reasonable doubt that the defendants permitted the removal of alcohol from the licensed premises contrary to the *Liquor Licence Act*. Our second submission is that if Your Worship finds that the Crown has met its burden in this case, we submit that the defendants took all reasonable steps to prevent the removal of alcohol from the licensed premises and should therefore be acquitted of the charges.

The facts of this case are as follows:

The defendant, Victoria Levens, runs a catering business called Treetop Catering Inc. Ms. Levens is the sole shareholder, director, and officer of Treetop Catering Inc. She organized and managed a party for the members of the Simpson Academy

Advocacy Club at the Simpson Academy student lounge on May 16, 2016. The defence does not dispute that she was solely responsible for this event. The evidence has shown that Treetop Catering Inc. held a Liquor Sales Licence and had a caterer's endorsement for the event, allowing it to serve and sell liquor in the indoor lounge and the outdoor patio. Both the Crown and the defendants agree that the defendants provided a light buffet, beer, wine, and soft drinks at the event for about 40 guests, and that the licensed boundaries of the event were the indoor lounge and outdoor fenced patio. The grassy area beyond the outdoor patio was not licensed for alcohol. There is undisputed evidence that the defendants complied with the provisions of their liquor licence and catering endorsement in that Ms. Levens notified the appropriate authorities of the event by sending a catering endorsement notification form in accordance with the *Liquor Licence Act*. On May 16, 2016 shortly after 11:30 p.m., Police Constable Matthew Lee arrived at the event to investigate a noise complaint. While on scene, the officer observed what he described as empty beer bottles and plastic wine glasses on the grassy area beyond the licensed patio.

This situation is governed by the *Liquor Licence Act*, RSO 1990, chapter L.19. Section 61(1)(c) provides as follows:

> 61(1) A person is guilty of an offence if the person, …
>   (c) contravenes any provision of this Act or the regulations.

The applicable regulation is RRO 1990, regulation 719: *Licences to Sell Liquor*. The relevant sections are as follows:

> 8(1) The following classes of licences to sell liquor are established:
>   1. A liquor sales licence authorizing the sale and service of liquor for consumption on the premises to which the licence applies. …
>
> 8(2) The following endorsements to liquor sales licences are established: …
>   3. A caterer's endorsement authorizing the applicant to sell and serve liquor for an event held on premises other than the premises to which the liquor sales licence applies. …
>
> 34(1) The licence holder shall not permit a patron to remove liquor from the premises to which the licence applies.

According to the 1978 Supreme Court of Canada decision of *R v Sault Ste Marie*, which Your Worship will find at Tab 4 of the defendants' Book of Authorities, the Crown must prove beyond a reasonable doubt that the defendants committed the *actus reus* of the offence, namely, the act of permitting the removal of alcohol from the licensed area of the premises.

Our first submission is that the Crown has not met its burden in this case. While Police Constable Lee testified that he saw and inspected empty beer bottles and plastic wine glasses on the grass outside the licensed area and that they smelled of alcohol, the Crown has not proven beyond a reasonable doubt that the alcohol came from the bar inside the student lounge that evening or that guests left the patio with alcohol. While a number of guests did leave the fenced patio through a gate onto the grassy area, not a single witness testified that he or she saw guests with alcohol standing on the grass beyond the enclosed patio—not Mr. Elder, not Police Constable Lee, not the defendant, Victoria Levens, and not the security guard, Mr. Hobbs. In fact, Mr. Hobbs testified that he stood on the patio all evening long and never saw any guests leave the patio with alcoholic beverages.

I will now move onto my second submission, which is that if Your Worship finds that the Crown has met its burden in this case, the defendants submit that they took all reasonable steps to prevent the removal of alcohol from the licensed premises. According to the Supreme Court of Canada decision of *R v Sault Ste Marie*, it is open to the defendant to prove, on a balance of probabilities, that she took all reasonable steps in the circumstances to comply with the law.

The evidence has shown that Ms. Levens did everything she could to prevent alcohol from leaving the licensed area. You heard her testify that as part of her preparation for the event, she made a site visit on May 1, 2016 to inspect the facilities and determine the licensed areas for service. You also heard Ms. Levens testify how she hired Mr. Hobbs, a licensed security guard, for an event with only 40 guests. Ms. Levens also testified that she did so for the purpose of ensuring that guests did not take alcoholic beverages beyond the patio, a patio that was only 30 feet by 30 feet in size. The evidence has shown that Mr. Hobbs stood on the patio for the entire duration of the event monitoring guests. He did not leave the patio once. You heard Mr. Hobbs testify how he stood next to the only gate leading to the grassy area and told every single guest who left the patio that alcoholic beverages were not permitted to leave the patio area. The evidence has also shown that there was a fence enclosing the entire perimeter of the outdoor patio to keep guests inside the patio. Signs were also posted on the premises advising guests that no alcoholic beverages were permitted outside the patio. These signs were clearly visible to all guests. You heard Police Constable Lee testify that he saw one of these signs on the gate door when he walked onto the patio that evening.

The defence therefore submits that the defendants should be found not guilty and ask that Your Worship acquit them of the charge.

Box 14.3 contains a sample closing argument for the tenants in the Landlord and Tenant Dispute. You'll get a chance to prepare a closing argument for the landlord as an exercise at the end of this chapter.

BOX 14.3

Tenants' Closing Argument in the Landlord and Tenant Dispute

Madam Adjudicator, the issue in this case is whether the landlord gave notice of termination to the tenants in good faith, and we submit that he did not.

The facts of this case are as follows:

Both parties agree that the tenants were tenants of the landlord under a one-year lease ending April 30, 2016 at a monthly rent of $1,250, and that on March 1, 2016 the landlord served the tenants with a form N12, terminating their tenancy as of April 30, 2016 on the basis that the landlord's daughter would be moving into the unit. Both parties also agree that, after serving the landlord with a form N9, the tenants moved out of the unit on March 31, 2016. The uncontradicted evidence of the tenants is that they moved into a new apartment at a rent of $1,350 per month and incurred moving costs of $750.

The landlord testified that when he served the notice of termination, he believed his daughter would be moving into the apartment after graduating from university in the spring. However, the landlord's daughter testified that she told her parents only that she would *probably* be moving back to Toronto. Both parties agree that the landlord's daughter did not move into the unit, and the landlord instead offered the apartment for rent at a monthly rent of $1,375.

The issue in this case is whether the landlord acted in good faith in giving the notice of termination, and we submit that the evidence shows he did not.

This situation is governed by the *Residential Tenancies Act, 2006*, SO 2006, chapter 17. Section 48(1)(c) provides as follows:

> 48(1) A landlord may, by notice, terminate a tenancy if the landlord in good faith requires possession of the rental unit for the purpose of residential occupation by, …
>
> (c) a child or parent of the landlord or the landlord's spouse.

If you conclude that the notice of termination was given in bad faith, the provisions of section 57 apply. Under section 57(1)(a), a former tenant may apply to the Landlord and Tenant Board if

> the landlord gave a notice of termination under section 48 in bad faith, the former tenant vacated the rental unit as a result of the notice … and no person referred to in clause 48 (1) … (d) occupied the rental unit within a reasonable time after the former tenant vacated the rental unit.

In such a case, the Landlord and Tenant Board may, under section 57(3), order that the landlord pay a specified sum to the former tenant for

> i. all or any portion of any increased rent that the former tenant has incurred or will incur for a one-year period after vacating the rental unit, and
>
> ii. reasonable out-of-pocket moving, storage and other like expenses that the former tenant has incurred or will incur.

In addition, Interpretation Guideline G12 of the Landlord and Tenant Board, *Eviction for Personal Use*, deals with interpretation questions respecting eviction applications under section 48. Under the heading "Requirement of good faith," it states, "The issue that arises in some cases is whether the landlord or a family member has a real intention to reside in the rental unit." Under the heading "The landlord requires the unit—test to be applied," it provides as follows:

> The burden of proof is on the landlord. It is relevant to the good faith of the landlord's intention to occupy the unit to determine the likelihood that the intended person will move into it.
>
> Based on the evidence of the landlord's daughter, it was by no means certain that she would be moving into the unit at the time the landlord served the notice to terminate. We therefore submit that the landlord has not satisfied the burden of proof that he acted in good faith.
>
> We therefore submit that the landlord should be ordered to pay the tenants their increased rent for one year of $1,200 and their moving expenses of $750 for a total of $1,950.

REVIEW QUESTIONS

1. What is the purpose of the closing argument?

2. When should you prepare your closing argument?

3. What is the recommended format for a closing argument? Briefly describe what should be included in each step.

4. How and why should you adjust the language of your closing argument so that it is appropriate for an oral presentation?

5. Why is it important to practise delivering your closing argument?

DISCUSSION QUESTION

You are a licensed paralegal representing the defendant in a provincial offences case. The defendant is charged with the offence of driving with a hand-held communication device contrary to section 78.1(1) of the *Highway Traffic Act*. The evidence is that a police officer observed the defendant driving along Sullivan Street in the City of Toronto with a cellphone between her left ear and shoulder. The defendant does not dispute this. In closing argument, the defendant's advocate states as follows:

> Your Honour, I believe that the defendant should be acquitted of the charge. While the defendant does not dispute the fact that she was speaking on her cellphone while her phone was between her left ear and her shoulder, I do not think that this constitutes "holding" a communication device under the *Highway Traffic Act*. In my opinion, the prosecutor has brought this bogus charge for the purposes of wasting court time and resources and because he has nothing better to do.

Identify three problems with this passage of your closing argument. Explain each problem and what you should say instead.

EXERCISES

1. Review the evidence in the Kitchen Renovation Case (the direct examinations can be found in Chapter 11 and the cross-examinations in Chapter 12) and the plaintiff's closing argument (found in this chapter). Then, prepare a closing argument for the defendant in the Kitchen Renovation Case.

2. Review the evidence in the Liquor Licence Case (the direct examinations can be found in Chapter 11 and the cross-examinations in Chapter 12) and the defendant's closing argument (found in this chapter). Then, prepare a closing argument for the Crown in the Liquor Licence Case.

3. Review the evidence in the Landlord and Tenant Dispute (the direct examinations can be found in Chapter 11 and the cross-examinations in Chapter 12) and the tenants' closing argument (found in this chapter). Then, prepare a closing argument for the landlord in the Landlord and Tenant Dispute.

CHAPTER 15

Additional Submissions

After closing arguments, the judge, justice of the peace, or adjudicator will give a decision in the case. After delivery of the decision, you may be called upon to make additional submissions on costs, interest, or sentence, depending on the nature of the matter.

Costs

If you are successful at your hearing or trial, your client may be able to recover fees and expenses incurred in the conduct of your case by way of an award of **costs**. Sometimes the judge or other decision-maker may simply fix costs, without requiring either advocate to make any submissions. For example, in Small Claims Court, the judge will typically award as costs the court fees (filing fee, set-down fee) and a preparation fee. At the Landlord and Tenant Board, the adjudicator will award a successful applicant the fees that the applicant paid to file the application.

The judge or other decision-maker may, however, ask both parties to make submissions on the issue of costs. These submissions are usually made right after the judge or other decision-maker delivers the decision. You should therefore be prepared to speak to costs.

Small Claims Court

Section 19 of the *Rules of the Small Claims Court* sets out the costs recoverable by a successful party. Generally speaking, the winning party is entitled to have reasonable disbursements paid by the losing party. If the amount claimed in the action is over $500, exclusive of interest and costs, and the successful party is represented by a lawyer, student-at-law, or agent, the court may also award the party a reasonable representation fee at trial. Under section 29 of the *Courts of Justice Act*, an award of costs in the Small Claims Court, other than disbursements, cannot exceed 15 percent of the amount claimed.

---

costs: monetary award made to the successful party for fees and expenses incurred in the conduct of a case

Before preparing your submission as to costs, you should review the relevant provisions of the Act and the Rules, so that you may refer to the rules on which you rely in support of your claim for costs. You should also prepare a **bill of costs**. A bill of costs is a detailed list of all the procedural steps taken at each stage of the proceeding and the legal fees and disbursements incurred at each stage. Make sure you keep a copy of all your receipts, invoices, or cancelled cheques to prove that you paid the amounts claimed.

After the judge makes a decision (and if you are the successful party), wait for the judge to ask you whether you would like to speak to costs. Then, stand up and state the amounts you are seeking and the authority for those amounts. At this time, you may also wish to present the judge with your bill of costs.

Provincial Offences Court

Under the *Provincial Offences Act*, a person who is convicted of an offence may be ordered to pay costs in addition to any fine. The regulations to the Act set out the amount of costs payable. For example, if convicted, the defendant must pay costs in the amount of $5 for service of the offence notice or summons. Although the amount of costs payable is fixed by the regulations, the parties are given an opportunity to make submissions about costs. If your client has financial difficulties, you should ask to make submissions about costs to try to minimize the costs (and fine payable) as much as possible. You may also want to ask that the time given to pay the costs (and fine) be extended beyond the deadline imposed by the legislation.

Tribunals

The *Statutory Powers Procedure Act* allows a tribunal to make its own rules about costs. At the Landlord and Tenant Board, costs are dealt with in the *Residential Tenancies Act, 2006* and the *Rules of Practice of the Landlord and Tenant Board*. Costs are also dealt with in an Interpretation Guideline. Review the Interpretation Guideline and Rules when you prepare your submissions.

Interest

Generally speaking, a party who is awarded money at a trial or hearing is entitled to interest on the amount awarded. There are two kinds of interest: **pre-judgment interest** is calculated from the date the cause of action arose to the date of judgment; **post-judgment interest** is calculated from the date of judgment to the date payment

---

bill of costs: a detailed list of all the procedural steps taken at each stage of the proceeding and the legal fees and disbursements incurred at each stage

pre-judgment interest: interest on the amount awarded calculated from the date the cause of action arose to the date of judgment

post-judgment interest: interest on the amount awarded calculated from the date of judgment to the date payment is made

is made. Both types of interest may be awarded at the Small Claims Court; only post-judgment interest may be awarded at the Landlord and Tenant Board.

The interest rate for both types of interest is set by law. However, there is discretion to change the interest rate or the period of time for which interest is allowed. For example, interest may be awarded at a lower rate than that prescribed by law if a party can establish that the circumstances of the case warrant it. As an advocate, you should be prepared to speak to the amount of interest awarded.

No interest is payable on fines imposed by the Provincial Offences Court. If payment is not made by the due date, the defendant's driver's licence can be suspended.

Sentence

If a person is convicted of an offence at Provincial Offences Court, he or she will be sentenced by the justice of the peace. The **sentence** is the penalty imposed for the offence committed. The sentence could be, for example, a set fine with or without costs, probation, licence suspension, or imprisonment. Before the sentence is imposed, the justice of the peace must ask both the prosecutor and the advocate for the defendant whether they have anything to say about the sentence.

You should be prepared to make submissions about the penalty that may be imposed. For example, if your client cannot afford to pay a fine, you can ask the court to reduce or waive the fine. If a minimum penalty is prescribed for an offence that includes imprisonment, you can ask the court to impose a fine of not more than $5,000 in lieu of imprisonment. When a fine is imposed, the defendant is given 15 days to pay it. If you think that your client will not be able to pay the fine on time, you should ask the court for more time to pay.

sentence: penalty imposed for an offence

KEY TERMS

bill of costs, 221
costs, 220
post-judgment interest, 221
pre-judgment interest, 221
sentence, 222

REVIEW QUESTIONS

1. How can a successful party recover the fees and expenses incurred in the conduct of his or her case?

2. What costs are recoverable by a successful party at the Small Claims Court?

3. What should you do when preparing your submissions as to costs in Small Claims Court?

4. When do you speak to costs in Small Claims Court?

5. How do you speak to costs in Small Claims Court?

6. How are costs dealt with at the Provincial Offences Court?

7. In what situation should you make submissions about costs at the Provincial Offences Court?

8. How are costs dealt with at the Landlord and Tenant Board?

9. How is pre-judgment interest calculated?

10. How is post-judgment interest calculated?

11. Why should you be prepared to speak to the amount of interest awarded?

12. What types of sentences may be imposed by the justice of the peace upon conviction in the Provincial Offences Court?

13. Briefly describe the submissions that can be made about sentencing in Provincial Offences Court.

DISCUSSION QUESTION

You are a licensed paralegal representing Amita Khan, a defendant in a provincial offences case. Amita was charged with the offence of failing to stop for a school bus contrary to section 175(12) of the *Highway Traffic Act*. She was found guilty at trial. The set fine for this offence is $400. Amita is a full-time student at an Ontario college. She also works part-time at a minimum-wage job to help pay for her housing, food, and education expenses. Amita is worried about her ability to pay the $400 fine in a short period of time. She does not have any savings. The justice of the peace asks you and the prosecutor to make submissions as to sentence. What should you say?

CHAPTER 16

Objections

LEARNING OUTCOMES

After reading this chapter, you will understand

▪ the purpose of objections

▪ how objections are made

▪ when objections are made

A trial or hearing is a highly structured proceeding in which each party's advocate addresses the court or tribunal at a specified time. Under the rules of courtroom etiquette, an advocate is required to listen quietly and respectfully when the opposing advocate is speaking. However, an advocate is permitted to speak out of turn, as it were, when making an objection.

This chapter discusses the purpose of objections, how they are made, and when they are made.

Purpose of Objections

Objections are used primarily to prevent improper evidence from being presented and considered by the court or tribunal. For example, objections may be made with respect to

- questions asked by an advocate,
- a witness's testimony, and
- the introduction or use of exhibits.

Less commonly, objections may also be used to object to the behaviour of the other advocate.

When made with respect to evidence, the purpose of the objection is to draw the decision-maker's attention to the impropriety of the evidence and to ask him or her to rule on its admissibility. If the decision-maker agrees with the objection, the objection is sustained and the evidence is excluded. If the decision-maker disagrees with the objection, the objection is overruled and the evidence is admitted.

How to Object

Make an objection by providing both notice of your objection and the grounds for it. Always direct your objection toward the judge or other decision-maker, not to the other advocate. It is important to be polite and respectful at all times, and not to shout or become argumentative.

Stand up and say, "I object, Your Honour" or "Your Worship, I have an objection." Then, state the reason for your objection, keeping it simple, yet specific. For example, "I object, Your Honour. The question is leading." The other side is given an opportunity to respond to your objection, and finally you have the opportunity to reply to that response. Remain standing until the judge or other decision-maker has made a ruling on the objection, and then sit down. Thank the decision-maker whether or not he or she rules in your favour.

Types of Objections

As stated earlier, objections are used primarily to prevent improper evidence from being presented and considered by the court or tribunal. As a result, most objections are made during the examination of witnesses. Some objections are based on the form in which the question is asked. Other objections are based on the substance of the evidence that the witness is being asked to give.

Objections to the Form of the Question

It is possible to object to the form in which a question is asked by the opposing advocate, even though the information being sought may be perfectly admissible. For example, you might object because a question is

- *leading* (on direct examination)—the question suggests the desired answer or assumes facts not in evidence;
- *compound*—the question asks two or more questions;
- *vague, ambiguous, or confusing*—the question is too general, has more than one meaning, or is confusing;
- *argumentative*—the question is an attempt to get the witness to agree with the questioner's conclusions or inferences rather than to agree with a statement of fact—the question is asked not to elicit information but rather to persuade the judge; or
- *repetitive*—the question has already been asked and answered (by the same witness).

These types of objections may be corrected by rephrasing the question.

Objections to the Substance of the Evidence

Objections to the substance of the evidence are based on the admissibility of evidence being asked for, and not on the question itself. The most common admissibility grounds are

- *hearsay*—the witness is stating what another person has said as proof of the truth of a relevant fact;
- *opinion*—the witness is not a qualified expert and is stating an opinion;
- *relevancy*—the evidence is not relevant to the issues of the case;
- *speculation*—the witness does not know the answer and is speculating about what the answer might be; and
- *privilege*—the evidence is protected by solicitor–client privilege.

Sometimes it is apparent from the question itself that the answer will contain evidence that should be excluded as inadmissible. For example, the question "What did your partner tell you about the quality of the goods your partnership sold?" is clearly asking for hearsay evidence if the quality of the goods is at issue in the proceeding. You may object to the question without waiting for the answer. Other times, the question is appropriate, but the answer given includes inadmissible evidence. For example, the question "What do you know about the quality of the goods your partnership sold?" is an acceptable question. However, if the witness responds, "My partner told me that the quality was high," that is hearsay, and you may object to the answer. In other words, you may object to a question if it clearly calls for inadmissible evidence; you may object to an answer if it contains such evidence.

If you are going to object, you should do so as soon as you realize that an objection is called for. For example, if you are objecting to a leading question, object as soon as the question is asked—don't wait to hear the answer! You should generally not interrupt the questioner unless the question is objectionable because of what it asserts. For example, if the questions starts, "When you signed the contract," you may object before the question is finished if there has been no evidence that a contract was signed. In this case, the question asserts the existence of a contract. If the question is objectionable only because of what it asks, then you should wait until the question is complete before making your objection. For example, the question "What do you think he meant by that?" is objectionable because it calls for an answer that is speculative.

When Objections Are Raised

As stated earlier, objections are used primarily to prevent improper evidence from being presented and considered by the court or tribunal. As a result, most objections are made during the examination of witnesses, although they can be made at other times as well, including during an opening statement and a closing argument.

Direct Examination

During direct examination by the opposing advocate of that advocate's witnesses, objections are made to limit the admission of evidence that is helpful to the other side. Objections may be made to either the question asked or the evidence given. The most common objections are

- the question is leading;
- the question calls for hearsay evidence, or the witness is giving hearsay evidence; and
- the question calls for an opinion, or the witness is giving opinion evidence and is not a qualified expert.

Cross-Examination

During cross-examination of your witness by the opposing advocate, objections are designed to prevent your witness from giving evidence that is harmful to your case or to protect your witness from mistreatment. Objections may be made to the question asked, not to the answer given. The most common objections are that the question is

- argumentative;
- repetitive;
- compound;
- vague, ambiguous, or confusing;
- seeking privileged information; or
- seeking evidence that is not relevant.

Re-Examination

During re-examination by the opposing advocate of that advocate's witnesses, again, objections are designed to limit the admission of evidence that is helpful to the other side. Objections are generally made to the question asked. The most common objections are

- the question is leading;
- the question is asking for information already given on direct examination; and

- the question is asking for information that should have been dealt with in direct examination.

Introduction of Exhibits

You should object to the introduction of an exhibit by the opposing advocate if the witness cannot authenticate the exhibit.

Opening Statement and Closing Argument

Objections are rarely made during the opening statement and the closing argument. However, during the opening statement it is possible to object if the opposing advocate is presenting legal argument, referring to inadmissible evidence, or stating his or her personal opinion. During the closing argument, it is possible to object if the opposing advocate is misstating the law or the evidence, arguing facts that have not been entered into evidence, or expressing his or her personal opinion.

The Wisdom of Objecting

Certainly you should never object unless your objection deserves to be sustained. An objection must always have merit, and cannot be used simply as a tactic to stall the trial process. You will lose credibility with the judge or other decision-maker if you repeatedly make objections that are unfounded and are therefore overruled. Even if you have good grounds to object, you should consider whether it is wise to do so. Some objections will hurt, more than help, your case. An objection interrupts the trial or hearing and shifts the attention to the objectionable evidence. The other side is given an opportunity to explain this evidence when responding to your objection. The process may increase the decision-maker's focus on the evidence.

When deciding whether to object, think about your theory of the case, and consider how the objectionable evidence affects your theory. If exclusion of the evidence is required to support your theory of the case, then you should object. If the objectionable evidence does not hurt your case, you may be wiser not to object to it. This is not an easy decision to make, and you do not have a lot of time in which to make it.

Responding to Objections

Unless the judge or other decision-maker immediately overrules an objection made by the other side, you will be given the opportunity to respond. Your response should explain why the evidence is being presented to the court or tribunal and why it is admissible.

Part of trial or hearing preparation involves considering the admissibility of the evidence you intend to present to the court. You should also consider the form and substance of the questions you intend to ask during direct examination and cross-examination. For every question you ask, you should have a purpose; every question should support and advance your theory of the case. Reviewing these matters will prepare you to respond to objections at the trial or hearing.

When making and responding to objections, remember your professional and ethical obligations under the *Paralegal Rules of Conduct* as discussed in Chapter 2.

REVIEW QUESTIONS

1. What is the purpose of objections?

2. Give an example of what you might object to during a trial or hearing.

3. What happens if the decision-maker agrees with your objection?

4. What happens if the decision-maker disagrees with your objection?

5. What is the proper way to object?

6. List and briefly describe the types of objections that may be made to the form of the question being asked by the opposing advocate.

7. List and briefly describe the types of objections that may be made to the substance of the evidence that the witness is being asked to give.

8. When should you object?

9. What are the most common objections made during direct examination of the other side's witness?

10. What are the most common objections made during cross-examination of your witness by the opposing advocate?

11. What are the most common objections made during re-examination by the opposing advocate of his or her witness?

12. When should you object to the introduction of an exhibit by the opposing advocate?

13. When should you object during the opening statement and closing argument of the opposing advocate?

14. How do you decide whether or not to object?

15. How do you respond to an objection made by the other side?

EXERCISES

1. You are acting on a residential landlord and tenant matter for the landlord. The paralegal for the tenant is conducting a direct examination of her client, the tenant, and asks the following question: "You and the landlord orally agreed to the termination of your tenancy, isn't that correct?" Prepare an objection to that question.

2. You are acting for the plaintiff in a Small Claims Court matter. The plaintiff, Ms. Samson, is suing the defendant for breach of contract involving the quality of paint used by the defendant to paint her home. The paralegal for the defendant is conducting a direct examination of his client, the seller of the paint, and asks the following question: "What did your production manager tell you about the quality of the paint?" Prepare an objection to that question.

3. You are acting for the defendant in a provincial offences case involving a charge of careless driving under the *Highway Traffic Act*. The prosecutor is conducting a direct examination of a lay witness who observed the defendant driving erratically down Charles Street. The prosecutor asks the witness the following question: "Why was the defendant driving erratically?" The witness provides the following answer: "Probably because he was texting on his cellphone while driving." Prepare an objection to the witness's answer.

PART V

Final Preparation

CHAPTER 17

Final Preparation for the Trial or Hearing

LEARNING OUTCOMES

After reading this chapter, you will understand

- how to ensure that your witnesses will attend
- how to ensure that your documentary evidence will be admitted
- how to prepare a trial or hearing notebook
- how to prepare a book of authorities

Previous chapters have discussed the preparation for a trial or hearing from the development of your theory of the case through every stage of the actual trial or hearing itself—opening statement, submission of evidence, and closing argument. That part of your preparation should take place well in advance of the actual trial or hearing date. As the actual trial or hearing date draws closer, there are several additional matters to attend to:

- ensuring that your witnesses will attend,
- ensuring that your documentary evidence will be admitted,
- preparing a trial or hearing notebook, and
- preparing a book of authorities.

This chapter discusses these matters.

Ensuring That Your Witnesses Will Attend

It is essential to the success of your case that all of your witnesses show up at the trial or hearing. Advise your witnesses of the trial or hearing date as soon as you are advised of it, and confirm that they are willing and able to appear on that date. Make sure they know where the trial or hearing will take place. If a witness refuses or is unwilling to testify, ask the court or tribunal to issue a summons to compel the witness's attendance.

Often witnesses will agree to come to the trial or hearing when you ask them. However, unless you are 100 percent confident that a witness will attend, you should arrange to have a summons issued to protect your client in the event that the witness fails to appear.

A **summons** is a legal document requiring a person to attend a trial or hearing as a witness. It may also require that person to bring specified documents to the court or tribunal. A witness who receives a summons must appear in the court or

---

summons: a legal document requiring a person to attend a trial or hearing as a witness

tribunal on the date and time specified in the summons. A witness who fails to do so is subject to arrest.[1] A witness who is not served with a summons is under no legal obligation to attend at the trial or hearing, and you may be forced to proceed without the witness.

A summons to a witness is issued by the court or tribunal at the request of a party to the proceeding. You will need to obtain the appropriate form and attend at the court or tribunal office to have it properly issued. Once the summons is issued, you must serve it on the witness. If the witness does not attend the trial or hearing, you will be required to prove that you served the witness with the summons.

Ensuring That Your Documentary Evidence Will Be Admitted

If you are relying on any documentary evidence, you must comply with any procedural requirements of the court or tribunal as to disclosure or notice of those documents. For example:

- The *Rules of the Small Claims Court* provide that a document that has been served at least 30 days before the trial date shall be received in evidence, unless the trial judge orders otherwise.

- Under the *Landlord and Tenant Board's Rules of Practice*, an LTB member may order the disclosure or exchange of documents, in which case a party who breaches the order may not rely on the evidence that was not disclosed.

Preparing a Trial or Hearing Notebook

A **trial or hearing notebook** contains all the important information you will need at the trial or hearing in a secure and organized format. It allows you to find documents and information quickly and easily; as a result, you are more likely to remain calm and in control throughout the proceeding, and appear confident and ready for the trial or hearing to both the judge or other decision-maker and the other side.

Create your notebook using a three-ring binder with tabs or dividers to separate the sections. Do not simply place everything in a folder, because if you drop it, all of your papers can fall out. Your notebook should be organized so that you will be able to find any information or documents you need easily and quickly.

Your notebook should contain the following sections:

1. *Title page*—Set out the names of the parties to the case, your client's contact information, and the name and contact information of the advocate for the other side.

---

trial or hearing notebook: notebook prepared and used by each party, containing all important information needed at the trial or hearing in a secure and organized format

2. *Summary of the facts of the case*—If you have a busy practice, you may have several cases on the go at the same time for which you may have prepared a while before the actual trial or hearing date. The summary will help to refresh your memory of the case.

3. *Pleadings*—Insert all the court or tribunal documents in chronological order—for example, in a Small Claims Court trial, include the plaintiff's claim and the defence.

4. *Trial checklist*—List the facts you must prove at the trial or hearing to establish the necessary legal elements of your case (go back to your theory of the case). Next to each fact, set out the name of the witness you will call and any documentary evidence you will be relying on to establish that fact.

5. *Witness list*—List the witnesses in the order in which you plan to call them, including contact information for each witness.

6. *Documents/exhibits*—Insert copies of all documents you intend to use during the trial or hearing. If there are a lot of documents, you may want to include an index at the beginning of this section. Do not punch holes in the original documents or insert them into the notebook. Instead, keep them in a folder or sleeve, and insert the folder or sleeve into the binder. This section should also include several blank pages for you to make an exhibit list, setting out the number and a brief description of each exhibit as it is entered into evidence. This lets you keep track of exhibits so that when you need to use them, you can quickly and easily identify them by exhibit number.

7. *Opening statement*—Insert the notes you have prepared for the delivery of your opening statement.

8. *Direct examination*—For each witness, insert notes setting out the questions you will ask together with the answers you expect. Include some blank pages so that you can take notes, if necessary.

9. *Cross-examination*—For each witness, insert notes setting out the target areas you have identified and the questions you have prepared on a preliminary basis. Also insert blank pages so that you can take notes on the direct examination of each witness you will be cross-examining. Draw a vertical line two-thirds of the way down the page. To the left of the line, write down what the witness says. To the right of the line, make notes on how to tie those statements to questions you have already prepared and/or to any additional questions you should ask.

10. *Closing argument*—Insert the notes of the draft closing argument you have prepared. Insert blank pages so that you can make notes of any additions or revisions required if the evidence does not unfold exactly as you anticipated.

Preparing a Book of Authorities

During your closing argument you must provide the judge or other decision-maker with a copy of any case or statutory provision on which you are relying. If you are relying on only one or two cases or statutory provisions, you may simply provide the decision-maker with copies of each as you go. However, if you are relying on multiple cases or statutory provisions, you should prepare a **book of authorities** into which you insert a copy of each case or statutory provision, separated by numbered tabs. Insert a list of the authorities at the front of the book, setting out the full name and citation of each case and statute.

---

book of authorities: book containing a copy of each case and statutory provision relied on for a trial or hearing

NOTE

1 The power to issue a warrant for the arrest of a witness who does not appear at a Small Claims Court trial is given to the trial judge under the *Rules of the Small Claims Court*; the power to issue a warrant for the arrest of a witness at a provincial offences trial is given to provincial judges under the *Provincial Offences Act*; the power to issue a warrant for the arrest of a witness at a tribunal hearing is given to a judge of the Superior Court by the *Statutory Powers Procedure Act*.

KEY TERMS

book of authorities, 241
summons, 238
trial or hearing notebook, 239

REVIEW QUESTIONS

1. What should you do to ensure that all of your witnesses will show up at the trial or hearing?

2. What is a summons?

3. What should you do to ensure that your documentary evidence will be admitted?

4. What is a trial or hearing notebook?

5. How should you prepare a trial or hearing notebook?

6. Briefly describe the sections your notebook should contain.

7. When should you prepare a book of authorities, and what should you put in it?

APPENDIX A

Selected Paralegal Rules of Conduct*

---

* The Law Society of Upper Canada may add to or revise these Rules without notice.

Rule 2: Professionalism

2.01   Integrity and Civility

Integrity

2.01(1) A paralegal has a duty to provide legal services and discharge all responsibilities to clients, tribunals, the public and other members of the legal professions honourably and with integrity.

(2) A paralegal has a duty to uphold the standards and reputation of the paralegal profession and to assist in the advancement of its goals, organizations and institutions.

Civility

(3) A paralegal shall be courteous and civil, and shall act in good faith with all persons with whom he or she has dealings in the course of his or her practice.

Outside Interests and Public Office

(4) A paralegal who engages in another profession, business, occupation or other outside interest or who holds public office concurrently with the provision of legal services, shall not allow the outside interest or public office to jeopardize the paralegal's integrity, independence, or competence.

(5) A paralegal shall not allow involvement in an outside interest or public office to impair the exercise of his or her independent judgment on behalf of a client.

Acting as Mediator

(6) A paralegal who acts as a mediator shall, at the outset of the mediation, ensure that the parties to it understand fully that the paralegal is not acting as a representative for either party but, as mediator, is acting to assist the parties to resolve the issues in dispute.

[Amended—October 2014]

Rule 4: Advocacy

4.01 The Paralegal as Advocate

Duty to Clients, Tribunals and Others

4.01(1) When acting as an advocate, the paralegal shall represent the client resolutely and honourably within the limits of the law while, at the same time, treating the tribunal and other licensees with candour, fairness, courtesy and respect.

(2) This rule applies to appearances and proceedings before all tribunals in which the paralegal may appear.

(3) This rule does not require a paralegal, except as otherwise provided in these Rules, to assist an adversary or advance matters derogatory to the client's case.

(4) Without restricting the generality of subrule (1), the paralegal shall,

(a) raise fearlessly every issue, advance every argument, and ask every question, however distasteful, that the paralegal thinks will help the client's case;

(b) endeavour, on the client's behalf, to obtain the benefit of every remedy and defence authorized by law;

(c) never waive or abandon a client's legal rights, for example, an available defence under a statute of limitations, without the client's informed consent; and

(d) avoid and discourage the client from resorting to frivolous and vexatious objections, or from attempts to gain advantage from mistakes or oversights not going to the merits, or from tactics designed to merely delay or harass the other side.

The Paralegal and the Tribunal Process

(5) When acting as an advocate, the paralegal shall not,

(a) abuse the process of the tribunal by instituting or prosecuting proceedings which, although legal in themselves, are clearly motivated by malice on the part of the client and are brought solely for the purpose of injuring the other party;

(b) knowingly assist or permit the client to do anything that the paralegal considers to be dishonest or dishonourable;

(c) knowingly attempt to deceive a tribunal or influence the course of justice by offering false evidence, misstating facts or law, presenting or relying upon a false or deceptive affidavit, suppressing what ought to be disclosed, or otherwise assisting in any deception, crime or illegal conduct;

(d) deliberately refrain from informing the tribunal of any binding authority that the paralegal considers to be directly on point and that has not been mentioned by an opponent;

(e) appear before a judicial officer when the paralegal, a partner of the paralegal, a paralegal employed by the paralegal firm or the client has a business or personal relationship with the officer that gives rise to, or might reasonably appear to give rise to, pressure, influence or inducement affecting the impartiality of the officer, unless all parties consent and it is in the interests of justice;

(f) knowingly assert as true, a fact when its truth cannot reasonably be supported by the evidence or as a matter of which notice may be taken by the tribunal;

(g) make suggestions to a witness recklessly or knowing them to be false;

(h) endeavour or allow anyone else to endeavour, directly or indirectly, to influence the decision or action of the tribunal or any of its officials in any case or matter by any means other than open persuasion as an advocate;

(i) knowingly misstate the contents of a document, the testimony of a witness, the substance of an argument or the provisions of a statute or like authority;

(j) knowingly permit a witness or party to be presented in a false or misleading way or to impersonate another;

(k) knowingly misrepresent the client's position in the litigation or the issues to be determined in the litigation;

(l) needlessly abuse, hector, harass or inconvenience a witness;

(m) improperly dissuade a witness from giving evidence or suggest that a witness be absent;

(n) when representing a complainant or potential complainant, attempt to gain a benefit for the complainant by threatening the laying of a criminal charge or by offering to seek or to procure the withdrawal of a criminal charge;

(o) needlessly inconvenience a witness; and

(p) appear before a court or tribunal while under the influence of alcohol or a drug.

[Amended—October 2014]

Duty as Prosecutor

(5.1) When acting as a prosecutor, a paralegal shall act for the public and the administration of justice resolutely and honourably within the limits of the law while treating the tribunal with candour, fairness, courtesy, and respect.

[New—May 2010]

Incriminating Physical Evidence

(5.2) A paralegal shall not counsel or participate in the concealment, destruction or alteration of incriminating physical evidence or otherwise act so as to obstruct or attempt to obstruct the course of justice.

[New—April 2016]

Disclosure of Documents

(6) If the rules of a tribunal require the parties to produce documents, a paralegal, when acting as an advocate,

(a) shall explain to his or her client the necessity of making full disclosure of all documents relating to any matter in issue and the duty to answer to the best of his or her knowledge, information and belief, any proper question relating to any issue in the action;

(b) shall assist the client in fulfilling his or her obligation to make full disclosure; and

(c) shall not make frivolous requests for the production of documents or make frivolous demands for information.

Errors and Omissions

(7) A paralegal who does, or fails to do, something which may involve a breach of this rule, shall, subject to rule 3.03 relating to confidentiality, disclose the error or omission and do all that can reasonably be done in the circumstances to rectify it.

Agreement on Guilty Pleas

(8) Before a charge is laid or at any time after a charge is laid, a paralegal acting for an accused or potential accused may discuss with the prosecutor the possible disposition of the case, unless the client instructs otherwise.

(9) A paralegal, on behalf of his or her client, may enter into an agreement with a prosecutor about a guilty plea, if, following investigation,

(a) the paralegal advises the client about the prospects for an acquittal or finding of guilt;

(b) the paralegal advises the client of the implications and possible consequences of a guilty plea and particularly of the sentencing authority and discretion of the court, including the fact that the court is not bound by any agreement about a guilty plea;

(c) the client is prepared voluntarily to admit the necessary factual and mental elements of the offence charged; and

(d) the client voluntarily instructs the paralegal to enter into an agreement as to a guilty plea.

4.02   Interviewing Witnesses

Interviewing Witnesses

4.02(1) Subject to the rules on communication with a represented party at Rule 7.02, a paralegal may seek information from any potential witness, whether under subpoena or not, but shall disclose the paralegal's interest and take care not to subvert or suppress any evidence or procure the witness to stay out of the way.

[Amended—October 2014]

4.03   Communication with Witnesses Giving Testimony

Communication with Witnesses Giving Testimony

4.03(1) Subject to the direction of the tribunal, a paralegal shall observe the following rules respecting communication with witnesses giving evidence:

(a) During examination-in-chief, the examining paralegal may discuss with the witness any matter that has not been covered in the examination up to that point.

(b) During examination-in-chief by another licensee of a witness who is unsympathetic to the paralegal's cause, the paralegal not conducting the examination-in-chief may discuss the evidence with the witness.

(c) Between completion of examination-in-chief and commencement of cross-examination of the paralegal's own witness, the paralegal ought not to discuss the evidence given in chief or relating to any matter introduced or touched on during the examination-in-chief.

(d) During cross-examination by an opposing licensee, the witness's own representative ought not to have any conversation with the witness about the witness's evidence or any issue in the proceeding.

(e) Between completion of cross-examination and commencement of a re-examination, a paralegal who is going to re-examine the witness ought not to have any discussion about evidence that will be dealt with on re-examination.

(f) During cross-examination by the representative of a witness unsympathetic to the cross-examiner's cause, the paralegal may discuss the witness's evidence with the witness.

(g) During cross-examination by the representative of a witness who is sympathetic to that licensee's cause, any conversations ought to be restricted in the same way as communications during examination-in-chief of one's own witness.

(h) During re-examination of a witness called by an opposing licensee, if the witness is sympathetic to the paralegal's cause, the paralegal ought not to discuss the evidence to be given by that witness during re-examination. The paralegal may, however, properly discuss the evidence with a witness who is adverse in interest.

(2) With the consent of the opposing licensee or with leave of the tribunal, a paralegal may enter into discussions with a witness that might otherwise raise a question under this rule as to the propriety of the discussions.

(3) This rule applies, with necessary modifications, to examinations out of court.

4.04 The Paralegal as Witness

The Paralegal as Witness

4.04(1) A paralegal who appears as advocate shall not testify or submit his or her own affidavit evidence before the tribunal unless

(a) permitted to do so by law, the tribunal, the rules of court or the rules of procedure of the tribunal, or

(b) the matter is purely formal or uncontroverted.

[Amended—October 2014]

4.05 Dealing with Unrepresented Persons

Dealing with Unrepresented Persons

4.05 When a paralegal deals on a client's behalf with an unrepresented person, the paralegal shall,

(a) take care to see that the unrepresented person is not proceeding under the impression that his or her interests will be protected by the paralegal; and

(b) make clear to the unrepresented person that the paralegal is acting exclusively in the interests of the client and accordingly his or her comments may be partisan.

[New—January 2008]

Rule 7: Duty to Licensees and Others

7.01 Courtesy and Good Faith

Courtesy and Good Faith

(1) A paralegal shall avoid sharp practice and shall not take advantage of or act without fair warning on slips, irregularities or mistakes on the part of other licensees not going to the merits or involving the sacrifice of a client's rights.

(2) A paralegal shall agree to reasonable requests concerning trial dates, adjournments, waiver of procedural formalities and similar matters that do not prejudice the rights of the client.

(3) A paralegal shall not, in the course of providing legal services, communicate, in writing or otherwise, with a client, another licensee, or any other person in a manner that is abusive, offensive, or otherwise inconsistent with the proper tone of a professional communication from a paralegal.

(4) A paralegal shall not engage in ill-considered or uninformed criticism of the competence, conduct, advice or charges of other licensees, but should be prepared, when requested, to represent a client in a complaint involving another licensee.

(5) A paralegal shall answer with reasonable promptness, all professional letters and communications from other licensees that require an answer, and a paralegal shall be punctual in fulfilling all commitments.

(6) A paralegal shall not use any device to record a conversation between the paralegal and a client or another licensee, even if lawful, without first informing the other person of the intention to do so.

(7) A paralegal who receives a document relating to the representation of the paralegal's client and knows or reasonably should know that the document was inadvertently sent shall promptly notify the sender.

[Amended—October 2014]

7.02 Communication with a Represented Person, Corporation or Organization

Communication with a Represented Person, Corporation or Organization

(1) Subject to subrules (2) and (3), if a person is represented by a legal practitioner in respect of a matter, a paralegal shall not, except through or with the consent of the legal practitioner,

(a) approach or communicate or deal with the person on the matter, or

(b) attempt to negotiate or compromise the matter directly with the person.

(2) Subject to subrule (3), if a person is receiving legal services from a legal practitioner under a limited scope retainer on a particular matter, a paralegal may, without the consent of the legal practitioner, approach, communicate or deal directly with the person on the matter, unless the paralegal receives written notice of the limited nature of the legal services being provided by the legal practitioner and the approach, communication or dealing falls within the scope of the limited scope retainer.

(3) A paralegal who is not otherwise interested in a matter may give a second opinion to a person who is represented by a legal practitioner with respect to that matter.

(4) A paralegal retained to act on a matter involving a corporation or organization that is represented by a legal practitioner in respect of that matter shall not, without the legal practitioner's consent or unless otherwise authorized or required by law, communicate, facilitate communication with or deal with a person

(a) who is a director or officer, or another person who is authorized to act on behalf of the corporation or organization,

(b) who is likely involved in decision-making for the corporation or organization or who provides advice in relation to the particular matter,

(c) whose act or omission may be binding on or imputed to the corporation or organization for the purposes of its liability, or

(d) who supervises, directs or regularly consults with the legal practitioner and who makes decisions based on the legal practitioner's advice.

(5) If a person described in subrule (4)(a), (b), (c) or (d) is represented in the matter by a legal practitioner, the consent of the legal practitioner is sufficient to allow a paralegal to communicate, facilitate communication with or deal with the person.

(6) In subrule (4), "organization" includes a partnership, limited partnership, association, union, fund, trust, co-operative, unincorporated association, sole proprietorship and a government department, agency, or regulatory body.

(7) This rule applies to communications with any person, whether or not a party to a formal adjudicative proceeding, contract, or negotiation, who is represented by a licensee concerning the matter to which the communication relates.

(8) The prohibition on communications with a represented person applies if the paralegal has direct knowledge of the representation or if he or she should be able to infer the representation from the circumstances.

Source: Law Society of Upper Canada, *Paralegal Rules of Conduct* (adopted by Convocation 29 March 2007), online: <http://www.lsuc.on.ca/list.aspx?id=1072>.

APPENDIX B

Selected Paralegal Professional Conduct Guidelines*

---

* The Law Society of Upper Canada may add to or revise these Guidelines without notice.

Guideline 1: Professionalism— Integrity & Civility

General

Rule Reference: Rule 2.01(1) & (2)

1. A paralegal should inspire the respect, confidence and trust of clients and the community.

2. Public confidence in the administration of justice and in the paralegal profession may be eroded by a paralegal's unprofessional conduct. A paralegal's conduct should reflect favourably on the legal professions, inspire the confidence, respect and trust of clients and of the community, and avoid even the appearance of impropriety.

3. A paralegal has special responsibilities by virtue of the privileges afforded the paralegal profession and the important role it plays in a free and democratic society and in the administration of justice. This includes a special responsibility to recognize the diversity of the Ontario community, to protect the dignity of individuals and to respect human rights laws in force in Ontario.

Integrity and Civility

Rule Reference: Rule 2.01(1) & (2)

4. Acting with *integrity* means that a paralegal will be honest and will act with high ethical and moral principles. *Integrity* is the fundamental quality of any person who seeks to provide legal services. If integrity is lacking, the paralegal's usefulness to the client and reputation within the profession will be destroyed regardless of how competent the paralegal may be.

5. Acting with *civility* means that a paralegal will communicate politely and respectfully and act in a manner that does not cause unnecessary difficulty or harm to another.

6. The obligation to show courtesy and good faith extends to clients, opposing parties, other paralegals and lawyers, support staff, adjudicators, court and tribunal officers and staff and representatives of the Law Society. This obligation applies regardless of where the paralegal may be appearing or at what stage of the process the matter may be.

Guideline 12: Advocacy

Definitions

Rule Reference: *Rule 4*

   Rule 1.02 definition of "tribunal"

1. An *advocate* is someone who speaks and acts on behalf of others. Rule 4 outlines a paralegal's duties when appearing as an advocate before a tribunal. Rule 4 applies to all appearances and all proceedings before all tribunals. A *tribunal* can be either an administrative board or a court of law. An *adjudicator* is any person who hears or considers any type of proceeding before a tribunal and renders a decision with respect to that proceeding.

General

Rule Reference: *Rule 4*

2. The paralegal has a duty to represent his or her client diligently and fearlessly. Generally, the paralegal has no obligation to assist an opposing party, or to advance matters harmful to the client's case. However, these general principles do not mean that, when acting as advocate for a client before a tribunal, the paralegal can behave as he or she likes or, in some cases, as his or her client may instruct. Rule 4 describes the professional obligations that a paralegal owes to opposing parties, other paralegals and lawyers, the tribunal and the administration of justice. These obligations are paramount, and must be met by the paralegal in each and every tribunal proceeding in which the paralegal acts as advocate for a client.

Candour, Fairness, Courtesy and Respect

Rule Reference: *Rule 4.01(1), 4.01(4)(d)*

   Rule 4.01(5)(o)

   Rule 7.01(3)

3. A paralegal should not engage in rude and disruptive behaviour before a tribunal, or uncivil correspondence, language or behaviour towards opposing parties or their advocates.

Malicious Proceedings

Rule Reference: Rule 4.01(5)(a)

4. A paralegal should not help a client to bring proceedings that have no merit. Claims that have no merit waste the time of the tribunal and its officers, and do not further the cause of justice.

Misleading the Tribunal

Rule Reference: Rule 4.01(5)(c), (d), (f), (i), (j), (k)

5. A paralegal must ensure that neither the paralegal nor his or her client(s) misleads the tribunal. For a tribunal to decide a matter effectively and appropriately, the tribunal must have access to everything that is relevant to the issues to be decided.

Improperly Influencing the Tribunal

Rule Reference: Rule 4.01(5)(e) & (h)

6. For the public to have respect for the administration of justice, tribunals must be fair, objective, independent and neutral. There should be no personal connection between an adjudicator and any of the parties to a proceeding or their advocates.

7. The only appropriate way to influence the tribunal's decision is through open persuasion as an advocate. This is done by making submissions based on legal principles and offering appropriate evidence before the tribunal in the presence of, or on notice to, all parties to the proceeding, or as otherwise permitted or required by the tribunal's rules of procedure. A paralegal should not communicate directly with the adjudicator in the absence of the other parties, unless permitted to do so by the tribunal's rules of procedure.

Dishonest Conduct

Rule Reference: Rule 4.01(5)(b), (c) & (f)

8. Acting with integrity before a tribunal means being honest and acting with high ethical principles.

Admissions by the Client

Rule Reference: Rule 4.01(5)(b), (c) & (f)

9. When defending an accused person, a paralegal's duty is to protect the client from being convicted, except by a tribunal of competent jurisdiction and upon legal

evidence sufficient to support a conviction for the offence with which the client is charged. Accordingly, a paralegal may properly rely on any evidence or defences, including "technicalities," as long as they are not known to be false or fraudulent.

10. However, admissions made by a client to a paralegal may impose strict limitations on the paralegal's conduct of the client's defence. The client should be made aware of this by the paralegal. Where the client has admitted to the paralegal any or all of the elements of the offence with which the client is charged, a paralegal must not do or say anything before the tribunal, including calling any evidence, that would contradict the facts admitted by the client to the paralegal. This would be misleading the court.

11. Where the client has admitted to the paralegal all the elements of the offence, and the paralegal is convinced that the admissions are true and voluntary, the paralegal may properly take objection to the jurisdiction of the tribunal, or to the form, admissibility or sufficiency of the evidence. The paralegal could not suggest that someone else committed the offence, try to establish an alibi or call any evidence which, by reason of the admissions, the paralegal believes to be false. Admission by the client to the paralegal of all of the elements of the offence with which the paralegal is charged also limits the extent to which the paralegal may attack the evidence for the prosecution. The paralegal may test the evidence given by each witness for the prosecution and may argue that the evidence, as a whole, is not enough to prove the client guilty. The paralegal should go no further than that.

Witnesses

Rule Reference: *Rule 4.01(5) (g), (i), (j), (l), (m) & (n)*

Rule 4.02

Rule 4.03

Rule 7.01(6)

12. As an advocate, a paralegal may contact all possible witnesses for both sides of a matter, (subject to Rule 7.02 regarding communications with a represented person, corporation, or organization,) but the paralegal must be fair and honest when dealing with them. This includes the paralegal speaking to the opposing party or co-accused. The paralegal must make it clear to the witness who is the paralegal's client(s) and that that [*sic*] the paralegal is acting only in the interests of his or her client(s). As part of this disclosure, the paralegal should give the witness his or her name, tell the witness that he or she is a paralegal, the name of the client(s) he or she represents in the matter, and his or her status in the proceeding. A paralegal should make an extra effort to be clear when the witness does not have legal representation. Note that, although a paralegal may ask to speak to a potential witness, the witness does not have to speak to the paralegal.

13. During a hearing, a paralegal's ability to speak with a witness giving testimony is limited. This ensures that the paralegal does not influence the evidence the witness will give. A comment made by the paralegal to the paralegal's own witness during court recess, for example, may result in a breach of the *Rules*. The witness may return to the witness box and, as a result of the communication with the paralegal, offer evidence that is slanted to benefit the paralegal's client. Such evidence is no longer neutral and could mislead the tribunal.

Disclosure of Documents
Rule Reference: Rule 4.01(6)

14. The rules of procedure of the tribunal may require parties to produce documents and information to the tribunal or to the other parties in the matter. Timely, complete and accurate disclosure helps settlement efforts and makes the hearing process more effective and fair.

Agreement on Guilty Pleas
Rule Reference: Rule 4.01(8) & (9)

15. As an advocate for a person accused in a criminal or quasi-criminal matter, the paralegal should take steps reasonable in the circumstances to satisfy himself or herself that the client's instructions to enter into the agreement on a guilty plea is informed and voluntary. The paralegal should ensure the client's instructions to enter into an agreement on a guilty plea are in writing.

The Paralegal as Witness
Rule Reference: Rule 4.04

16. As an advocate, the paralegal's role is to further the client's case within the limits of the law. The role of a witness is to give evidence of facts that may or may not assist in furthering the case of any of the parties to a proceeding. Because these roles are different, a person may not be able to carry out the functions of both advocate and witness at the same time.

17. Unless permitted by the Tribunal, when acting as an advocate for his or her client before a tribunal, the paralegal should not express personal opinions or beliefs or assert as a fact anything that is properly subject to legal proof, cross-examination, or challenge, or otherwise appear to be giving unsworn testimony. This is improper and may put the paralegal's own credibility in issue.

17.1 Unless permitted by the tribunal, the paralegal who is a necessary witness should testify and entrust the conduct of the case to another licensee. A paralegal who has appeared as a witness on a matter should not act as an advocate or legal representative in any appeal of that matter.

17.2 There are no restrictions on the advocate's right to cross-examine another licensee, however, and the paralegal who does appear as a witness should not expect to receive special treatment because of professional status.

Dealing With Unrepresented Persons

Rule Reference: Rule 4.05

18. The paralegal has a special duty when representing a client and an opposing party is not represented by a paralegal or a lawyer.

19. To avoid misunderstandings, it will be helpful for the paralegal to confirm in writing the steps he or she takes to fulfill the requirements of Rule 4.05.

Withdrawal and Disclosure Obligations

Rule Reference: Rule 4.01(7)

Rule 3.08

20. If, after explanation and advice from the paralegal, the client persists in instructing the paralegal to engage in or continue a type of conduct prohibited by Rule 4, the paralegal must withdraw from representing the client in the matter. (See Guideline 11: Withdrawal of Representation.)

Guideline 17: Duty to Paralegals, Lawyers and Others

General

Rule Reference: Rule 2.01(3)

Rule 7.01

1. Discourteous and uncivil behaviour between paralegals or between a paralegal and a lawyer will lessen the public's respect for the administration of justice and may harm the clients' interests. Any ill feeling that may exist between parties, particularly during adversarial proceedings, should never be allowed to influence paralegals or lawyers in their conduct and demeanour toward each other or the parties. Hostility or conflict between representatives may impair their ability to focus on their respective clients' interests and to have matters resolved without undue delay or cost.

Prohibited Conduct

Rule Reference: Rule 7.01

2. The presence of personal animosity between paralegals or between a paralegal and a lawyer involved in a matter may cause their judgment to be clouded by emotional factors and hinder the proper resolution of the matter. To that end, Rule 7.01 outlines various types of conduct that are specifically prohibited.

3. One of the prohibitions in Rule 7.01(1) refers to sharp practice. Sharp practice occurs when a paralegal obtains, or tries to obtain, an advantage for the paralegal or client(s), by using dishonourable means. This would include, for example, lying to another paralegal or a lawyer, trying to trick another paralegal or a lawyer into doing something or making an oral promise to another paralegal or lawyer with the intention of reneging on the promise later. As another example, if an opposing paralegal were under a mistaken belief about the date of an upcoming trial, a paralegal would be obligated to tell the opposing representative about the error, rather than ignoring the matter in the hope the opposing representative would not appear at the trial.

Limited Scope Retainer

Rule Reference: Rule 7.02(2)

3.1 Where notice as described in Rule 7.02(2) has been provided to a paralegal, the paralegal is required to communicate with the legal practitioner who is representing the person under a limited scope retainer, but only to the extent of the matter(s) within the limited scope retainer as identified by the legal practitioner. The paralegal may communicate with the person on matters outside the limited scope retainer.

Source: Law Society of Upper Canada, *Paralegal Professional Conduct Guidelines* (adopted by Convocation October 2008), online: <http://www.lsuc.on.ca/paralegal-conduct-guidelines>.

Glossary

administrative tribunal: quasi-judicial body dealing with matters under a specific statute

advocacy: process of presenting a case or defence at a trial or hearing

advocate: person who pleads the cause of another before a court or tribunal

applicant: party who files an application with a tribunal

application: document filed by an applicant that starts a proceeding at a tribunal

bill of costs: a detailed list of all the procedural steps taken at each stage of the proceeding and the legal fees and disbursements incurred at each stage

book of authorities: book containing a copy of each case and statutory provision relied on for a trial or hearing

claim: a document in prescribed form setting out the facts that the plaintiff intends to rely on to prove his or her case

closing argument: summary of a party's case, including a discussion of the relevant law

corroborate: confirm or support with additional evidence

costs: monetary award made to the successful party for fees and expenses incurred in the conduct of a case

courtroom etiquette: a set of customary rules of behaviour for individuals appearing before a judge, justice of the peace, or adjudicator

cross-examination: questioning of a witness by the advocate of the opposing party

defence: a document in prescribed form setting out the facts that the defendant intends to rely on to prove his or her defence

defendant: person against whom relief is sought in an action

direct examination: questioning of a witness by the advocate of the party who called that witness

endorse: make note of a decision

examination-in-chief: also known as a direct examination of a witness, it is the questioning of your own witness(es) under oath

exhibit: an object that is introduced as evidence at a trial or hearing

expert witness: a witness who is permitted to testify at a trial or hearing because of special knowledge or proficiency in a particular field that is relevant to the case

guilty plea: a voluntary admission, by a defendant in a criminal or quasi-criminal case, of the essential factual and mental elements of an offence, thereby giving up the right to a trial

hearsay: a statement, originally made out of court, that is repeated in court for the truth of its contents

law of evidence: the law that determines the way in which the facts are to be proved, as required by substantive law

Law Society of Upper Canada: a self-governing body created by statute that educates, licenses, regulates, and disciplines paralegals and lawyers in Ontario in accordance with the *Law Society Act*, its regulations, by-laws, and rules

leading question: question that suggests a desired answer or that assumes a fact in dispute that has not yet been proven

motion: an interim step in a proceeding in which a party makes a request to the court for an order or directions

notice of hearing: tribunal document served on a respondent along with an application

notice of intention to appear: form to be filed by the defendant with the provincial offences office notifying the court of the defendant's intention to dispute the charge

objection: statement directed to the decision-maker that a question asked, an answer given, or an object introduced by the opposing party is improper

offence notice: document that starts some types of provincial offence processes

offer to settle: formal written offer made by one party to another, outlining the terms by which the party making the offer agrees to settle an issue or all issues in the proceeding

Paralegal Professional Conduct Guidelines: Guidelines created by the Law Society of Upper Canada to assist paralegals with the interpretation of their professional obligations under the _Paralegal Rules of Conduct_

Paralegal Rules of Conduct: set of rules created by the Law Society of Upper Canada that establish ethical and professional standards of conduct for licensed paralegals in Ontario

permitted scope of practice for licensed paralegals: areas of law in which licensed paralegals may represent clients as set by the Law Society of Upper Canada in its by-laws and rules

plaintiff: person who brings a civil action against another

plea bargain: negotiate a resolution to a criminal or provincial offence matter

pleadings: court documents setting out the nature of the plaintiff's and defendant's cases

post-judgment interest: interest on the amount awarded calculated from the date of judgment to the date payment is made

pre-judgment interest: interest on the amount awarded calculated from the date the cause of action arose to the date of judgment

probative value: is sufficiently useful to prove something in a trial

procedural law: the law that deals with the way a dispute comes to a court or tribunal and then continues to its final resolution

provincial offences: non-criminal offences arising under provincial statutes

re-examination: questioning of a witness by the advocate of the party who called the witness after the opposing advocate has cross-examined

reply evidence: plaintiff's opportunity to introduce new evidence to respond to new matters raised by the defendant

respondent: party against whom an applicant files an application with a tribunal

sentence: penalty imposed for an offence

serve: provide a copy of a party's court or tribunal documents to the opposite party

settlement conference: informal and confidential meeting during which the parties try to resolve or simplify issues in dispute

substantive law: the law that defines legal rights and obligations

summons: a legal document requiring a person to attend a trial or hearing as a witness

sympathetic witness: a witness who gives evidence that is favourable to your client's case

trial or hearing notebook: notebook prepared and used by each party, containing all important information needed at the trial or hearing in a secure and organized format

unrepresented persons: individuals involved in a legal proceeding without legal representation by a lawyer or paralegal

unsympathetic witness: a witness who gives evidence that is unfavourable to your client's case

without prejudice: cannot be referred to in court or used as evidence against a party in a legal proceeding

Index

Credits

CHAPTER 11

Publications Ontario Tenant's Notice to End the Tenancy (Form N9): http://www.sjto.gov.on.ca/documents/ltb/Notices%20of%20Termination%20&%20Instructions/N9.pdf. © Queen's Printer for Ontario. Modified and reproduced with permission.

Publications Ontario Notice to End Your Tenancy Because the Landlord, a Purchaser or a Family Member Requires the Rental Unit (Form N12): http://www.sjto.gov.on.ca/documents/ltb/Notices%20of%20Termination%20&%20Instructions/N12.pdf. © Queen's Printer for Ontario. Modified and reproduced with permission.

Catering Notification Form http://search.agco.on.ca/?q=Catering+Notification. © Queen's Printer for Ontario. Modified and reproduced with permission.

APPENDIX A

Paralegal Professional Conduct Guidelines Rule 2.01, Rule 4, Rule 7. Copyright 2007-2016, The Law Society of Upper Canada. Reprinted with permission of the Law Society of Upper Canada.

APPENDIX B

Guidelines 12 and 17. Copyright 2008-2016, The Law Society of Upper Canada. Reprinted with permission of the Law Society of Upper Canada.